AMERICA'S NATURAL PLACES

Regional Volumes in *America's Natural Places*

East and Northeast, Donelle Nicole Dreese

Pacific and West, Methea Kathleen Sapp

Rocky Mountains and Great Plains, Kelly Enright

South and Southeast, Stacy Kowtko

The Midwest, Jason Ney and Terri Nichols

AMERICA'S NATURAL PLACES

THE MIDWEST

Jason Ney
Terri Nichols

Stacy Kowtko, General Editor

GREENWOOD PRESS
An Imprint of ABC-CLIO, LLC

A B C • C L I O

Santa Barbara, California • Denver, Colorado • Oxford, England

Library of Congress Cataloging-in-Publication Data

Ney, Jason.
   America's natural places. The Midwest / Jason Ney, Terri Nichols.
      p. cm. — (Regional volumes in America's natural places)
   Includes bibliographical references and index.
   ISBN 978-0-313-35088-7 (set hardcover : alk. paper) — ISBN 978-0-313-35089-4 (set ebook) — ISBN 978-0-313-35316-1 (alk. paper) — ISBN 978-0-313-35317-8 (ebook)
1. Protected areas—Middle West.   2. Endangered ecosystems—Middle West.   I. Nichols, Terri.
II. Title.
   S932.M43N49   2010
   333.720977—dc22   2009032381

14   13   12   11   10   1   2   3   4   5

This book is also available on the World Wide Web as an eBook.

Visit www.abc-clio.com for details.

ABC-CLIO, LLC
130 Cremona Drive, P.O. Box 1911
Santa Barbara, California 93116-1911

This book is printed on acid-free paper ∞
Manufactured in the United States of America

CONTENTS

SERIES FOREWORD

The United States possesses within its borders some of the most diverse and beautiful natural wonders and resources of any country on earth. Many of these valuable natural places exist under a constant threat of damage from environmental pollution, climatic change, and encroaching civilization, just to name a few of the more destructive forces. Some natural areas enjoy the care and protection of neighboring human societies, but some have fallen to the wayside of concern. This series of reference volumes represents a collection of distinct areas of preservation concern in the following five geographical divisions of the United States: the East and Northeast, the Pacific and West, the Rocky Mountains and Great Plains, the South and Southeast, and the Midwest. The goal is to present representative challenges faced across the country, providing information on historical and ongoing preservation efforts through the process of identifying specific sites that representatively define the United States as an environmental entity. Individual entries were chosen based on the following criteria: biodiversity, ecology, rare or endangered species habitats, or unique environmental character. Many of the entries are nature preserves, state or national parks, wildlife habitats, or scenic vistas. Each selection focuses on a particular area and describes the site's importance, resident flora and fauna, and threats to the area's survival, along with historical and current information on preservation efforts. For sites that are physically accessible, there is information on location, access methods, and visiting tips. Although each volume is organized by state, many natural places cross state borders, and so the larger focus is on environmental ecosystem representation rather than state definition. The goals are to inform readers about the wide variety of natural places across the country as well as portray these natural places as more than just an exercise in academic study. The reality of natural preservation in the United States has an immediate impact on everyone.

Each volume contains a short introduction to the geographical region, including specific information on the states' natural environments and regionally specific concerns of restoration and preservation. Content entries represent one or more of the following criteria: ecological uniqueness; biodiversity; rare or endangered species habitat; exceptional natural beauty; or aging, fragile, or disappearing natural environs. By reading the various entries in each volume, readers will gain understanding concerning environmental issues of consequence as demonstrated by the representative entry choices. The audiences especially suited to benefit from this series are high school and undergraduate students as well as hobbyists and nature enthusiasts. Readers with an interest in local, regional, and environmental health will find easily accessible, useable information throughout the series. The following paragraphs offer short excerpts from the introductions of the regional volumes in *America's Natural Places*.

The East and Northeast United States is a corridor, a doorway to America that has facilitated movement and migration into the continent. The subject of corridors is revisited frequently in the East and Northeast volume as it covers natural areas beginning as far west as Kentucky, as far south as Virginia, and voyages up the coast to Maine. Smaller corridors are described here as well, because many of the places featured in this book have their own respective passageways, some more wild than others. This volume is also about larger corridors—those that connect the past to the present and the present to the future. These natural areas are storytellers chronicling the narratives of cultural and ecological histories that not only have much to tell about the region's past, but also are microcosmic indicators of the earth's current global health. They are corridors into our future as they tell us where our planet is going—toward the loss of countless native species, archeological treasures, and ecosystems that are vital for a sustainable planet. These natural areas are themselves guided paths, passageways into a healthier future as they teach us what is happening within their fragile ecological significance before their lessons are lost forever.

The American Pacific and West is a place of legendary proportions; its natural resources have beckoned to entrepreneurs, prospectors, immigrants, adventurers, naturalists, writers, and photographers, thereby deeply embedding the region into U.S. history, culture, commerce, and art. J. S. Holliday wrote. "I think that the West is the most powerful reality in the history of this country. It's always had a power, a presence, an attraction that differentiated it from the rest of the United States. Whether the West was a place to be conquered, or the West as it is today, a place to be protected and nurtured. It is the regenerative force of America." Over the course of its history, the ecosystems of the Pacific and West have been subject to a variety of forces, both restorative and destructive. Individual entries in the Pacific and West volume seek to not only detail the effects of these forces but to describe the flora, fauna, and topography that make each entry unique. As a cumulative effect, the volume offers an inclusive depiction of the region as a whole while echoing the famous call to "Go West."

"The western landscape is of the wildest variety," Wallace Stegner wrote of his homeland. "There is nothing in the East," he continued, "like the granite horns of Grand Teton or Teewinot, nothing like the volcanic neck of Devil's Tower, nothing like the travertine terraces of Mammoth Hot Springs." Consisting of deserts, grasslands, alpine mountains, plateaus, canyons, cliffs, and geyser basins, the Rocky Mountains and Great Plains is a region of great biodiversity and natural beauty. From the 100th meridian over the peaks of the Rocky Mountains, this landscape has been the source of frontier legends, central to the nation's geography as well as its identity. Home to the world's first national park and some of the most extractive industries in the nation, this landscape displays the best and worst of human interactions with the natural world. Fossils in Colorado are evidence of ancient inland seas. Tall-grass prairies reveal pre-Anglo American ecology. This volume teaches students to read natural landscapes as products of interacting dynamics between culture and nature. People of many backgrounds, ethnicities, and cultures have contributed to the current state of the environment, giving readers a strong, provocative look at the dynamics of this ever-changing landscape.

"The American South is a geographical entity, a historical fact, a place in the imagination, and the homeland for an array of Americans who consider themselves southerners. The region is often shrouded in romance and myth, but its realities are as intriguing, as intricate as its legends." So states Bill Ferris. This volume explores the variable, dynamic South and Southeast through the details of its ecoregions and distinct areas of preservation. Individual entries provide the elements necessary for examining and understanding the threats, challenges, and promises inherent to this region. State partitions serve as geographical divisions for regional treatment, but the overall goal of this work is to present representative examples of the varying ecosystems across the area rather than focusing on the environmental character of individual states. When combined, the sections present a total picture of the South and Southeast through careful selections that portray not only the coastal wetlands and piedmont areas characteristic of the region but also the plateaus, mountains, highlands, plains, and woodlands that define the inland South and Southeast. The goal is to produce a comprehensive picture of the South and Southeast natural environs as they combine to present a unique character and quality that shapes Southern reality today.

The Midwest stands historically as the crossroads of America, the gateway to the West. The region is incredibly diverse, long shaped by geological forces such as the advance and retreat of glaciers. It is a transitional region, where the eastern temperate forests meet the Great Plains of the West and where the southern extent of the northern forests transitions from the mixed-wood plains to the Ozark forests and southeastern plains of the South. Human presence and interaction, however, have greatly reduced and currently threaten this diversity. The Midwest's rich soils and forests, along with its abundant lakes and streams, make this region's natural resources some of the county's most desirable for farming, logging, and development. As a result, little of the once-vast prairies, forests, and wetlands remains. Nonetheless, many efforts, both public and private, are underway to restore and protect the diversity of the Midwest. By taking a holistic approach, individual entries in this volume exemplify the varied ecosystems of the region with the volume as a whole covering all the major Midwest ecoregions. As readers explore the various entries, a comprehensive understanding of the natural systems of the Midwest will emerge, grounded in the region's natural and cultural history and shaped by its current and future challenges.

PREFACE

America's Natural Places: Midwest is intended for high school through college-level readers as well as those who wish to learn more about the ecological diversity, environmental challenges, and natural resource management approaches being undertaken throughout the Midwest.

This volume covers eight states: Illinois, Indiana, Iowa, Michigan, Minnesota, Missouri, Ohio, and Wisconsin. The number of entries is roughly the same for each state, and the areas are geographically dispersed within each state. Natural places were selected with the desire to expose readers to the depth and breadth of the ecological and geographical diversity as well as the conservation issues and management strategies in each state. After exploring all the entries for a state, readers will have a good feel for the terrestrial and aquatic ecosystems particular to that state and the corresponding environmental and conservation challenges and strategies being undertaken.

Because natural places were selected with the intent to expose readers to the ecological diversity across the Midwest, the Environmental Protection Agency (EPA) ecoregion model was used as the basis for delineating and describing this diversity. The EPA ecoregions model was chosen because of its holistic approach. Ecoregions comprise regions where there is similarity in the type, quality, and quantity of environmental resources. For the purpose of this work, EPA Level III was used as the foundation for describing diversity throughout the Midwest. Level III ecoregions are at a level descriptive of the general characteristics of that region and at a level that can emphasize the important characteristics that make the region different from other regions in the Level III ecoregion hierarchy. The EPA framework takes into account terrestrial and aquatic biotic and abiotic components as well as considers humans as part of the biota (i.e., humans' use of and influence on the land and water). More importantly, the EPA approach is designed to serve as a framework for "research, assessment, monitoring, and management of ecosystems and ecosystem components." In other words, ecoregions as defined by the EPA are meant to not only define and map ecoregions but also to address ecosystem management as opposed to the more traditional approach of individual natural resource management. Contemporary resource management considers the protection and restoration of entire ecosystems rather than focusing on only specific areas such as fish, wetlands, or forests, for example. The EPA approach also attempts to eliminate bias toward particular characteristics as might be the case with an ecoregion map developed by a governmental agency responsible for managing a particular natural resource. For this reason, we feel that the EPA ecoregion framework provides one of the most unbiased descriptions of biological diversity across state lines for the purpose of implementing ecosystem management strategies.

Natural places were chosen for three reasons: (1) to be representative of the ecoregions within each state; (2) to thus be descriptive of the environmental challenges faced by the organisms characteristic of each ecoregion; and (3) to illustrate the interconnectiveness of ecosystems across geographical and political boundaries. Inevitably, some natural places were chosen that are not typical of their region but are nonetheless significant because they are representative of historical, geological, or ecological systems of their respective ecoregions in addition to being descriptive of the ecoregions that they more closely represent elsewhere in the Midwest. There is at least one natural place that is representative of and within nearly all ecoregions represented in each state. All significant ecoregions in the Midwest are represented by at least one entry. Although natural places were not chosen because they have endangered species or resources, they often contain significant habitats and species, and many preserves are recognized at the state, national, and, in some cases, international level.

After completing all entries for a state, readers will have an appreciation for the ecological and geographic diversity of that state, the notable environmental challenges faced by those particular ecosystems, and the management and restoration strategies that have been implemented. After reading about the states in this volume, readers will begin to develop a picture of environmental patterns and corresponding ecosystem management strategies that cross political boundaries. The hope is that readers will begin to view natural places in a larger context not bounded by property lines or by political-geographical distinctions but by an interconnectedness based on ecosystems.

America's Natural Places

The Midwest

THE MIDWEST

INTRODUCTION

The Midwest is a region of transitions, boundaries, edges. It is a region that links ecologically and culturally the two coasts and the north and the south. It is the region where the Eastern Temperate Forest meets the Great Plains and the Northern Forests, and it is where the Central Plains meet the Southeastern Plains. It is where the United States physically and psychologically saw the beginning of the vast unexplored and untamed West. These boundaries, where people and environment meet, have resulted in an extraordinarily diverse region. The United States as a whole supports a greater diversity of ecosystems than any other nation and is home to a large percentage of the world's broadleaf forests, temperate grasslands, and Mediterranean-climate vegetation. The nation is surprisingly rich in aquatic life, including fishes, turtles, salamanders, and mussels. The Midwest has the greatest concentration of natural lakes in the nation, most formed from past glaciers, as well as many very high-quality rivers and streams.

This diversity is in no small part the result of varied ecological components—geology, soil, climate, vegetation, wildlife, lakes, and streams—coming together. From these meetings of north, south, east, and west, the Midwest offers a sample of not only its own unique ecosystems but representative species and ecological communities of regions much further away. From the boreal forest relicts isolated in the cool algific talus slopes in Iowa and Illinois to the Atlantic coastal species along Lake Michigan and the southern forest communities and animals in Missouri and southern Illinois, to the western plants, insects, and reptiles found in the sandy prairies of Minnesota, Iowa, and Wisconsin, the Midwest holds representatives of surrounding states as well as its own distinct systems. In the meeting of dissimilar communities in the Midwest, one discovers the most diverse environments.

This varied natural landscape has been historically shaped by geological natural processes and especially the relatively recent glaciations. Since the beginning of the current

ice age a little more than two and a half million years ago, the ice over the polar caps has
advanced and retreated with the warming and cooling of the earth in what are called glacial stages. We are technically still in an ice age, because there are still extensive permanent ice sheets on the earth, though they are now confined to the polar caps. However,
during the glacial advances, ice more than a mile thick reached as far south as northern
Missouri. As the glaciers retreated, they shaped the land in various ways. Organisms
that were displaced recolonized the land, only to repeat the process with each glacial
advance and retreat. So in this sense we are in an interglacial period that ended about
12,000 years ago, after the greatest advance of the last glaciation about 18,000 years
ago. It is evident from an exploration of the various natural places in this volume that
the effects of the latest glacial advance—which in human terms seems so long ago (in-
deed, the last glacial advance ended before the beginning of human civilization)—are
still present in the topography, hydrology, and both biotic (living things) and abiotic
(no living things) environment, despite the massive influence humans have had on the
land and aquatic environments. In fact, even after all this time, for instance, there are
ice age relict communities still present as far south as Missouri. These are not always the
most rare plants and animals, being well represented in the northern parts of the United
States and Canada, but these ecosystems so far south are now extremely rare. They serve
as reminders of the past.

We have a tendency to expect to some degree that things will always be the way
they are. The recent glacial stages in North America remind one of the dramatic changes
that have taken place over the past two million years. However, the continental-scale
natural processes, which have occurred collectively over the past tens of thousands of
years, humans have effected, on a continental scale, in only a little over 100 years. By
primarily individual effort, with local and national policies, we have dramatically altered
the landscape. In the Midwest, the change has been most dramatic in the clearing of
forests for timber, the draining of wetlands, and the channelization of natural and artificial waterways to make the land arable. It also comes as no surprise that the most altered
landscapes are those that have the most economic potential, and those landscapes that
remain the most intact are the most inhospitable and of least economic value. Places like
the vast patterned peatlands of northern Minnesota, which have no timber and are not
practical to farm, remain virtually untouched, while the prairies of southern Minnesota
and Wisconsin and of the greater part of Illinois and Iowa, whose fertile soils may run
more than two feet deep, are the most altered places in America. There is a reason why
Illinois and Iowa rank respectively as 49th and 50th among states in the percentage of
their land remaining in its original state—that is uncut, unplowed, or drained. For instance, of the possible 22 million acres of prairie that existed in Illinois prior to European
settlement, only 2,300 acres of high-quality prairie remain today. This means that there
are 2,300 acres of remnant prairie—never plowed—that are still biologically intact.

Nonetheless, the changes humans have made, though profound, are within our
power to further alter for the benefit of both humans and nature. Our relationship with
nature can be mutually beneficial, and the bountiful land and water can continue to
provide for us if we use sustainable management techniques. The entries in this volume

present various methods for preserving and managing natural places. Also important are the alliances, partnerships, and cooperative efforts by public agencies and private groups—and in particular with individual landowners—forged not only to protect natural places but improve the environment for all, for the entire system. Consider, for instance, the management of prairies, once so prevalent in the Midwest but which now have all but vanished. It has only been within the past few decades that prescribed burning, the deliberate and controlled burning of dead vegetation for specific management purposes, has been used as a widespread forest and grassland management technique. Even more recently, patch-burn grazing has been utilized for managing native grasslands. The idea is that native prairie plants have adapted to tolerate fires ignited by natural occurrence or set by Native Americans. Prairie plants actually need fires to control the invasion of shrubs and fire-intolerant plants such as sugar maples. Although this goes a long way toward managing American grasslands, the introduction of grazers such as cows or American bison further mimics natural processes. The grazers prefer the fresh growth of newly burned patches. Over three years, different patches are burned, moving the grazers from one part of the field to the other. This allows forbs—or nongrass flowering perennials—to thrive without competition from grasses in the initial year after a burn, when grazers select the tender grass shoots over the forbs. This practice can be duplicated on pasturelands with native plants. The benefit to the farmer or rancher is reduced need for herbicides, because the fires control nonnative weeds that are toxic to cattle or, at the very least, are unusable forage. It reduces overall time spent managing the pasture and eliminates a good portion of fencing, because larger areas can be used. A practice that benefits natural systems also benefits humans.

This example also illustrates an important point: Natural process is about the process of change. No natural place is in equilibrium or stays the same in a conventional sense. Whether in geological time—think of the dramatic change to the landscape with a mile-thick ice sheet—or with the seasonal changes, the natural areas of the United States are in constant flux. Change is what natural places in the United States have adapted to and need to survive. Thus, the protection and management of natural places is not about preventing change within the preserves and natural landscapes but managing it. This goes counter to many years of conservation efforts. It is only since the late 1960s that preserve managers have begun to embrace this approach. A good example of this is in Wisconsin. In the late 1940s and early 1950s, John T. Curtis conducted an extensive survey of Wisconsin's plant communities that included natural sites as well as disturbed sites. When the same sites were revisited decades later, some of the most degraded places were those being managed as preserves. This illustrates the limitations of past practices and attitudes that nature is best when best left alone. Through research and action, we are beginning to understand otherwise.

The reason is twofold. U.S. ecosystems are generally fire dependant. Ravines and low, damp areas were, for the most part, protected from fires, and the eastern forests were subjected to less frequent fires. Disturbance is natural in the American landscape. Second, we have altered the landscape so dramatically by draining the land, altering habitat, fragmenting the remaining intact natural habitats, plowing under and clear-cutting vast tracts of land, and, most importantly, preventing natural disturbances such as fire that natural processes are not and cannot occur with a similar frequency and pattern and on the same scale as they historically had occurred. Furthermore, natural processes will occur regardless of the conditions, but these changes, though natural, do not necessarily represent the natural areas we are trying to preserve or the landscapes we wish to save. This realization has resulted in a fundamental shift in environmental management from managing natural resources such as forests, grasslands, lakes, wildlife, and agriculture to managing ecosystems. This change occurred around the 1980s, as government agencies began redirecting their efforts toward a holistic approach to ecosystem management. The natural areas highlighted in this volume are a testament to the strides made in just a few decades. All ecological components are interconnected; understanding to what degree and how the biotic, abiotic, terrestrial, aquatic, and human influences interact and affect one another is crucial to better managing the environment for the benefit of the earth and our species.

But this approach also makes painfully evident the deficiencies of past and current practices. Different agencies and programs have different responsibilities and different missions, often within the same region. Conflicting management practices are the result of having disparate goals for the same region. For instance, the best management practices for agriculture can be at odds with improving stream and lake habitat for fishing. A common geographic framework is therefore necessary to facilitate management by ecosystems and ecological regions rather than by purely administrative or political regions such as county or state. A framework is needed to show the patterns in the capacity and potential of ecological systems.

A hierarchical framework of ecological regions, or ecoregions, allows for disparate objectives to be placed in a larger context. Because natural resources are currently being managed with a more holistic approach, it seems appropriate that the entries for the Midwest volume should reflect this approach. Rather than highlight the rarest organisms or atypical environments, this volume attempts to represent the diversity and breadth of the Midwest by choosing natural places that exemplify the historical natural environment of the region. Entries were also chosen that demonstrate the difficulties and challenges particular to the various ecosystems in the Midwest and the approaches being used to meet these challenges. Hence, ecoregions are used as the framework for presenting and organizing in a coherent and holistic manner the ecological diversity of the Midwest.

There are many ecoregion frameworks in the literature—some with specific objectives, such as the World Wildlife Fund's Terrestrial Ecoregions of North America, which was developed to identify places of unique biodiversity. This volume aims to present the broadest view of the ecological diversity of the Midwest; therefore, U.S. Environmental Protection Agency (EPA) ecoregion mapping is used. The EPA ecoregions are qualitative (weight of evidence) rather than quantitative (rule based) and hierarchical (four levels of ecoregions are each nested within the preceding one), with the objective, according to James M. Omernik of the EPA, of representing "the mosaics of all ecosystems and their components. . . . They [ecoregions] are intended to show patterns in the capacities and potentials of ecological systems." The approximate boundaries of the EPA ecoregions are not based on a single characteristic such as vegetation, soil, or aquatic environments, which is usually applied to serve a particular purpose. Ecoregions, by nature, are not precise and rarely are ecological regions distinct, more often blending from one into another over large areas. By looking at patterns in all environmental and ecological instances, the EPA ecoregions are defined by the weight-of-evidence approach, which looks at the quality and quantity of environmental resources and the way they interrelate in order to determine similar regions in the diversity of ecosystems and their components: abiotic, biotic, terrestrial, and aquatic. The benefit of this approach is to not favor one characteristic over another. The importance of characteristics varies by region and at all scales. Where the geology, for example, may strongly influence the other systems such as aquatic and terrestrial in one ecoregion, it may not be as important as aquatic systems in another. Using this framework for organizing the entries presents a holistic picture of the ecological diversity and interconnectedness of all the ecological components that make up the Midwest today. Ecoregions also present the region at various scales appropriate for such a survey. The EPA ecoregion framework represents current conditions and not what the land was like before human intervention. For this reason, the framework is also dynamic and is continually being updated by the EPA as conditions change and new information is acquired.

A brief description of the characteristics and environmental challenges of each of the ecoregions of the Midwest, starting from the east and moving west, will provide the background to help contextualize the entries of natural places, thereby seeing them as part of the region and not separate entities.

Because ecosystems are complex and do not respect political boundaries, their management, protection, and restoration are challenging. However, just as no component of an ecosystem exists in a vacuum, preserve managers are finding that the most successful projects are those of collaboration. With the vast majority of natural lands being held in private hands, it is critical that government agencies and private organizations encourage private landowners to become partners in the preservation of natural areas. Many state agencies have set up departments to specifically address these needs and facilitate the protection and management of natural areas. Programs such as conservation easements allow private landowners to continue ownership of their property while permanently setting aside a portion for perpetual protection from development and committing to manage it for its natural value. Private organizations are also important in the conservation of natural areas, particularly in not being politically encumbered. Such groups do not have the same pressures to extensively develop recreational activities in addition to passive activities within a natural area.

Ultimately, success in the protection and management of natural areas will depend on our ability to balance human needs with the natural system. It is becoming clear that this requires a focus not only on individual natural resources but rather a more holistic ecosystem management approach.

Due to space considerations and the difficulty of giving simple-to-follow directions to the natural areas, many which do not have addresses, the authors have posted the locations of all the natural areas in a collection on the map search engine www.maps.

live.com. By zooming to the Midwest and typing the keywords "America natural places Midwest" (not case sensitive), readers will see a selection of natural places from the Midwest volume. Opening the collection will display all the natural places in this volume. (If this does work, try adding a keyword of one of the entries.) Follow the Web site directions for navigating around the maps. Aerial photography is an invaluable complement to the entries. Some places, such as the patterned peatlands of Big Bog Recreation Area in Minnesota, for instance, whose variety of repeating peatland landscape patterns can only truly be grasped on a landscape scale and can only be fully appreciated through aerial photography. Because many of the threats to natural places come from outside the preserves—from agriculture, urban and industrial development, and upstream pollution—aerial photography allows one to quickly grasp the physiographic relationships not possible from the ground. Aerial photography also reinforces the importance of managing entire systems and not individual resources to successfully protect the remaining natural areas.

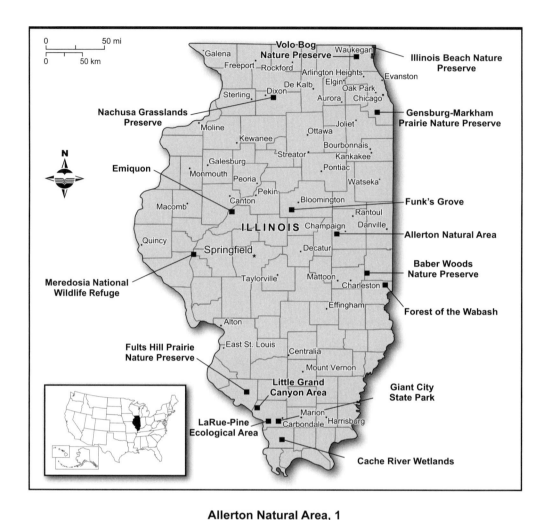

Allerton Natural Area, 1

Baber Woods Nature Preserve, 3

Cache River Wetlands, 5

Emiquon, 6

Fults Hill Prairie Nature Preserve, 9

Forest of the Wabash, 11

Funk's Grove, 12

Gensburg-Markham Prairie Nature Preserve, 14

Giant City State Park, 15

Illinois Beach Nature Preserve, 17

LaRue-Pine Ecological Area, 19

Little Grand Canyon Area, 21

Meredosia National Wildlife Refuge, 22

Nachusa Grasslands Preserve, 24

Volo Bog Nature Preserve, 26

ILLINOIS

Illinois ranks next to last in the amount of remaining natural places—only Iowa has fewer remnant natural places. With some of the richest soils for farming in the United States, nearly all of Illinois's once vast prairies and wetlands have been converted to farmland. The past glaciations left much of the state relatively flat. When settlers first encountered this level terrain, it was in many places poorly drained. However, with the installation of enough drain tile to encircle the globe six times, the land was made arable. Much of the remaining natural places were historically relegated to wood lots and hedge rows. The river systems provide bottomland and lowland habitat and are where many of the present-day forests are found. The Mississippi River forms the western boundary of the state, where, along with the particular ecosystems along this major waterway, many political, environmental, social, and economic factors come together.

Agriculture has a significant impact on natural places and systems in Illinois. And population density is of great consequence, particularly in the Chicago region. Urban development provides its own set of challenges. A number of the entries feature the issues of restoration, preservation, hydrology, and urban pressures in the context of a populous landscape.

ALLERTON NATURAL AREA

The Allerton Natural Area encompasses 1,000 acres of floodplain and upland forests along the Sangamon River. Located in the University of Illinois's Allerton Park in the town of Monticello, it represents a relatively intact river valley ecosystem—an anomaly along this stretch of the Sangamon, where nearly 75 percent of the land has been converted to agriculture and just 10 percent remains forested. Designated a national natural landmark in 1971, the area hosts diverse hardwood tree species and the state-endangered eastern massasauga rattlesnake.

The Sangamon River, like many area waterways that flow along relatively flat topography, is prone to flooding, particularly in the spring. During flood events, the river deposits nutrient-rich silt, sand, and clay soils that nurture vegetation along its banks. This same flooding, however, also can be damaging to plants, rotting their roots and covering their leaves with sediment. For this reason, the flora of the Allerton Natural Area, like other northern floodplain forests, is highly adapted to such conditions.

Sandbar willow, a shrub species that can tolerate being partially buried by sediments, typically occupies areas closest to the water's edge, while cottonwoods, box elder, elms, and ash species are common floodplain tree species just beyond. Below the forest canopy, the ground is bare immediately after annual floodwaters recede, but, by late summer, such flora as sedges, smartweeds, asters, red cardinal flower, and the state-threatened decurrent false aster begin sprouting. These are among the few plant species that can tolerate frequent flooding.

The Sangamon's wide banks encourage the growth of such trees as bur oak, black walnut, and hickory at the edges of the floodplain, where floods are less frequent and shorter in duration. Gooseberry and elderberry shrubs, grape vines, and such wildflowers as bluebells, violets, phlox, and buttercups grow in this area as well. Beech trees, along with more oak and ash, are among the most common tree species in Allerton's upland forests above the floodplain. In all, the Allerton Natural Area and the surrounding park host 31 tree species and more than 1,000 flowering plants.

Allerton also harbors a wide array of animals, including the state-endangered eastern massasauga rattlesnake, which feeds on prairie voles residing in a 50-acre restored tall-grass prairie just outside the natural area boundaries. Other animals within the area include rat snakes, painted box turtles, foxes, white-tailed deer, herons, kestrels, red-shouldered hawks, and many butterfly species.

With native predatory mammals extinct from the region, an explosion in the local deer population has become one of the biggest threats to the natural area's ecosystem. Biologists estimate that 20 or fewer deer per square mile is optimal for an area such as Allerton; in 2004, the park had about 163 deer per square mile. Browsing by such large numbers of deer took a major toll on the natural area's vegetation, especially hardwood saplings, reducing plant diversity and making it difficult for many species to regenerate.

In response, the University of Illinois has allowed tightly controlled deer hunting within the natural area and the larger park since fall 2004. Hunters must first volunteer 40 hours in the park and must kill at least one doe before they can kill a buck. This program has reduced the deer population by more than half in recent years. Park officials also have planted oak and hickory seedlings in large enclosures, protected from deer browsing, along with control groups of the same seedlings outside the enclosures to research the future effects of deer on park vegetation. Invasive plants, especially garlic mustard, also pose a serious threat to native vegetation here.

The Allerton Natural Area, along with the larger, 1,517-acre park that surrounds it, is open to the public year-round. There are 14 miles of hiking and cross-country ski trails. Bicycles are allowed on designated trails or on roadways that also allow cars.

Further Reading

Illinois Department of Natural Resources, Office of Realty and Environmental Planning. "Lower Sangamon River Valley: An Inventory of the Region's Resources." March 2003. http://dnr.state.il.us/orep/pfc/assessments/LSV/toc.htm.

Illinois State Museum. "Illinois Forest Types: Floodplain Forests." http://www.museum.state.il.us/muslink/forest/htmls/pr_flood.html.

Rosenblatt, Daniel L., et al. "Forest Fragments in East-Central Illinois: Islands or Habitat Patches for Mammals?" *American Midland Naturalist* (University of Notre Dame), January 1999, 115–23.

BABER WOODS NATURE PRESERVE

In the early nineteenth century, much of eastern and central Illinois and parts of western Indiana were dominated by bluestem prairies and oak-hickory forests. Oak-hickory forests consist predominantly of black oak (*Quercus velutina*), white oak (*Quercus alba*), and shagbark hickory (*Carya ovata*), which are typically found on dryer slopes. The mesic, or moist, sites in this region contained maple-oak forests dominated by red oak (*Quercus rubra*), sugar maple (*Acer saccharum*), and American elm (*Ulmus americana*). The oak-maple forest association is found scattered throughout eastern Illinois, becoming more common into central Indiana as well as being one of the dominant forests of the eastern United States. Historically, though, moisture and soil were not the only factors in forest composition, particularly in this region. The oak-history forests were supported primarily by periodic fires started by Native Americans, lightning, or other natural means. The thin, slightly furrowed bark of sugar maples is easily damaged by fire, confining this and other fire-intolerant species in this region to streams, ravines, and topographies protected from fire. The thick, deeply furrowed bark of many of the oaks, conversely, is adapted to withstand fires. Baber Woods is one of the best remaining examples of an oak-hickory forest in this ecoregion. However, with over a century of fire suppression, Baber Woods, as well as other oak-hickory forests in the Midwest, have been gradually converting to a sugar maple–dominated forest. The traditional conservation strategy of leaving nature to take its course—that is, not allow cutting or fire—is actually counter to the natural ecological processes in this region. Thus, new strategies are needed to preserve this increasingly rare ecosystem.

Since 1974, the 59-acre preserve has been owned and managed by The Nature Conservancy. With the exception of three acres of land once cleared for cabins, the land has remained virtually untouched since 1835, when the Baber family acquired the land. This lack of disturbance has been both good and bad. It is exceedingly rare to find land untouched by plow or chainsaw in the Midwest, because much of the land has rich topsoil—prime land for conversion to agriculture. The lack of human intervention at Baber Woods has supported a great diversity of plants, insects, and animals, which have thrived. But a general policy of preventing all fires has meant that the historically open parklike Baber Woods, and other fire-dependent ecosystems, have gone through a natural succession to a forest dominated by sugar maples. Human intervention, preventing and suppressing fires, has favored fire-intolerant ecosystems, not the natural habitat in this region, resulting in fire-tolerant ecosystems becoming increasingly rare.

We know this change has occurred in Baber Woods because it is one of only a few Illinois forests that has been extensively documented and inventoried. Over 40 years of plant surveys reveal dramatic changes at Baber Woods as a result of fire suppression. The first survey in 1965 recorded white oaks to be the dominant and largest trees. By 1998 (the last survey), sugar maples dominated more than half of the canopy trees. The variety of understory plants had diminished, as well as the variety of animals the woods historically supported. Having evolved to withstand fires, oak-hickory savannas and forests are also dependent upon it. Without periodic fires, particularly slow-burning low-intensity fires, less fire-resistant and more shade-tolerant species, such as sugar maple, have gradually come to dominate Baber Woods. This is true of other fire-dependent ecosystems throughout the Midwest.

Fire suppression allows oak seedlings that are injured or killed by fires to proliferate shading the once-open parklike savanna. As a result, soil moisture is increased, allowing less drought-tolerant but shade-tolerant species, particularly sugar maples, to begin to invade the woods. At Barber Woods, the sugar maples that now dominate came from nearby ravines. As of the last survey, there were no oaks regenerating.

A concerted effort has been made in the past few years to remove at least 80 percent of the sugar maples. Cutting down trees and girdling, or removing a ring of the bark and tissue underneath in order to kill a tree, has been the first step in managing the woods. Reintroducing fire is the next step. The considerable debris from the dead and felled trees, however, would provide too much fuel, burning considerably hotter than historical fires and damaging even the thick-barked oaks. As a result, in 1999, The Nature Conservancy received authorization from the Illinois Nature Preserve Commission to barter or sell the larger sugar maples. This approach not only has saved money but also makes use of a valuable natural resource and eliminates excessive fuel when future burns are made. It was an unusual measure and at first questioned because of the typically high value placed on sugar maples. But the rarity of the historical oak-hickory ecosystem made such actions necessary.

The efforts at Baber Woods are being closely monitored and are of great educational value. The lack of experience restoring such landscapes makes Baber Woods a test case. As is being discovered in many natural areas throughout the country, taking a hands-off approach is not necessarily the best preservation management practice for a healthy ecosystem.

The preserve, open to the public, is located five miles southeast of Kansas, Illinois.

Further Reading
Abrams, M.D. "Fire and the Development of Oak Forests." *Bioscience* 42 (1992): 346–53.
McClain, W.E., and S.L. Elzinga. "The Occurrence of Prairie and Forest Fires in Illinois and other Midwestern States." *Erigenia: Journal of the Illinois Native Plant Society* 13 (1994): 79–90.

CACHE RIVER WETLANDS

Named a wetland of international importance by the United Nations' Ramsar Convention, the Cache River Wetlands host ancient cypress-tupelo swamps as well as upland forests and barrens. Located in the southernmost tip of Illinois, along the Cache River's lower watershed, the swamp provides critical shelter to migratory shorebirds and waterfowl. More than 40,000 acres are protected in a combination of preserves owned by the Illinois Department of Natural Resources, the U.S. Fish and Wildlife Service, and The Nature Conservancy.

The Cache River valley lies at a juncture of the nation's distinct southern, northern, eastern, and western ecological regions. Such a convergence of landforms, bedrock types, and soils are the basis for the area's unique and highly diverse flora and fauna. Atop this landscape, the nearby Ohio River carved a wide floodplain at the end of the last ice age, when it was fueled by huge volumes of glacial melt water. When the Ohio later shifted its course to the south, it left the much smaller Cache River to meander across a flat landscape of rich glacial till.

These permanently flooded bottomlands are now home to massive bald cypress and tupelo gum trees more commonly found in the Deep South. Many of the cypress are more than 1,000 years old, including the state's largest bald cypress tree, which has a base trunk width of more than 40 feet. These towering trees can survive the constant flooding of their roots, but their saplings cannot; for this reason, cypress can only reproduce during droughts and other unusual periods when the soil surface is not covered with water. Such swamp shrubs as Virginia willow and swamp rose also cannot tolerate submersion in water, so they have adapted to grow atop the bald cypress's knees—vertical root outgrowths likely developed to give the trees stability in saturated soils. Other swamp vegetation includes duckweed, buttonbrush, Virginia creeper, and poison ivy.

At the edges of the swamp grow bottomland hardwood forests of overcup oak, pin oak, cherrybark oak, sweet gum, and pumpkin ash. Such forests occur primarily at the base of the Lesser Shawnee Hills that rise above the river valley. These trees in turn give way to more mesic hardwood forests of red oak, white oak, shagbark hickory, and pignut hickory at higher elevations. An unusual example of this upland forest type occurs in the Cache River State Natural Area—atop a rare sandstone knob such as those more commonly found in the Greater Shawnee Hills to the north.

In the thin, dry soils of the highest ridgelines above the river is the barrens plant community. Here, small, stunted post oak and blackjack oak trees are scattered across open grasslands. The trees, grasses, and forbs of the barrens are normally found within dry prairie and oak savanna habitats much further north and west.

The Cache River Wetlands are known for their abundant bird life, which includes great blue herons, great egrets, little blue herons, green herons, least bitterns, wood ducks, mallards, snow geese, sora rails, woodcocks, quail, mourning doves, red-headed woodpeckers, pileated woodpeckers, prothonotary warblers, black vultures, red-tailed hawks, and great horned owls. The swamplands also host a wide array of amphibians, including bird-voiced tree frogs, southern leopard frogs, spring peepers, western chorus frogs, bullfrogs, and American toads. Snakes in the area include copperheads, cottonmouths, and timber rattlesnakes. Among the fish living in the waters of the Cache River are such species as bowfin, needlenose gar, grass pickerel, and yellow bullhead catfish, along with the state-endangered pygmy sunfish and cypress minnow—both found only in forested swamplands. Common mammal residents include white-tailed deer, raccoons, beavers, gray foxes, red foxes, opossums, skunks, and mink; rare species include river otters, bobcats, and the federally endangered Indiana bat. Such large animals as wolves, bears, and elk once roamed the area as well, but they were extirpated in the region by the mid-1800s due to habitat loss.

Logging and agriculture both have taken their toll on the wetlands. Attempts to drain the swamps with numerous canals and diversions have greatly altered the river's natural flow, and significant portions of the forest in the lower watershed have been cleared. Due to erosion from cleared land and from tillage on farms upstream, up to 150 tons of soil per acre now washes into the Cache and its wetlands annually, threatening aquatic life.

Plans are underway, however, to protect and restore a 50-mile stretch of the river corridor—60,000 acres in all, compared with the 40,000 currently in public and private preserves. The Cache River Joint Venture Program is a collaborative effort among the state, federal, and nonprofit agencies that own and manage lands along the river. The Nature Conservancy has taken on one of the largest and most ambitious portions of this effort: reconnecting the Upper and Lower Cache rivers, which are currently separated by an artificial diversion near the conservancy's Grassy Slough Preserve.

Grassy Slough Preserve, the Cypress Creek National Wildlife Refuge, and the Cache River State Natural Area all are open to the public, with permitted activities varying by agency and location. Access is easiest, and trails most numerous, within the NRA and at Grassy Slough. All of these protected areas lie west of the town of Belknap, off Routes 37 or 51.

Further Reading

Illinois Department of Natural Resources. "Cache River State Natural Area: South Region." http://dnr.state.il.us/lands/landmgt/parks/r5/cachervr.htm.
Illinois State Museum. "Illinois Forest Types: Swamps." http://www.museum.state.il.us/muslink/forest/htmls/pr_wet.html.

EMIQUON

Once home to tall-grass prairie, hardwood forest, wetlands, and lakes, all sustained by the backwaters of the Illinois River, Emiquon is now the site of a massive restoration effort. The Nature Conservancy is rebuilding this ecosystem from scratch, replacing the corn and soybean fields that have grown here since the area was drained in the 1920s. Encompassing more than 7,000 acres along the west bank of the Illinois River, about an hour south of Peoria, the Emiquon reclamation is one of the nation's largest such projects outside the Florida Everglades and the largest in the Midwest. It is seen as a cornerstone in the restoration of the wider Illinois River ecosystem and has been touted as a model for river floodplain restoration worldwide.

Historically, the Illinois River floodplain included hundreds of backwater lakes that filled with floodwaters each spring. After the river receded, they remained isolated for the rest of the year as large pools of standing water with muddy bottoms of silt and decomposing plant matter. Among these backwater lakes were Thompson and Flagg lakes on the current Emiquon property. Their waters and those of the receding river supported surrounding wetlands, as well as snapping turtles, painted turtles, various frogs, calico crawfish, grass shrimp, giant floater mussels, and numerous other animal species. In surrounding upland areas, tall-grass prairies of big bluestem, Indian grass, black-eyed Susan, coreopsis, and a wide array of other vegetation grew. Hardwood forests of mainly oak and hickory trees, with wildflowers growing in the understory, also dotted the landscape.

Such diversity also supported human communities for more than 12,000 years. With more than 149 known archaeological sites at Equimon and hundreds more on surrounding lands, this area is considered one of the nation's best for Native American settlement discoveries and research. Among the findings here are former Native American villages, ceremonial sites, and burial mounds.

Emiquon's environment experienced a drastic change in 1923, when a series of levees, ditches, and pumping projects drained the site for agricultural use. Along with similar conversions throughout the Illinois River floodplain, these actions essentially halted seasonal flooding and either eliminated or drastically altered the ecosystems that depended upon it. At Emiquon, the former lakes, wetlands, and prairies gave way to cropland, and most of the hardwood trees were felled.

In 2000, as plans for preserving and reclaiming the Illinois River's natural watershed gained steam, The Nature Conservancy purchased more than 7,000 acres of farmland along the river at Emiquon. The group set forth a goal to remake the entire ecosystem and established a scientific research station on site to implement the plan and study its results.

In March 2007, at the start of spring flooding, the conservancy turned off the pumps that had kept the land dry for 80 years. Within two months, Thompson Lake was 650 acres in size, and eight native wetland plants had begun to grow on their own—likely from seeds that had remained dormant for many years. By the following year, the lake had grown to 1,900 acres, and Flagg Lake, its smaller neighbor, was returning as well.

Since then, the conservancy and the Illinois Department of Natural Resources have stocked the lakes with 24 species of native fish, including bluegill, largemouth bass, and pumpkinseed sunfish. As of December 2008, the conservancy also was raising red-spotted sunfish, a state-threatened species, for introduction to the lakes within two years. Tens of thousands of waterfowl have returned to the area, including coots, northern harriers, and long-billed dowitchers. Pied-billed grebes, black-crowned night herons, and bald eagles now inhabit the property as well. To provide further habitat by restoring Emiquon's hardwood forests and prairies, the conservancy has planted hundreds of thousands of native hardwood trees and plans to plant native grasses and other prairie vegetation as well.

Emiquon. (Jane Ward)

If restoration efforts continue successfully, conservationists expect that many more native animals will return to the Illinois River floodplain, including Henslow's sparrows, eastern bluebirds, orioles, and migrating warblers. Reptiles and amphibians native to the area include prairie king snakes, western ribbon snakes, diamondback water snakes, bullfrogs, slider turtles, and plains leopard, northern cricket, and green frogs. Among potential returning mammals are river otters, muskrats, beavers, mink, raccoons, short-tailed weasels, and meadow-jumping mice.

Emiquon is open to the public for observation and research, and the conservancy already has constructed a parking lot and a boardwalk across wetland areas. There are plans to build hiking trails as well, and the conservancy is working with the nearby Dickson Mounds Museum to preserve and display archaeological findings from the site. Emiquon is just east of the museum, outside Lewistown, off Route 78/97.

Further Reading

Hosner, John F., and Leon S. Minckler. "Bottomland Hardwood Forests of Southern Illinois: Regeneration and Succession." *Ecology* 44, no. 1 (January 1963): 29–41.

Howard, Claire. "Value in the Land." *Peoria Journal-Star*, January 13, 2008.

University of Illinois at Springfield. "The Emiquon Field Station Project." http://www.uis.edu/emiquon/index.html.

FULTS HILL PRAIRIE NATURE PRESERVE

Along the Mississippi River bluffs of southwestern Illinois, Fults Hill Prairie Nature Preserve encompasses the state's largest intact loess hill prairie ecosystem. An unusual prairie type due to its rolling hills and islands of prairie flora amid otherwise wooded slopes, hill prairies are shrinking in size throughout the state. In an effort to protect and manage Fults Hill, the state made the area a nature preserve in 1970; its designation as a national natural landmark followed in 1986. Fults Hill's 532 acres also include savannas, upland forests, and limestone glades with sinkhole ponds.

Of the four main types of hill prairies in Illinois, loess hill prairie, found primarily along the Illinois and Mississippi rivers, is the most common and is the type found at Fults Hill. (Sandhill prairies, glacial drift hill prairies, and gravel hill prairies are the other three types.) Glacial deposits of fine, loamy soils shaped by wind erosion compose the basis of the loess hill landscape, which, in the case of Fults Hill, formed atop bluffs overlooking the Mississippi River.

Such hills typically harbor woodlands, with dry upland forests at higher elevations and mesic (intermediate moisture) forests in the valleys and ravines below, and Fults Hill has its share of such vegetation. On steep south- or southwest-facing slopes, however, islands of prairie vegetation thrive in the harsh, dry conditions where trees have difficulty taking root. Here, wildfires—essential to the health of prairie flora and detrimental to young trees—are more common than on wetter, more sheltered slopes, creating the perfect environment for sun-loving prairie grasses and wildflowers to grow and reproduce.

Among the most common flora in the Fults Hill Prairie are side-oats grama, little bluestem, big bluestem, and Indian grass. Among the preserve's wildflowers are false boneset, pale purple coneflower, flowering spurge, hairy petunia, butterfly milkweed, tickseed coreopsis, and prickly pear cactus. In general, most hill prairie vegetation is similar to that found on more typical flatland prairies, including those with different soil types. However, a few species are restricted mainly to loess hill prairie habitat; among these are blue hearts, marbleseed, scurf-pea, scented lady's tresses, and the state-threatened narrow-leaved green milkweed.

Limestone glades, along with limestone cliffs and the sinkhole ponds common to both types of terrain, occur in areas of the preserve where soils are more shallow than elsewhere and sit atop easily eroded limestone outcroppings. Here vegetation is scarce—both more sporadic and generally smaller than the same plants growing on the loess prairie—but includes little bluestem, side-oats grama, American aloe, purple prairie clover, false boneset, and the state-endangered Missouri orange coneflower.

The Fults Hill woodlands include upland forests composed mainly of white oak, black oak, post oak, and black hickory; and mesic ravine forests are dominated by red oak, sugar maple, white ash, and black walnut. Wildflowers that bloom in the forests include bloodroot, spring beauty, bellwort, false Solomon's seal, may apple, Dutchman's-breeches, trout lily, wild geranium, wild columbine, phlox, violets, jack-in-the-pulpit, and bluebells. At the interface between the preserve's hill prairies and its upland forests are savannas dominated by prairie grasses but interspersed with scattered trees, mainly oak species.

The preserve supports a large number of animals, including foxes, coyotes, and many more common mammals. Such unusual species as the plains scorpion, coachwhip snake, and narrow-mouth toad also reside here. Migrating birds present in spring include such warbler species as Tennessee, Kentucky, blue-winged, yellow-winged, yellow-rumped, black-throated, prairie, and worm-eating warblers. American redstart, rose-breasted grosbeak, and wood thrush are also common in spring. Migrating raptors frequent Fults Hill in the fall and include osprey, northern harriers, red-tailed hawks, broad-winged hawks, and Cooper's hawks. Bald eagles visit in winter.

Frequent wildfires and those set by Native Americans and early European settlers once maintained the balance between prairie and woodland species in Fults Hill and other similar habitats. However, since the advent of coordinated fire suppression efforts in the 1930s, forests have advanced on prairies throughout the region by shading out prairie species. Between 1962 and 1988, Fults Hill lost one-third of its pre-1940 prairies to forest encroachment. This rate compares favorably, however, with the overall loss of hill prairie habitat in the state, which has been above 60 percent on average. The Illinois Department of Natural Resources has conducted regular, controlled burns in the Fults Hill preserve since it was created in 1970, but scientists speculate that these may not be as frequent as the previous cycle of natural and human-started fires.

Due to their topography, hill prairies in general have not been converted to farmland on nearly the same scale as their flatland counterparts, but many have been used for grazing domestic livestock. Such use has reduced species diversity in general.

The Fults Hill Prairie Nature Preserve lies within the larger Fults Hill Prairie State Natural Area, which also encompasses Kidd Lake Marsh. It is open to the public year-round and can be accessed off Bluff Road, near the town of Fults about 25 miles south of the St. Louis suburbs.

Further Reading

Anderson, R. C. 1991. "Illinois Prairies: A Historical Perspective." In *Our Living Heritage: The Biological Resources of Illinois*, edited by L. P. Page and M. R. Jeffords, 384–91. *Illinois Natural History Survey Bulletin* 34, no. 4 (1991): iv + 357–477.

Evers, R. A. "Hill Prairies of Illinois." *Bulletin of the Illinois Natural History Survey* 26, no. 5 (1955): 367–466.

Illinois Department of Natural Resources. "Fults Hill Prairie and Kidd Lake Marsh State Natural Areas." http://dnr.state.il.us/lands/Landmgt/PARKS/R4/fhp.htm#Limestone.

Robertson, Kenneth R., et al. "50 Years of Change in Illinois Hill Prairies." *Erigenia: Journal of the Illinois Native Plant Society*, no. 14 (January 1996): 41–52.

Forest of the Wabash

One of the last virgin deciduous forests east of the Mississippi River, the Forest of the Wabash harbors upland and northern floodplain woodlands along the Wabash River. A remnant of the extensive forests that once covered the valley, the 329-acre preserve lies along the west bank of the lower Wabash. Its old-growth trees are among the largest in Illinois, with many over 120 feet tall and more than 3 feet in diameter. Also known as the Beall Woods Nature Preserve, the Forest of the Wabash is one of the state's oldest preserves and has been named a national natural landmark.

The second-largest tributary to the Ohio River, the Wabash has long fed a thriving bottomland ecosystem with its annual flood waters, depositing fine particles of silt and clay on the floodplain as it recedes each year. While younger floodplain forests generally subsist on sandy, low-nutrient soils, the roots of old-growth trees in the preserve have collected large amounts of silt and decomposed organic matter that now compose deep, fertile soils.

As a result, the willow and cottonwood tree species common to younger floodplains are much less common in the Forest of the Wabash. Instead, three forest types dominate: silver maple–pecan, hackberry–sweet gum–kingnut hickory, and elm–sweet gum–oak. All of these tree species have adapted to tolerate having their roots completely submerged. The ground below the forest canopy remains bare for a time after flood waters recede, but, by late summer, flowering vegetation begins to sprout. Common understory plant species within northern floodplains include sedges, smartweeds, asters, and red cardinal flower.

Compared with the bottomlands, upland forests on the well-drained, mesic soils just above the floodplain contain much more diverse tree species. Here 6 kinds of hickory and 11 kinds of oak grow alongside sugar maples, silver maples, sweet gums, American elms, and ashes. The state's largest sugarberry, mockernut hickory, pecan, and black gum trees all reside within the forest.

Overpopulation of white-tailed deer in the area due to a lack of native predators has had a major negative impact on the forests. Young saplings and shrubs are particularly vulnerable to overbrowsing by deer. In an effort to reduce the deer population, the Illinois Department of Natural Resources now allows hunting in the preserve during archery season only.

With its combination of still pools and fast-moving currents over shallow, rocky areas, the lower Wabash River hosts a wide variety of fish, including carp, channel catfish, white bass, freshwater drum, sauger, golden redhorse, gravel chub, long-ear sunfish, rock bass, river chub, and mooneye. The river bed—a mixture of sand, gravel, and rock—historically provided habitat for 27 state-threatened or state-endangered species of mussels, 8 of which are on the federal endangered species list. However, mussel populations dropped sharply through the 1800s and 1900s, due mainly to excess sediment runoff from nearby farms. Chemical and fertilizer runoff also has affected aquatic species. Most notably, polychlorinated biphenyls (PCBs) remain at high levels in several fish species;

even though their use and manufacture in the United States was banned in the late 1970s, PCBs were widely used prior to that time and take many years to break down.

Cropland now covers two-thirds of the lower Wabash valley through Lawrence, Wabash, Edwards, White, and Gallatin counties. Just 18 percent of the area remains wooded, and some nonforested wetlands also remain. As a result, the Forest of the Wabash is considered a fragment, isolated from other upland and floodplain forests in the region. The Beall family had owned the forest since the mid-1800s and left it intact within a larger, 635-acre farm. After the last remaining heir died, a proposed timber harvest met with outrage from a group of local individuals and conservation organizations. This prompted the state to purchase the land in 1965 and establish Beall Woods State Park, with the Forest of the Wabash at its core.

The park and preserve are open year-round from sunrise to 10 P.M. Five short trails run through the old-growth forests, and camping, picnicking, and fishing are allowed elsewhere in the park. The park is located six miles south of the town of Mt. Carmel, off Route 1.

Further Reading

Gammon, James Robert. *The Wabash River Ecosystem*. Bloomington: Indiana University Press, 1998.

Lindsey, Alton A., Robert O. Petty, David K. Sterling, and Willard Van Asdall. "Vegetation and Environment along the Wabash and Tippecanoe Rivers." *Ecological Monographs* 31, no. 2 (1961): 105–56.

McClain, William E., Richard L. Larimore, and John E. Ebinger. "Woody Vegetation Survey of Beall Woods Nature Preserve, Wabash County, Illinois." *Proceedings of the Indiana Academy of Science*, January 1, 2001.

Phillippe, Philip E., and John E. Ebinger. "Vegetation Survey of Some Lowland Forests along the Wabash River." *Castenea* 38, no. 4 (1973): 339–49.

Sullivan, Janet. 1995. "Northern Floodplain Forest." In *Fire Effects Information System*, U.S. Department of Agriculture, Forest Service, Rocky Mountain Research Station, Fire Sciences Laboratory (Producer). http://www.fs.fed.us/database/feis/kuchlers/k098/all.html.

FUNK'S GROVE

Funk's Grove harbors the largest intact prairie grove in central Illinois and one of the largest tracts of virgin forest in the state. Representing a transitional zone between western prairie and eastern woodland habitats, its scattered groves of white and bur oaks are a remnant of a once-vast natural landscape that now covers just one percent of the state. Eighteen acres of Funk's Grove are designated as a state nature preserve, and other areas include a registered state land and water reserve and a national natural landmark. The Sugar Grove Nature Center also lies within these protected areas.

Lying atop the Grand Prairie Natural Division, a vast expanse of fertile plains that covers central and east-central Illinois, Funk's Grove is a forested island in a sea of tall-grass prairie—the vast majority of which has been converted to farmland. Moderate moisture levels and well-drained soils with high nutrient content support the white and bur oaks that dominate groves of mesic woodlands throughout the property. Other common trees found in prairie groves include other oak species, American elm, chokecherry, wild black cherry, and basswood. Shrub species include gray dogwood, silky dogwood, smooth sumac, wild plum, nannyberry, and several species of hawthorn.

These forested patches have never been logged at Funk's Grove, but the old-growth white and bur oaks are dying out, giving way to sugar maples and beech species. Oaks require a relatively open forest canopy and large amounts of sunlight to reproduce, but maple and beech species do not. Historically, the fire-tolerant oaks relied on wildfires—as well as those intentionally set by Native Americans and early European settlers—to keep the understory clear and to kill off the saplings of competing tree species. However, fire suppression efforts during the past century have changed this delicate balance, paving the way for maples and beech trees that cannot survive frequent fires. As the grove's oak trees aged and grew, they gradually blocked out sunlight, harming the regrowth of their own species while aiding the succession to sugar maple forest.

Outside the more heavily wooded groves, oak savannas also contain bur oaks and white oaks, but in much fewer numbers. Here conditions are drier, and the trees are scattered across large areas of tall-grass prairie. Typical vegetation in oak savannas includes such grasses as big bluestem, Indian grass, and autumn bentgrass, along with prairie wild onion, yarrow, goldenrod, clover, and numerous wildflowers.

The Grand Prairie Natural Division that includes Funk's Grove once hosted large numbers of bison, Blanding's turtles, and Franklin's ground squirrels, but the first is now locally extinct, and the other two are in danger of extinction. Critical avian species include the northern harrier, short-eared owl, Henslow's sparrow, Nelson's sharp-tailed sparrow, prairie warbler, woodcock, short-billed dowitchers, red-headed woodpecker, savanna sparrow, and dickcessel. Among reptiles native to the area are the ornate box turtle, western hognose snake, smooth green snake, and the state-endangered eastern massasauga rattlesnake. Common mammals include white-tailed deer, cottontail rabbits, fox squirrels, and coyotes.

Although Funk's Grove has been protected in one form or another for more than 160 years, it still faces threats from lack of fires and invasive weeds. In addition to the impact of fire suppression on the composition of forested groves, lack of fire also has resulted in forest encroachment on the native tall-grass prairie and savannas, changing the balance of this patchwork ecosystem. Invasives are overtaking habitat from native vegetation. To help mitigate such threats, volunteers help the state Department of Natural Resources remove nonnative plants, collect and plant native seeds, and conduct controlled burns throughout the grove.

Funk's Grove lies southwest of Bloomington off Interstate 55 and can be accessed from exits 145 or 154. Along with the Sugar Grove Nature Center, it is open year-round. There are walking trails throughout the grove.

Further Reading

Illinois Department of Natural Resources. "The Illinois Comprehensive Wildlife Conservation Plan & Strategy: The Grand Prairie Natural Division." Division of Wildlife Resources. http://dnr.state.il.us/orc/wildliferesources/theplan/final/pdf/Grand_Prairie. pdf.

Rosenblatt, Daniel L., et al. "Forest Fragments in East-Central Illinois: Islands or Habitat Patches for Mammals?" *American Midland Naturalist*. January 1999, 115–23.

GENSBURG-MARKHAM PRAIRIE NATURE PRESERVE

Located within the Chicago suburb of Markham, the Gensburg-Markham Prairie Nature Preserve is a restored sandy loam grassland with characteristics of both sand prairie and black loam prairie ecosystems. It also hosts wetland meadows. This 106-acre prairie remnant was restored to health after its discovery in the 1960s and is now one of the Indian Boundary Prairies, four properties covering a total of 271 acres—all in the suburbs of one of the nation's largest cities.

The Gensburg-Markham Prairie sits atop the former lakebed of ancient Lake Chicago. Formed by melting glaciers at the end of the last ice age, Lake Chicago later receded, leaving behind deposits of clay and sand, as well as a low but distinct ridge similar to larger dunes closer to today's Lake Michigan. Wet sedge meadows eventually developed in low-lying areas atop the poorly drained clay soils, while the more abundant drier prairie habitats formed on sandy and sandy loam soils at incrementally higher elevations.

Sandy loam prairie habitat such as that found in the preserve is unusual in that it hosts both the mesic vegetation of black silt loam prairies and the dryland vegetation more common in true sand prairies. At Gensburg-Markham, species belonging to the former habitat include nodding wild onion, cream wild indigo, prairie coreopsis, and prairie alum root. Species common to the latter include colic root, yellow-eyed grass, screwstem, and huckleberry. The dominant grasses throughout the prairie—growing on both types of soil—are big bluestem, Indian grass, and prairie dropseed. Sedge meadows occur in depressions where water collects and host cord grass, bluejoint grass, and various sedges.

When a Northeastern Illinois University biochemist discovered this small fragment of forgotten prairie amid suburban homes in the 1960s, it was partly covered by trees and shrubs that normally do not occur in a prairie landscape. Native prairie grasses still grew in patches, however, and a group of scientists and conservationists set out to restore the property by cutting trees and shrubs; pulling invasive weeds; planting native species from seed; and conducting controlled burns. In 1971, the Gensburg family, which owned 60 acres of the prairie, donated the land to The Nature Conservancy. The larger site is now jointly owned and managed by the conservancy, the university, and the Natural Land Institute as part of a larger effort to restore and protect prairie remnants throughout the area. It became a state nature preserve in 1980.

The Gensburg-Markham Prairie began rebounding after only a few years, with the return of such native plants as prairie betony, pink phlox, white prairie clover, and wild quinine. Other rare grasses and wildflowers later returned as well, including small sundrops, narrow-leaved sundew, yellow-eyed grass, and the endangered white-fringed orchid. Controlled burns—designed to mimic the wildfires that formerly kept the prairie free from invaders—now help the fire-dependent flora thrive while keeping exotic weeds at bay.

Northeastern Illinois University biologists have successfully reintroduced several native animals, including the rare Franklin's ground squirrel and the state-endangered rattlesnake-master borer moth. Others have returned on their own, including the state-threatened Henslow's sparrow and the gray fox. The preserve hosts more than 350 insect species, including the Aphrodite fritillary, bunchgrass skipper, and dreamy dusky wing, and 13 amphibian and reptile species, including the eastern milk snake and the smooth green snake. Nearly 100 bird species have been observed, including the short-billed marsh wren, the swamp sparrow, the Virginia rail, savanna sparrows, sandpipers, and the rare bobolink, whose numbers have declined 97 percent since 1958 due mainly to habitat loss.

Threats to the Gensburg-Markham Prairie remain from invasive weeds and from feral and domesticated cats that kill native birds. Even when combined with the larger Indian Boundary Prairie ecosystem, the preserve remains a small fragment of the vast grasslands that once covered the region, with its plant and animal species genetically isolated. Still, by all accounts, the prairie is thriving and has become an oasis for native flora and fauna in metropolitan Chicago.

The preserve is open to the public for hiking, bird-watching, and other passive, non-motorized activities. Located in the town of Markham off Interstate 57, it is on Whipple Avenue two blocks north of 159th Street.

Further Reading
Greenberg, Joel. *A Natural History of the Chicago Region*. Chicago: University of Chicago Press, 2004.
Wiggers, Ray. "Classic Prairie Restoration: Gensburg-Markham Prairie." *Chicago Wilderness Magazine*, Summer 2000. http://www.chicagowildernessmag.org/issues/summer2000/gensburg.html.

GIANT CITY STATE PARK

With its towering sandstone bluffs and lush forests, Giant City State Park is typical of southern Illinois's Greater Shawnee Hills. This rock-strewn terrain, covered with large fern communities, oak-hickory forests, and floodplain forests along Indian Creek, lies within Shawnee National Forest, just south of Carbondale. The 4,000-acre park includes the smaller Fern Rocks Nature Preserve within its boundaries.

The sandstone formations underlying Giant City were formed about 320 million years ago beneath an inland sea that once covered most of the state along with western Indiana and western Kentucky. Over millions of years, sediments carried to the sea by ancient rivers settled along the sea floor and shoreline and compacted into layers of rock thousands of feet thick. Later tectonic uplifting raised the area well above sea level, fracturing bedrock and molding the region's unusual rock formations.

When glaciers scoured through the Great Lakes region during the last ice age, they stopped just north of the present-day cities of Carbondale and Harrisburg, leaving southern Illinois as a remnant of sedimentary hills in a now largely flat state. Over time, erosion by wind, rain, and annual freeze-thaw cycles all have shaped the Giant City geological formations, creating fault lines, crevices, and steep cliffs.

Within the drylands at the top of the bluffs, forests of oak and hickory trees dominate, though, as they age, they are being replaced by maples that can grow below the increasingly shady canopy. Along Indian Creek, bottomland forests are nourished by annual flood waters, which deposit nutrient-rich sediments in the floodplain. Common floodplain tree species include willows, cottonwoods, American elm, green ash, and silver maple.

The steeper slopes of Giant City's cliffs and bluffs harbor smaller, specially adapted vegetation—much of which is unusual or absent elsewhere in the state. Most notable are the large number of ferns growing mainly in areas where water seeps through cracks in the rock. These include Christmas fern, marginal fern, lady fern, several types of spleenwort ferns, and maidenhair. Mosses, liverworts, and other shade-loving vegetation dominate north-facing slopes, and the many rock crevices host such specially adapted species as small alumroot, partridgeberry, and Forbes' saxifrage. The Fern Rocks Nature Preserve is a major refuge for the park's ferns as well as an abundance of wildflowers, including Forbes' saxifrage and French's shooting star. In all, more than 75 types of trees and hundreds of wildflower species grow within the Giant City ecosystem.

Wildlife abounds in the Giant City area, with 48 mammals, 52 reptiles, 57 amphibians, 237 birds, and 109 species of fish living either within the park or in the surrounding national forest. Among these are the common white-tailed deer, fox and gray squirrels, eastern cottontail rabbits, and wild turkeys. More rare and critical species include the alligator snapping turtle, timber rattlesnake, black king snake, Fowler's toad, slimy salamander, Indiana bat, and Rafinesque's big-eared bat. Among the many birds that depend upon Giant City and the Shawnee Hills are Henslow's sparrows, Bachman's sparrows, hooded warblers, ovenbirds, worm-eating warblers, pileated woodpeckers, red-bellied woodpeckers, Carolina wrens, Louisiana water thrushes, summer tanagers, and red-eyed vireos.

Native Americans also lived in the area as early as 10,000 years ago. In addition to its natural features, Giant City State Park also contains many archeological sites, including stone-walled buildings and rock shelters worn into cliff sides.

Giant City State Park is open year-round for fishing, boating in Little Grassy Lake, camping, horseback riding, and hunting during the fall season. Many miles of hiking trails also wind through the park and the surrounding national forest. The park is located on Giant City Road, just east of Route 51 and the town of Makanda.

Further Reading
Illinois Department of Natural Resources. "Regional Assessment of the Shawnee Hills Natural Division." http://dnr.state.il.us/orc/wildliferesources/theplan/final/pdf/Shawnee_Hills.pdf.
Wiggers, Raymond. *Geology Underfoot in Illinois.* Missoula, MT: Mountain Press, 1997.

ILLINOIS BEACH NATURE PRESERVE

Lying within the highly developed Chicago metropolitan area, the Illinois Beach Nature Preserve protects ecologically rich lakeshore habitat. The 829-acre preserve represents the state's last remaining beach dune shoreline and encompasses sand dune, sand prairie, savanna, and various wetland communities. Located within Illinois Beach State Park in Lake County, the preserve provides critical habitat for migrating birds and several threatened and endangered plant species. Named the state's first nature preserve in 1964, the beach was later designated a national natural landmark as well.

The dune and swale complex at the heart of Illinois Beach was formed and shaped over thousands of years by the retreat of former Lake Chicago. An ancient body of water formed by glacial melt waters about 14,000 years ago, Lake Chicago receded over thousands of years. As water levels dropped, winds shaped each newly exposed beach into a line of sand dunes, and linear depressions formed in between. Over time, small vegetation and, later, trees grew up on the older dunes, stabilizing them, while the newer dunes closer to shore remained largely bare and continued to shift with the winds. Between the dunes, low-lying areas filled with water to form ponds and such wetland types as fens, pannes, and sedge meadows. This same process created the much larger dunes of Indiana and Michigan on Lake Michigan's eastern shore, but, in Illinois, which is on the west side of the lake, the dunes remained much smaller (rarely rising above 10 feet) because prevailing winds blow sand deposits back toward the lake.

Beginning at the current shoreline, the youngest sand dunes of Illinois Beach host hardy, low-lying vegetation, including bearberry, trailing juniper, sea rocket, and Waukegan juniper. As such plants grow, their roots eventually stabilize the sand dunes, making way for other species. The next stage in the Illinois dunes' development is the sand prairie, where a much thicker carpet of grasses has taken hold. Among the most common are little bluestem, switch grass, Indian grass, and sand reed grass. Prickly pear cactus and various wildflowers also grow in the sand prairie.

Further inland, the ridges support larger shrubs, including sand cherry, willow, New Jersey tea, shrubby cinquefoil, and larger numbers of cactus. Here also are the beginnings of forested sand dunes, with oak savannas dominating. Savannas consist mainly of prairie species, with scattered trees. Black oaks are the most common tree species, but several kinds of pine introduced about 100 years ago also grow here.

Between the dunes lies a complex wetland ecosystem, much of which is nurtured by the seasonal fluctuations of the Dead River. Actually a small stream that flows toward Lake Michigan, this waterway is blocked for much of the year by a sandbar, causing a backflow of water into the marshes. Eventually, however, heavy rains or spring snowmelt raise water levels until the river breaks through the sandbar, draining the marshes. Among the wetland plants that rely on this annual cycle are cattails, bluejoint grass, prairie cordgrass, reed grass, big bluestem, and sedges. These grow mainly in the sedge meadows at the edges of marshes, which are flooded only seasonally; wetter areas host red-osier dogwood, Kalm's Saint-John's-wort, sundew, wood lilies, gentians, Indian paintbrush, and a wide array of orchids. The wetlands also harbor several plants that are threatened or endangered in Illinois, including the marsh speedwell, speckled alder, Crawford's oval sedge, and prairie white-fringed orchid. This last flower is also on the federal threatened species list.

Specialized wetlands within the marshy areas include fens and pannes. Fens form atop peat, a thick mat of partly decomposed vegetation and, unlike bogs, obtain water from both precipitation and underground aquifers. Because the groundwater percolates through mineral soil, fens are just slightly acidic or almost neutral despite the normally acidic peat. Pannes are much more alkaline, since the sandy soils on which they form are rich in calcium. Plants common to these alkaline marshes include sedges, Ohio goldenrod, fringed gentian, Kalm's lobelia, and shrubby cinquefoil. There are just 57 acres of panne habitat remaining in the state—all found between the sand dunes of Lake County.

Illinois Beach is an important nesting ground and migratory rest area for numerous bird species, including ducks, shorebirds, gulls, herons, rails, songbirds, hawks, and falcons. Red-tailed hawks and great horned owls are common. Deer, mink, beaver, red fox, and even the rare gray fox live within the preserve as well.

The northeastern corner of Illinois, where the Illinois Beach Nature Preserve sits, hosts the state's greatest biodiversity as well as its largest urban area. Alongside such a major human population, the beach, like other natural habitat in the area, is under constant threat from pollution, increased development, and urban sprawl. Wetlands throughout the region have been damaged by chemicals, fertilizers, road salt (used for melting ice in winter), and sediments in urban runoff, as well as municipal wastewater discharge. The preserve is a small fragment of the dune system that once covered the state's entire shoreline, and its species remain isolated, reducing genetic diversity. Invasive species, including red canary grass, purple loosestrife, carp, and mute swans, threaten to outcompete native plants and animals, and both feral and domesticated cats prey on native birds.

Despite such threats, restoration efforts and the comparatively large numbers of protected areas along the lakeshore continue to provide an oasis of intact habitat. State management and conservation has left Illinois Beach Nature Preserve with many acres of largely undisturbed, pristine habitat.

The preserve, along with the larger Illinois Beach State Park, is open to the public year-round. Hiking is allowed on trails within the preserve, but cross-country skiing, biking, and fishing are prohibited. (Biking and fishing are allowed elsewhere in the park.) The park and preserve can be accessed off Wadsworth Road, just north of Waukegan and the larger Chicago metropolitan area.

Further Reading

Illinois Department of Natural Resources. "The Chicago River/Lakeshore: An Inventory of the Region's Resources." Office of Realty and Environmental Planning. http://dnr.state.il.us/OREP/pfc/assessments/LMW/.

Larson, Chris. "Into the Wild: Watch Migrating Birds, Hike and Camp Near Dunes, and Swim at Popular State Park." *Chicago Wilderness Magazine*, Winter 1998. http://www.chicagowildernessmag.org/issues/winter1998/IWillinoisbeach.html.

Suloway, Liane, Mark Joselyn, and Patrick W. Brown. "Inventory of Resource Rich Areas in Illinois: An Evaluation of Ecological Resources." Center for Wildlife Ecology, Illinois Natural History Survey. 1996. http://www.inhs.uiuc.edu/cwe/rra/rra.html.

LaRue-Pine Ecological Area

Encompassing a swamp remnant below towering limestone bluffs, the LaRue-Pine Ecological Area of the Shawnee National Forest is one of the most biologically diverse places in Illinois. Together, the intertwined ecosystems of the Pine Hills and the LaRue Swamp harbor 43 percent of all the state's known plant species; dozens of rare, threatened, or endangered plants and animals; and several unusual species more common to the southern United States. The area also experiences a major biannual migration of snakes between their winter hibernation grounds in the rocky bluffs to their summer habitat in the swamp.

The limestone cliffs of the Pine Hills (also known as the Illinois Ozarks) stretch along Illinois's southwestern border, east of the Mississippi River. Like the rest of southern Illinois, the area's bedrock was formed about 320 million years ago from mud and sand below an ancient sea that once covered most of the state, along with western Indiana and Western Kentucky. These deposits were compacted over millions of years into layers of sedimentary rock thousands of feet thick. Later uplift in the earth's crust raised the area well above sea level and formed its prominent rock outcroppings. For thousands of years, the Mississippi River also took its toll, running directly alongside today's Pine Hills and eroding the limestone cliffs.

During the last ice age, the glaciers that scoured the rest of the state flat stopped just north of the present-day cities of Carbondale and Harrisburg. However, the last glacier's southern lobe impacted the southwest corner of the state in other ways, forcing the Mississippi to shift several miles west, to its present course. Another river, the meandering Big Muddy, formed in its place and ran across the alluvial flats for many years until the Mississippi's Grand Tower Bend intersected it. However, the Big Muddy River left behind several oxbow lakes that eventually became the current LaRue Swamp, which now lies between the Pine Hills and the Mississippi River.

Today, runoff from the Pine Hills and numerous springs flowing from the base of the bluffs supply water to the swamp, which has been designated a National Natural

Landmark. (The springs also support spring cavefish within some of the many caves carved into the lower cliffs.) The floodplain forest, shrub swamp, and pond communities of the LaRue Swamp host such trees as swamp oak, swamp hickory, pumpkin ash, sweet gum, bald cypress, and water tupelo. The last two especially are more commonly found in southern swamps. American lotus, swamp iris, and other aquatic plants from the bur-reed, bladderwort, mud plantain, and featherfoil genera also grow here. Green tree frogs, beavers, mink, muskrats, and the much rarer bobcat and freshwater otter all live within the swamp, along with the rice rat—far north of its usual range through the southeastern states.

Rising nearly 400 feet straight up from the swamp, the cliff face hosts lush vegetation around springs and seepages. Ferns, club mosses, sphagnum moss, and other species all cling to the sheer rock. The cliffs also provide winter shelter to many of the approximately 20 snake species that live in the area—mainly aquatic snakes that spend their summers in the swamp, including cottonmouths, diamondback water snakes, and green water snakes, which are an endangered species. Copperheads, timber rattlers, and black rat snakes also migrate to the cliffs each year. Because many of the migrating snakes must cross a road that borders the swamp at the base of the cliffs, the U.S. Forest Service closes it to traffic for a few weeks each spring and fall.

On the hills and bluffs above the cliffs, dry and mesic forests dominate, but small patches of prairie vegetation—including Indian grass, false boneset, white prairie clover, little bluestem, and side-oats grama-grass—also grow in open areas atop the rocky slopes. Supported by thick, fertile loess soils in most areas, about 1,040 plant species, including 40 designated as rare, grow here. Just east of the bluffs, where soils are thickest, silver maple, sweet gum, red oak, beech, and tulip poplar are among the most common trees of the mesic forest. Closer to the upper slopes of the Pine Hills, where soils are thinner and drier, blackjack oak and shortleaf pine are the dominant tree species.

Shrews, least shrews, gray foxes, bobcats, and white-tailed deer are among the forest's mammalian residents. Common birds in the area include red-shouldered hawks, pileated woodpeckers, common turkeys, and bald eagles; Mississippi kites, Kentucky warblers, ovenbirds, wood thrush, and Swainson's warblers also can be found. Among the rare animal species within the LaRue-Pine Hills area are the golden mouse, eastern wood rat, and Indiana bat (a federally endangered species), along with such fish as the blue-headed shiner, banded pygmy sunfish, spotted sunfish, and bantam sunfish in the swamp ponds.

Located southwest of Carbondale along Route 3, the LaRue-Pine Ecological Area of the Shawnee National Forest is open to visitors year-round, with the exception of the seasonal road closure between the swamp and cliff areas.

Further Reading

Evers, Robert A., and Lawrence M. Page. *Some Unusual Natural Areas in Illinois*. Urbana: Illinois Natural History Survey, 1977.

Fliege, Stu. *Tales & Trails of Illinois*. Champaign: University of Illinois Press, 2002.

Hutchinson, Max D. "Establishment Record for the Larue Pine Hills—Otter Pond Research Natural Area within the Shawnee National Forest, Union County, Illinois."

Unpublished report, Northern Research Station, Rhinelander, and the Shawnee Supervisor's Office, Harrisburg, IL, 1987.

"LaRue-Pine Hills Ecological Area." *Outdoor Illinois*, May 1973.

U.S. Forest Service. "Research Natural Area: LaRue Pine Hills—Otter Pond." Northern Research Station. http://www.nrs.fs.fed.us/rna/il/shawnee/larue-pine-hills-otter-pond/.

LITTLE GRAND CANYON AREA

The Little Grand Canyon hosts a mixture of semidesert, forest, cliff wall, and floodplain habitat that is unique in Illinois. Located in the state's southwestern corner, the canyon boasts cliffs and steep, tree-covered slopes rising nearly 400 feet from its floor. Such drastic variations in topography and elevation have made the area a sanctuary for extremely diverse flora and fauna and prompted its designation as a national natural landmark.

Running east to west and ranging from 100 to 300 feet wide, the Little Grand Canyon is an example of a box canyon, with an entrance on its west side but no corresponding outlet to the east. Carved over time by erosion, the sedimentary rock of its cliffs, like the hills found throughout southern Illinois, were formed about 320 million years ago. Over millions of years, deposits of sand and mud collected at the bottom of a large inland sea that once covered most of the state; these were then compacted into rock layers thousands of feet thick. Much later tectonic shifting of the earth's crust raised the area well above sea level and shaped many of its most prominent features. The glaciers that scoured across most of present-day Illinois during the last ice age stopped just north of the towns of Carbondale and Harrisburg, leaving far southern Illinois as a rugged anomaly in an otherwise flat state.

Dissected by a small, gravel-bottomed stream, the canyon floor is a lush landscape fed by seasonal waterfalls and partly shaded by sandstone overhangs and towering deciduous trees. American beech, sugar maple, and tulip poplar dominate the forest canopy, while such shrubs as spicebush, bladdernut, and poison ivy grow below. Beginning in June, a vast array of wildflowers bloom here, including giant white trillium, bluebells, squirrel corn, Dutchman's-breeches, blue cohosh, celandine poppy, goat's rue, pencil flower, and American columbo.

Near the mouth of the canyon, on its western end, the floodplain of the Big Muddy River is evident with a shift to bottomland forest species, including sweet gum, river birch, and box elder. This area is seasonally flooded, and fewer plant species can survive here. Floodplain wildflowers have adapted to the floods and bloom later in the year, after the soil has dried out.

The canyon's north-facing cliffs host a wide array of moisture-loving vegetation. Clinging to the walls around the many seepages and waterfalls are numerous fern species, including marginal shield fern, maidenhair spleenwort, and Christmas fern. Wild hydrangea and shadbush trees are among the shrubs that find purchase on wider ledges, but trees grow only on more gradual slopes. Mesic (intermediate moisture-level) forests of red maple, flowering dogwood, and shagbark hickory dominate the northern slopes. In the upland forest above the canyon, black oak and pignut hickory are the dominant trees, and common shrubs include low bush blueberry and coralberry.

In the dry conditions and thin, acidic soils of the south-facing slopes and cliff tops, slow-growing post oak and winged elm are the dominant tree species. Such shrubs as farkleberry and aromatic sumac also grow here, along with tiny bluet, wild petunia, and succulent widow's cross—all wildflowers that bloom in the warmth of early spring. Conditions are even more arid along the south-facing cliff's exposed rim, where prickly pear cactus, Illinois agave, and other desert plants are the only species to survive.

Among the animals that make the Little Grand Canyon Area their home are a large number of poisonous and nonpoisonous snakes, including timber rattlers, copperheads, cottonmouths, diamondback water snakes, and black rat snakes. Many snake species hibernate in small caves or on overhangs in the canyon's north-facing cliffs, migrating each year from their summer homes along the canyon floor or in nearby swampland. Other animals in the canyon area include bobcat, deer, fox, mink, raccoon, and numerous amphibians and reptiles. Many migratory songbirds can be seen in spring and fall, while common year-round birds include hawks and turkey vultures.

Like the rest of the Shawnee National Forest, the Little Grand Canyon is open to visitors year-round for hiking and wildlife viewing. A 3.6-mile loop trail follows both the canyon rim and its rocky creek bed. Hunting is permitted in season. The area and the trailhead are located along Hickory Ridge Road, south of the town of Murphysboro off Illinois Route 127.

Further Reading

Illinois Department of Natural Resources. "Regional Assessment of the Shawnee Hills Natural Division." http://dnr.state.il.us/orc/wildliferesources/theplan/final/pdf/Shaw nee_Hills.pdf.

Mohlenbrock, Robert H. "Little Grand Canyon." *Natural History,* June 1997. http://fin darticles.com/p/articles/mi_m1134/is_n5_v106/ai_19752779/.

MEREDOSIA NATIONAL WILDLIFE REFUGE

Nearly all of the original forest, prairies, and marshes along the floodplains of the Mississippi River and its major tributaries have been drained and converted to farmland and pasture. Dams and levees have permitted more predictable farming and more habitable land. However, much natural habitat has been lost or fragmented as a result of these hydrological changes. The Meredosia Refuge, which is located on the floodplains of the Illinois River, a major tributary of the Mississippi River, is an important sanctuary for wildlife, especially migratory birds.

The broad floodplain of the sluggish Illinois River is characterized by its oxbow lakes, islands, and scattered dunes. In fact, the lower Illinois River has more backwater lakes than the Mississippi River. The Meredosia National Wildlife Refuge, presently covering over 5,200 acres, is a microcosm of the broad floodplain ecosystems that once covered this ecoregion. As one of four areas of the Illinois River National Wildlife Refuge Complex, Meredosia Refuge forms a vital link within the Illinois River complex and the Mississippi Flyway, a corridor used by migrating birds. The numerous backwater lakes, bottomland and upland forests, and wet and dry prairies provide habitat for various animals, including woodpeckers (*Picidae* family), wild turkey (*Meleagris gallopavo*), grasshopper sparrow (*Ammodramus savannarum floridanus*), and white-tailed deer (*Odocoileus virginianus*).

Periodic flooding, particularly along low rivers, was part of the natural wet and dry cycle in which forests and land flooded, renewing and maintaining natural habitat. Flood control measures along the Illinois River, such as locks and dams, permanently flooded wetland habitat while leaving other areas dry. Predictability of the river, good for agriculture and human habitation, has dramatically changed the cyclical nature of river habitat to which plants and animals had adapted.

Because control measures of the Illinois River have moderated the natural ebb and flow of the river, the most significant management practices today involve re-creating the cyclical nature of the refuge's floodplain. By draining water from shallow wetlands in the refuge in early summer, wading and shoreline birds have increased habitat. This also serves to stimulate vegetation regrowth. The seeds and tubers produced by the plants are then available in the fall when the areas are flooded. Burning of the more than 100 acres of prairie has reduced invasive species in addition to keeping down shrubby growth and trees that would eventually shade the grassland. The major emphasis in the refuge has been on water management, re-creating the natural cycles that once characterized the river on a grand scale.

It is neither possible nor desirable, due to intense human habitation and development, to restore the dry and wet cycle along the entire Illinois River. But there are places along the river where the natural habitat has been recognized as necessary and integral to not only wildlife health but human health as well. Wetlands and floodplains purify the water and control flooding as well as provide habitat for birds, animals, and plants. With the recent acquisitions of over 2,000 acres by The Nature Conservancy being deeded to the U.S. Fish and Wildlife Service, as well as possible future acquisitions, the Meredosia National Wildlife Refuge is being restored to a high-quality floodplain ecosystem.

The refuge is open to the public and located one mile north of Meredosia on Beach Road.

Further Reading

Clark, Jeanne. *America's Wildlife Refuges: Lands of Promise*. Portland, OR. Graphic Arts Center, 2003.

Jeffords, Michael, Susan Post, and Kenneth Robertson. *Illinois Wilds*. Urbana, IL: Phoenix, 1995.

Nachusa Grasslands Preserve

One of Illinois's largest remaining prairies, the Nachusa Grasslands Preserve stretches across more than 2,800 acres in north-central Illinois. The property includes little bluestem prairie, oak savanna, and wetland habitats that provide sanctuary to 600 native plant species and 180 types of birds. Owned by The Nature Conservancy, the preserve connects with the nearby Lowden Miller State Forest, forming a critical corridor for migrating animals.

Less than one-tenth of one percent of the state's original prairies remain, largely because their fertile, well-drained soils were ideal for farming. Even at Nachusa, the majority of the landscape had been converted to fields of corn and soybeans before restoration efforts began in the 1980s. Native grasses and wildflowers survived on large swaths of the property, however, because of its rocky topography. Steep sandstone outcrops, rocky meadows, and several streams discouraged plowing and left many prairie remnants intact. Although the glaciers of the most recent, or Wisconsonian, ice age scoured much of Illinois flat, variations in the glacial lobes, advances, and deposits left behind varied topography in the area.

Little bluestem dominates the grasses of Nachusa's prairie habitat. Other common plants include prairie dropseed, pale purple coneflower, shooting star, cream indigo, prai-

Nachusa Grasslands Preserve. (Justin Meissen)

rie smoke, bird's-foot violet, and rough blazing star. The grasslands also host one of the state's largest concentrations of prairie bush clover, a federally threatened species.

The same irregular topography that protected the prairie ecosystem also encouraged the growth of scattered patches of oak-hickory forest. Such groves grew up primarily on hills or other areas of slightly higher elevation, where wildfires were less frequent than on the prairie's flat expanses. Oak savannas—grasslands with scattered trees, mainly bur oak—also occur within the preserve. Wildfires and fires intentionally set by Native Americans and early European settlers helped prairie vegetation thrive while it killed off young saplings of many tree species.

Wetlands developed in low-lying areas, often at the base of rocky outcrops and small hills. Water collecting in such depressions lingered to provide a habitat for sedges, rushes, and other moisture-loving vegetation. Also growing within the Nachusa Grasslands are the rare downy yellow painted cup, fame flower, Hill's thistle, kittentails, and forked aster.

Many rare and threatened animals live within the preserve, including Blanding's turtles, badgers, grasshopper sparrows, dickcessels, and Henslow's sparrows. Another is the rare gorgone checkerspot butterfly, which was reintroduced to Nachusa after several years of habitat restoration. Bluebirds, wild turkeys, upland sandpipers, and bobolinks are among the other native birds that thrive here.

Since The Nature Conservancy purchased the first portion of the Nachusa Grasslands in 1986, native species have been slowly returning due to a large-scale restoration effort including controlled burning, invasive plant elimination, native seed collection, and reseeding of degraded areas. In addition to the main property, which has been expanded in recent years with additional land purchases, nearby landowners have dedicated another 725 acres as conservation easements. Like many of Illinois's intact prairies, the Nachusa Grasslands remain a habitat fragment. However, recent expansions, the establishment of easements, and the corridor linking it to Lowden Miller State Forest have made it a very large one, with sufficient land to support a healthy prairie ecosystem.

The preserve is open to the public for hiking, bird-watching, and other passive, nonmotorized activities. Located northwest of the town of Franklin Grove, it lies along Lowden Road between Flagg and Naylor roads.

Further Reading

Nachusa Grasslands ECO. no. 1, May 1989. http://www.nachusagrasslands.org/PSmoke/Issue1May1989.pdf.

Sullivan, Janet. "Mosaic of Bluestem Prairie and Oak-Hickory Forest." In *Fire Effects Information System*, U.S. Department of Agriculture, Forest Service, Rocky Mountain Research Station, Fire Sciences Laboratory (Producer). 1995. http://www.fs.fed.us/database/feis/kuchlers/k082/all.html.

Weaver, J. E., and F. W. Albertson. *Grasslands of the Great Plains*. Lincoln, NE: Johnson, 1956.

VOLO BOG NATURE PRESERVE

Representing all the stages of bog succession, Volo Bog is Illinois's only quaking bog with open water at its center. Designated a state nature preserve in 1970 and a national natural landmark in 1974, the bog hosts five wetland types—graminoid bog, low shrub bog, forested bog, tall shrub bog, and sedge meadow—in concentric circles around a pond. The Volo Bog Nature Preserve comprises 161 acres in all and is surrounded by the larger Volo Bog State Natural Area, 45 miles northwest of Chicago.

Originally, Volo Bog was a poorly drained, 50-acre lake—one of many created when the Wisconsin glacier retreated from the area at the end of the last ice age. Lobes of this most recent glaciation had deposited varied glacial till, including clay, sand, gravel, and boulders, throughout present-day northeastern Illinois. Also left behind were large chunks of ice, which later melted to form lakes and wetlands in depressions within the landscape. Volo Bog was among these glacial lakes until about 6,000 years ago, when vegetation, including sphagnum moss, cattails, and sedges, began growing along its edges. As the plants died and decomposed, they formed increasingly thick mats of peat, which, along with the stagnant water conditions, created the acidic conditions necessary for a bog community.

Volo Bog has been evolving ever since, with one plant group succeeding the next as the peat mat expanded toward the center of the pond and thickened around its edges. Today, the pond has shrunk to around 10,000 square feet (less than a quarter of an acre) and averages just nine inches deep. The floating peat mat at its edges is the source of the quaking bog designation, since it shakes and quivers if walked upon. Known as a graminoid bog, this area hosts a tangle of sphagnum moss intertwined with red-rooted spike rush, porcupine sedge, bottlebrush sedge, sensitive fern, marsh shield fern, cinnamon fern, buckbean, and broad-leaved cattail. Two carnivorous plants—the round-leaved sundew and the pitcher plant—also grow here, along with rare orchids, including the rose pogonia.

As the peat mat thickens further out, the low shrub community takes over in an irregular and often poorly defined zone that frequently blends into adjoining habitat zones. Dwarf birch, leatherleaf, and poison sumac are the most common plant species here; pussy willow, bog willow, beaked willow, buckbean, and marsh cinquefoil also grow in this zone.

Next is the forested bog, dominated by tamarack trees. Growing below the forest canopy are starflower, water arum, highbush blueberry, three-seeded bog sedge, common fox sedge, smooth white violet, winterberry holly, glossy buckthorn, and poison sumac. Several of these species blend into the next plant community, the tall-shrub bog, a more extensive shrub community where glossy buckthorn, winterberry holly, and red-osier dogwood dominate. Growing in the shade below the larger shrubs are poison sumac, marsh cinquefoil, sensitive fern, cinnamon fern, and marsh marigold.

Furthest from the pond is the marsh/sedge meadow community, where the peat mat has reached its thickest and most stable expression. Common vegetation includes reed canary grass, broad-leaved cattail, marsh bluegrass, and marsh shield fern.

Many waterfowl, wading birds, and songbirds stop to rest and feed in the bog during their spring and fall migrations. Among the bird species found at Volo Bog are veery, sandhill cranes, great blue herons, green-backed herons, and crossbills. Little brown bats, muskrat, beaver, weasel, red fox, and white-tailed deer make their homes here as well.

Although much of the region's former bogs have been cleared or drained, and tamaracks at the northern end of Volo Bog were logged some time before 1920, the preserve is now protected from any such alterations. The Illinois Department of Natural Resources has expanded the original preserve to include buffer zones and the larger Volo Bog SNA. As lower water levels and bark beetle infestations in recent years have taken their toll on the tamarack bogs, the state also is studying ways to preserve the ecosystem.

Volo Bog Nature Preserve and the larger SNA are open to the public year-round, with trails—including boardwalks over wet areas—for hiking, cross-country skiing, and wildlife viewing. The preserve lies off Brandenburg Road, northwest of the junction of Routes 12 (59) and 120.

Further Reading

Greenberg, Joel. *A Natural History of the Chicago Region.* Chicago: University of Chicago Press, 2004.

Illinois Department of Natural Resources. "Volo Bog State Natural Area." http://dnr. state.il.us/Lands/landmgt/parks/R2/VOLOBOG.HTM.

INDIANA

Glaciers have shaped central and northern Indiana, leaving behind fertile soils to create the eastern and central Corn Belt that covers most of the state except the southwestern corner. Crop agriculture is extensive in the Corn Belt, with livestock farms more common in the southern part of the state. Prairies were common on the glaciated plains but now are given over to primarily agriculture. Hardwood forests are found throughout the state, and along the river ways is bottomland habitat. Because of agriculture, urbanization, and strip mining (mainly in the southwestern part of the state) much of the stream habitat and quality in Indiana has been degraded. The following entries highlight some of the ecosystems of the state. These natural places demonstrate the variety of ecosystems in Indiana and the many challenges and efforts being made to preserve these places and, by extension, similar habitats throughout the state.

DAVIS-PURDUE RESEARCH FOREST

Located in northwest Randolph County, the 111-acre Davis-Purdue Research Forest is North America's oldest and largest mapped, temperate deciduous woodland. Fifty-one acres of virgin hardwoods within its boundaries also have been designated a national natural landmark. Originally mapped in 1926, the forest is now used by Purdue University for teaching and research. It is part of the 623-acre Davis-Purdue Agricultural Center, which also hosts 460 acres of farmland for agricultural research.

The forest grows atop the glacially deposited soils of the vast Tipton Till Plain that covers all of central Indiana. The glaciers of the last ice age scoured the area flat, filling bedrock valleys first with thick accumulations of sand, silt, clay, and boulders, and later with outwash sand and gravel from the melting ice. Poorly drained silty loam and silty clay loam soils now underlie the forest, where elevations vary by just 10 feet from the lowest to highest points.

In the old-growth portion of the forest, the dominant trees are very large oak species (mainly red, white, swamp white, and bur oaks) along with large ash and walnuts. Below the canopy of such mature hardwood forests dogwood, redbud, and ironwood are common species, while smaller shrubs and herbaceous plants occupy the forest floor. Old-growth woodlands in particular provide ideal habitat for myriad birds and mammals that depend on tree holes and hollow trunks for nesting. Among these are squirrels, raccoons, bats, wood ducks, and woodpeckers. Dead trees knocked over by the wind provide a thriving ecosystem of their own, harboring various fungi, bacteria, termites, ants, beetles, centipedes, millipedes, and other insects that eventually break down the wood and return it to the soil. Shrews, mice, and salamanders also live in Indiana's hardwood forests.

Within the Davis-Purdue Research Forest, however, the ecosystem's delicate balance is shifting as mature oaks fill in the canopy, unwittingly speeding their own demise. Shade-tolerant species, especially maples, are rapidly taking over the understory, while the sun-loving oaks are largely unable to reproduce beneath the thick canopy. Such forest succession has created a dilemma for the university's forestry department, which agreed to preserve "all native trees and plants in their natural condition" and to harvest no timber for commercial purposes in a 1917 agreement with the landowner who donated the forest and surrounding areas to Purdue. The agreement also requires the university to "endeavor to keep from becoming extinct our fine native wildflowers, medicinal plants, and trees." Such stipulations have proved contradictory in the midst of natural forest succession that threatens to wipe out the area's signature oak species. However, the university is continuing to work with researchers and forestry experts to maintain the health of the forest while upholding the spirit of the agreement, made with former landowner Martha F. Davis, for whom the woodlands were named.

In other portions of the forest, where past logging and more active management by the university have altered natural processes, the balance of tree species is different. Oak, hickory, maple, walnut, ash, basswood, and beech species all vie for dominance, and shade-intolerant ash and basswood trees are successfully regenerating due to selective tree removal that has opened up the canopy. Oaks, however, have declined here as well, with researchers observing minimal, if any, regeneration. Continuing research projects address oak and walnut regeneration, long-term forest dynamics, and biodiversity.

Another threat to forest regeneration is the area's overpopulation of white-tailed deer due to a lack of natural predators, most of which have been extirpated from the region. Excessive deer browsing is especially detrimental to young saplings and has contributed to the decline of many tree species. Because the Davis agreement also prohibits hunting, this issue has posed yet another point of debate on forest preservation and management.

The Davis-Purdue Research Forest is located 15 miles northeast of the town of Muncie, off Indiana Route 1. It is used primarily as a teaching laboratory and research site.

Further Reading

Aldrich, Preston R. et al. "Confirmation of Oak Recruitment Failure in Indiana Old-Growth Forest: 75 Years of Data." *Forest Science*, October 2005.

Carlson, Don. "Forest Management Plan for the Davis Purdue Agricultural Center." Purdue University, December 2004. http://www.fnr.purdue.edu/research/properties/mgmtplan/davis.pdf.

Peterken, George F. "Natural Woodland: Ecology and Conservation in Northern Temperate Regions." Cambridge: Cambridge University Press, 1996.

Spetich, Martin A., and George R. Parker. "Distribution of Bio-Mass in an Indiana Old-Growth Forest from 1926 to 1992." *American Midland Naturalist*, January 1, 1998.

DONALDSON CAVE AND DONALDSON'S WOODS NATURE PRESERVES

Donaldson Cave and Donaldson's Woods are two nature preserves that protect a limestone cave entrance and one of Indiana's last remaining old-growth forests, respectively. Located in Spring Mill State Park, the preserves together host woodlands, a limestone glade, streams, and sinkholes atop the jagged karst landscape of southern Indiana.

The Donaldson preserves lie atop the limestone bedrock of the Mitchell Plain region, which stretches from the Ohio River north into central Indiana. The area has one of the highest concentrations of sinkholes in the United States—100 per square mile on average—as well as numerous caves and underground streams. Water erosion formed this karst topography over many years, as groundwater combined with carbon dioxide in decomposing vegetation, soil, and air to form a weak acid that slowly dissolves limestone. This process creates cracks and, eventually, large caves and sinkholes.

Donaldson Cave is among the largest of several caves found within the state park and is part of the Donaldson-Bronson-Twin caves system, the source of much of the park's underground waterways. This six-acre nature preserve encircles the mouth of Donaldson Cave, encompassing a shallow stream that flows out of the cave and into a gorge before eventually feeding a small lake. A hardwood forest of white oak, black oak, and pignut hickory dominates the higher slopes of the gorge, where soils are thinner and conditions drier. On the shady lower slopes grow beech and maple trees.

Vegetation is sparse in the small limestone glade above the mouth of the cave. Those plants that have managed to survive on the dry, rocky terrain are more common to prairie habitats and include little bluestem, obedient plant, blue-eyed grass, prairie dock, shooting star, hoary puccoon, and New Jersey tea. Rare lady's slipper orchids and bird's-foot violets—two prairie wildflower species—also grow in the limestone glade community. The rocky banks of Donaldson Cave's stream also provide nesting habitat for Louisiana water thrushes. Eastern phoebes and northern rough-winged swallows typically nest in or around the cave entrance.

The 67-acre Donaldson's Woods, one of just a few virgin forests remaining in the state, has never been logged or seriously altered by humans. Many of the white oak, tulip, and black walnut trees that dominate the canopy are more than 200 years old. These woods are a combination of oak-hickory and beech-maple forest types, with an unusually high percentage of white oaks. However, forest succession has led to greater numbers of beech and maple trees in recent years, since these shade-tolerant species can regenerate on the dim forest floor while sun-loving oaks and hickories cannot. A lack of natural wildfires also has played a role in this forest shift, since fires kill off maple and beech saplings far more easily than oaks, which have evolved to depend on fire. Another unusual feature of the Donaldson's Woods Nature Preserve is the tendency of its runoff waters to drain through sinkholes rather than surface streams.

Both preserves host many common woodland birds, including pileated and red-bellied woodpeckers, eastern wood-pewee, Acadian flycatchers, wood thrushes, red-eyed vireos, summer and scarlet tanagers, Kentucky warblers, barred owls, and black vultures, along with numerous finch and sparrow species.

In an effort to protect and restore the Donaldson Cave and Donaldson's Woods habitats, state officials actively manage the preserves, along with the rest of Spring Mill State Park. Invasive plants—especially vinca minor (also known as periwinkle or myrtle) and garlic mustard—pose an ongoing threat to native vegetation, as do large populations of deer. Large numbers of visitors to the park also can cause damage to sensitive species, especially near the mouth of Donaldson Cave. Efforts by the Indiana Department of Natural Resources include monitoring of plant and animal populations, occasionally allowing hunting, removing invasive vegetation, and limiting the number of visitors to the caves.

Both Donaldson Cave and Donaldson's Woods are open to the public year-round. Donaldson Cave can be explored with just a flashlight, and several hiking trails run through both preserves. Spring Mill State Park is located in Lawrence County, south of the town of Bedford. It can be accessed off Indiana Route 60 east of the town of Mitchell.

Further Reading
Bloom, Phil. *Hiking Indiana*. Guilford, CT: Globe Pequot, 2000.
Goll, John. *Indiana State Parks*. Saginaw, MI: Glovebox Guidebooks of America, 1995.
Indiana Department of Natural Resources. "State Parks and Reservoirs: Resources for Teachers." http://www.in.gov/dnr/healthy/pdfs/TeacherBooklet06Web.pdf.

HARRISON SPRING

Harrison Spring is the largest spring in Indiana, pumping an average of 18,000 gallons per minute into the lower Blue River watershed. Located on private land in western Harrison County, the spring is a major water collection point along the path of extensive underground streams in area's karst landscape. It is considered one of the finest examples of an alluviated cave spring in the country and was designated a national natural landmark in 1980.

The Mitchell Plain region, of which Harrison Spring is a part, is an area of limestone bedrock stretching from the Ohio River north into central Indiana. Mitchell Plain hosts many caves and underground streams as well as one of the nation's highest concentrations of sinkholes—100 per square mile on average. Known as karst, this landscape formed over many years as groundwater combined with carbon dioxide in the air, soil, and decomposing vegetation to form a weak acid that slowly dissolves limestone. The water's corrosive effects have created the cracks, caves, sinkholes, solution channels, and springs that are now part of a complicated underground watershed.

Much of the waters that issue from Harrison Spring comes from surface water entering thousands of small cracks, sinkholes, and solution channels in north-central Harrison County. A significant portion originates in the nearby Indian Creek watershed. These waters travel through subterranean channels at a rapid rate; tests using dyes have shown that water from the sinks of Indian Creek can travel the more than four miles to Harrison Spring in as little as one hour.

These collected waters emerge from a large cavern buried by Pleistocene alluvial sediments, forming a pool at least 35 feet deep and covering about 800 square feet. The minimum discharge rate from Harrison Spring is more than three million gallons a day but can increase tenfold after heavy rains upstream. Harrison Spring flows from this pool about a half mile downstream and into the Blue River.

Around the spring's junction with the river, immature, second-growth deciduous forests of sycamore and beech dominate. Other common vegetation includes water willow and smartweed. Tree roots have helped stabilize the river banks and reduce erosion, maintaining the clarity of spring waters and providing critical habitat for three endangered darter fish (spotted, blue-breast, and variegate darters) as well as the more common banded darter. Other aquatic species include mussels, rock bass, and long-ear sunfish, all of which take shelter among the rock outcrops, root wads, and brush along the river's banks.

State and local officials have long discussed Harrison Spring's potential as a potable water source for local communities, but the watershed's vulnerability to runoff contamination has halted such plans. In general, karst landscapes are highly susceptible to pollutants—from leaking storage tanks and septic systems, pesticides, fertilizers, road salt, and other sources—because of their fast-flowing, interconnected waterways. The limestone bedrock atop which they flow also provides little opportunity for filtration of the waters through organic soils. Instead, pollutants, like the spring waters themselves, generally make their way rapidly through the system. This same hydrology leaves the aquatic plants and animals of the Blue River—and the larger watershed—vulnerable to contamination as well.

Harrison Spring is on private land and is not open to the public. However, the Blue River is accessible at a point downstream, off Route 62 on Harrison Springs Road. Nonmotorized boats are allowed along the river both upstream and downstream of the spring.

Further Reading

Indiana Department of Natural Resources. *Indiana: Our Hoosier State beneath Us.* Indiana Geological Survey. 1974–1984. Reprinted by Indiana University. http://www.indiana.edu/~librcsd/etext/hoosier/GM-13.html.

Unterreiner, Gerald A. "Hydrogeology of Harrison County, Indiana." Indiana Department of Natural Resources, Division of Water. 2006. http://www.in.gov/dnr/water/files/5361.pdf.

HEMMER WOODS NATURE PRESERVE

The old-growth forests of Hemmer Woods Nature Preserve are a remnant of the vast woodlands that once covered southwestern Indiana. Located in eastern Gibson County, the 73-acre preserve hosts both upland oak-hickory forest and bottomland mixed hardwoods. Among the fewer than 2,000 acres of virgin forests that remain intact from the state's original 20 million forested acres, the preserve has been designated a national natural landmark.

Hemmer Woods lies within the Wabash lowlands that extend across southwestern Indiana. Although the glaciers of the last ice age did not reach this far south, their melt waters had a major impact on this corner of the state. Located a few miles to the north, the glaciers sent torrents of water through the area at the end of the last ice age, carving out a low spot in the landscape that extends to the present-day Wabash River. Glacial till soils carried along this outwash plain provided the basis for Indiana's southwestern forests.

Bottomland forest covers the lowest elevations of Hemmer Woods, but, unlike similar forest types elsewhere in the region (especially those closer to the Wabash River), the forest floor is rarely flooded. The stream that runs through the forest is small and meandering, carrying low water volumes even after rains; thus, most flooding is relatively shallow and lasts only a short time. A recently built drainage ditch that redirects water from the stream to an adjacent farm also has lowered water levels. As a result, bottomland species here include vegetation that does not have a high tolerance for flooding.

The bottomland woods host many southern plant species growing at the far northern end of their range, most notably sweet gum and tulip trees. The two largest tulip trees in the state grow here, measuring more than 150 feet tall but just 5 feet in diameter. Other common trees in the bottomlands include river birch, sycamore, wild black cherry, and various oak species.

Hemmer Woods' much larger upland forest grows on slightly elevated land with mesic (intermediate moisture-level) soils. White oak and black oak are the dominant trees; other common species include white ash, red oak, sassafras, pignut, small-fruited hickory, and shagbark hickory. Typical understory tree species in this type of upland forest include dogwood, redbud, and ironwood. Various shrubs and wildflowers grow on the forest floor, and such vines as Virginia creeper and poison ivy are common.

Old-growth forests such as those at Hemmer Woods, which have never been logged, host diverse fauna, including squirrels, raccoons, bats, wood ducks, woodpeckers, and many other animals that rely on the hollowed trunks and tree holes of large, mature trees and dead snags. Many migrating birds, including warblers, also rely on the trees for shelter. Dead trees knocked over by wind or other disturbances become a haven for fungi, bacteria, and insects, including termites, beetles, centipedes, and millipedes. A great deal of windthrow occurred in the preserve during a major storm in 1999 that knocked down many large, older trees—not only standing snags but also living trees.

Forests throughout the Wabash Lowlands have been logged and cleared for agriculture during the past two centuries, but Hemmer Woods is now protected from such activities as part of the state nature preserve system. Water diversions are an ongoing threat, however, as area stream waters are used to irrigate nearby cropland.

The Hemmer Woods Nature Preserve is open to the public, with a short nature trail circling the upland forest. The preserve is located east of the town of Buckskin, off County Road 1050E.

Further Reading

Indiana Department of Natural Resources. "Indiana's Old-Growth Forests." Indiana Division of Forestry. http://www.in.gov/dnr/forestry/files/indianaoldgrowthforests.pdf.

Indiana Department of Natural Resources. "The Natural Heritage of Old-Growth Forests in Indiana." Natural Heritage of Indiana. http://www.naturalheritageofindiana.org/learn/oldforests.html.

Jackson, Marion T. "Forest Communities and Tree Species of the Lower Wabash River Basin." *Proceedings of the Indiana Academy of Science*. February 12, 2007.

HOOSIER PRAIRIE NATURE PRESERVE

A remnant of the vast sand prairies that once covered northwest Indiana, Hoosier Prairie Nature Preserve lies southwest of Gary in a heavily industrialized area. Varying moisture conditions within its rolling topography have created several grassland habitats: dry oak barrens; dry, mesic, and wet sand prairie; sedge meadows; and marshlands. Originally owned by The Nature Conservancy, Hoosier Prairie now has joint protection from the state (as a nature preserve) and by the National Park Service (as a unit of Indiana Dunes National Lakeshore.) It was named a national natural landmark in 1977.

The 430-acre preserve lies atop sandy soils deposited by glacial Lake Chicago as it retreated at the end of the last ice age. Although soils vary slightly throughout the prairie, with some clay and silt intermixed, topography is the biggest determining factor for plant communities in the area. Because the prairies' sandy soils are well drained, higher areas are the driest, and moisture levels increase on lower slopes until they reach their greatest concentration in low-lying depressions. This mixture of sandy uplands and wetlands is known as a dune and swale complex. Although elevation changes at Hoosier Prairie are much less pronounced than those in the sand dunes closer to Lake Michigan, they have a great effect on the overall ecosystem.

On low rises grow the Hoosier Prairie's only trees of note—black oaks—within dry oak savanna habitat, also known as barrens. Here, scattered trees grow above a dry sand prairie of grasses and wildflowers typical of those found in the dry sand prairies.

Below the oak barrens, in descending order, lie the preserve's dry sand prairie, mesic sand prairie, and wet sand prairie habitats. Typical dry sand prairie vegetation in this region includes little bluestem, big bluestem, June grass, and Pennsylvania sedge. Common flowering plants include goat's rue, bush clover, flowering spurge, Indian hemp, rough blazing star, plains puccoon, wild lupine, and showy goldenrod. Notable species growing in Hoosier Prairie's dry grasslands include white wild indigo, prairie parsley, Indian paintbrush, and rose pogonia.

Wet sand prairies host herbs, grasses, rushes, and sedges; dominant species here include prairie cordgrass, bluejoint, and various sedges. The mesic (intermediate moisture-level) sand prairies that lie between wet and dry areas typically include a mixture of prairie vegetation. Throughout the preserve, one habitat type blends into the next. Thus, the sedge meadows growing at the base of slopes (and the edges of the marshlands) contain many of the same plant species as the wet prairies and marshlands. These include numerous wetland sedges and rushes, including flat sedge and spike rush, all of which thrive under conditions of seasonal flooding.

Hoosier Prairie's true wetlands—the marshes—occur at its lowest points, which are constantly covered in standing water. Water depth varies seasonally and from year to year but is always present. Sometimes called flooded grasslands, these wetlands are the climax of the prairie's progression from dry to wet habitat. They host such vegetation as cattails, grasses, sedges, rushes, arrowhead, pickerel weed, and smartweed. Where deeper waters occur in larger depressions, lily pads, elodea, pondweed, and other aquatic plants may grow.

In all, more than 350 native plants have been found within Hoosier Prairie, including 43 that are rare within the state. Among the rarest are yellow wild indigo, wolf's spike rush, and hair bladderwort. Such floral diversity also provides habitat for a wide range of birds, from red-headed woodpeckers and sage wrens in the oak savanna to herons, cranes, rails, marsh wrens, and yellow warblers in the marshes. Eyed brown butterflies are found in the savanna and grasslands; various unusual amphibians and reptiles live in the marshes.

The Hoosier Prairie ecosystem is under constant threat from pollution, particularly runoff from nearby residential and industrial areas. Fertilizers, pesticides, road salt, sewage, and industrial waste are among the various contaminants that enter local watersheds via runoff. Fire suppression during the past century also has changed the balance of a typical prairie landscape, allowing more trees to grow and shade out the sun-loving grasses and wildflowers. In the past, frequent wildfires killed off most young trees while helping prairie plants to regenerate and thrive. Today, state and federal officials conduct controlled burns to mimic the natural wildfire cycle and keep woodlands at bay.

Hoosier Prairie is open to the public, with developed trails for hiking and wildlife observation. The preserve lies within the Chicago/Gary suburbs, just east of the Illinois-Indiana border and south of Interstate 94. It can be accessed off Griffith Road, east of U.S. Route 41.

Further Reading

Greenberg, Joel. *A Natural History of the Chicago Region.* Chicago: University of Chicago Press, 2004.

State of Indiana. Wetland Science Advisory Group. "Recommendations of the Wetland Science Advisory Group on Rare and Ecologically Important Wetland Type Definitions." July 28, 2005. www.in.gov/idem/files/rareecowetland.doc.

INDIANA DUNES NATIONAL LAKESHORE

Encompassing a wide array of ecosystems including sand dunes, forests, bogs, and sandy beaches, Indiana Dunes National Lakeshore lies just outside the city of Gary, on the shore of Lake Michigan. With the Chicago skyline visible from the tops of the highest dunes, the lakeshore's proximity to urban areas has made it a key battleground for protecting wildlife habitat. Established as part of the National Park system in 1966, Indiana Dunes National Lakeshore contains more than 15,000 acres of dunes, oak savannahs, forests, prairies, rivers, swamps, bogs, and marshes. Spanning 15 of the state's 45 miles of Lake Michigan shoreline, the lakeshore also protects the health of the larger riparian ecosystem.

The glaciers that formed Lake Michigan also created the dunes for which the national lakeshore is known. As the Wisconsin Glacier—the last to cover the Great Lakes region during the last ice age—began slowly melting about 11,000 years ago, it formed a series of successive shorelines, creating interspersed beaches, dunes, and wetlands from deposits of glacially eroded material. Today there are four major dune ridges, with the most recently formed rising closest to the lake and the oldest lying further inland, where they were pushed by wind and geologic forces over many years. The newer dunes move inland at an average rate of about four feet annually; Mount Baldy, which currently is 126 feet high, is the largest moving dune along the national lakeshore. Older dunes further inland are more stable, having evolved over time into oak forest. In between lie transition zones including oak savanna and tall-grass prairie. Such changes make the park an important geologic record of Lake Michigan's history.

Due to this ever-changing landscape, the lakeshore has the fourth-largest diversity of native plants per unit of land among all national parks. The Indiana Dunes National Lakeshore hosts more than 1,100 flowering plants and ferns, including bog shrubs, native tall-grass prairie species, white pines, and rare algae. With diverse habitats often side by side (large wetlands, for example, often fill the depressions between sand dunes), such varied plant species as Arctic bearberry and desert-loving prickly pear cactus can be found within a short walking distance. About 30 percent of the state's federally listed rare, threatened, endangered, and special concern plant species grow within the lakeshore's boundaries, including the threatened Pitcher's thistle.

Indiana Dunes National Lakeshore also is an important sanctuary for more than 350 species of birds, providing a permanent home for some and a feeding and resting area for others migrating through the area. Various species of loons, grebes, herons, swans, geese, ducks, cormorants, hawks, eagles, pheasants, coots, terns, sandpipers, owls, woodpeckers, and flycatchers are among the many birds that depend on the lakeshore. One part of the park receives special protection as a rookery for great blue heron. The lakeshore's other animals include 46 mammal species, 18 amphibians, 23 reptiles, 71 fish, and 60 butterflies, including the endangered Karner blue butterfly. Among the most common large mammals are coyotes and deer.

Increased development along the lakeshore—beginning with loggers and farmers in the 1800s and progressing with the growth of industry and residential communities after World War II—poses the greatest threats to the Indiana Dunes' ecosystems. Logging greatly altered the forested dunes and led to significant erosion; farmers and residential developers drained wetlands and killed off native predator species, including wolves and cougars. The introduction of industry, including steel mills and coal-fired power plants,

Indiana Dunes National Lakeshore. (Bach Q. Ha)

polluted the air and the waters of rivers, streams, and Lake Michigan. The establishment of Indiana Dunes National Lakeshore in 1966 was part of a local effort to preserve the lakeshore from further damage.

Today the health of the lakeshore has improved greatly, but threats remain, particularly in the areas of water quality and wetlands degradation. Lakeshore officials monitor water quality and have begun to restore part of the Great Marsh wetland complex in the park's southeastern corner. They also are working to reduce the presence of invasive plant species that have taken over habitat from native plants. Controlled burns aim to restore habitat damaged by decades of natural fire suppression. Another continuing problem is the existence of breakwaters and other erosion-control structures that have been built along Lake Michigan's shores east of the national lakeshore. Lake currents naturally move sand westward along the shore, but such structures have reduced this action, causing increased erosion of beaches and dunes.

Indiana Dunes National Lakeshore is easily accessed off Indiana Route 12, which runs parallel to Interstate 94 east of Gary. Chicago's South Shore Line commuter train stops in the park. The park's visitor and interpretive centers are open year-round, and activities include camping; swimming; fishing; boating; hiking; and, in winter, snowshoeing, and cross-country skiing.

Further Reading

Arzarian, Kenneth. "Birds of the Indiana Dunes National Lakeshore." (SuDoc I 29.6/3:IN 2/6) 1991.

National Park Service, Indiana Dunes National Lakeshore. "Nature & Science." http://www.nps.gov/indu/naturescience/index.htm

Save the Dunes. "Indiana Dunes—History." http://www.savedunes.org/history/.

KANKAKEE SANDS

Kankakee Sands is at the heart of a major effort to restore part of the sand prairie, black oak savanna, and marsh wetlands that once covered northwestern Indiana. The 7,800-acre preserve, owned by The Nature Conservancy, links a larger, 21,000-acre network of protected lands that stretches into neighboring Illinois along the Kankakee River. With 5,000 acres of former farmland restored to date, the preserve now hosts hundreds of native plants and animals, including numerous threatened and endangered species.

Underlying the area's sand prairie ecosystem is a broad outwash plain created by glacial melt waters at the end of the last ice age. As glaciers melted to the north, they sent forth torrents of sediment-filled water across the Valparaiso Moraine and on to the flatlands of present-day Newton County. Here the water slowed and deposited its coarsest sediments—largely sands. Finer mud and silt sediments, however, remained in solution and were mostly carried away to the west by the newly formed Kankakee River. Thus, the Kankakee Outwash Plain was left with well-drained, nutrient-poor soils that formed the basis of a unique ecosystem amid richer prairie landscapes found elsewhere.

Prior to European settlement, the ecosystem centered on Beaver Lake, a shallow body of water seven miles long and four miles wide that nurtured vast marshlands as well as the surrounding prairies. In 1873, a wealthy landowner dug what became known as the Big Ditch, diverting Beaver Lake's waters into the Kankakee River so its sandy bed could be used for growing crops. This was the first and largest of a series of diversions that eventually drained 87 percent of the lake's waters and forever altered the surrounding habitat.

Today, roads cross the former lake bed and marshlands, so a full restoration of the area is not possible. However, The Nature Conservancy and the Indiana Department of Natural Resources, which manages the 640-acre Beaver Lake Nature Preserve to the east and the 809-acre Conrad Savanna to the north, have restored significant portions of the area's hydrology, creating a range of soil moisture levels meant to mimic presettlement conditions. Along with the removal of invasive plants and the reseeding of more than 400 native plant species, the hydrological rehabilitation has so far converted 5,000 acres of farmland to a range of native habitats: oak savanna and dry sand prairie on the highest, driest slopes; wet sand prairie and marshland at lower elevations; and mesic sand prairie in between. Among the native plants that have returned to the area are little bluestem grass, blazing star, common mildweed, cardinal flower, blue-flag iris, willows, dogwood, and the federally threatened prairie flame flower.

Within the Kankakee Sands preserve, the conservancy has placed special emphasis on restoring wet sand prairie, since this habitat is most under threat, having been virtually eliminated within the region. Other surrounding parcels that are part of the larger restoration project include Conrad Savanna, a landscape of sparse black oak trees scattered across dry and mesic sand prairie, and the nearly 12,000-acre Willow Slough Fish and Wildlife Area, a federally managed preserve that harbors marshland and wet sand prairie habitat to the southwest. Another 2,480 acres of open marsh and prairie-covered sand dunes lie further west, in Illinois, within the Iroquois County Conservation Area.

The Nature Conservancy's purchase of Kankakee Sands from private landowners in 1997 effectively linked the state- and federally owned properties into one large ecosystem, repairing the formerly fragmented prairie landscape and providing a critical corridor to wildlife that requires vast tracts of open prairie or wetlands. Among the many animals to benefit from this expansion of habitat are grassland birds, including 13 listed as threatened or endangered within the state, and shorebirds. Among the rare species spotted at Kankakee Sands in recent years are the black rail, Henslow's sparrow, grasshopper sparrow, field sparrow, northern bobwhite, bobolink, piping plover, yellow-breasted chat, black-billed cuckoo, Bell's vireo, northern harrier, upland sandpiper, American bittern, and black tern. Migrating American golden plovers, marbled godwits, lesser yellowlegs, king rails, and short-eared owls also use the preserve as a stopover site. Kankakee Sands is currently the only known breeding ground in the state for Wilson's phalarope, another declining species.

Other rare and threatened animals living in the preserve include the plains pocket gopher, blue racer, grass lizard, six-lined racerunner lizard, and the regal fritillary butterfly. Numerous amphibians have returned to the preserve's restored marshes and wet prairies, including the northern leopard frog, western chorus frog, Fowler's toad, American toad, gray tree frog, spring peeper, bullfrog, green frog, and several salamanders.

Although there are no trails through Kankakee Sands, the entire preserve is open to the public for walking and wildlife observation. About 16 miles west of the town of Rensselaer in neighboring Jasper County, the preserve's headquarters is five miles north of State Road 114, off Route 41. Adjacent public lands also are accessible nearby.

Further Reading

Lucas, Marty. "Kankakee Sands." *Chicago Wilderness Magazine,* Summer 2005. http:// www.chicagowildernessmag.org/issues/summer2005/weekendexplorer.html.

The Nature Conservancy. "Grassland Birds at Kankakee Sands." http://www.nature.org/ wherewework/northamerica/states/indiana/work/art23658.html.

Schoon, Kenneth J. *Calumet Beginnings: Ancient Shorelines and Settlements at the South End of Lake Michigan.* Bloomington: Indiana University Press, 2003.

PINE HILLS NATURE PRESERVE

At Pine Hills Nature Preserve, both the topography and the native forests are unusual for the region, remaining as relics of the last ice age. Stands of white pine, hemlock, and Canada yew—first established after the last glaciers had retreated and area temperatures were much colder than today—continue to grow in the cool shade of glacially incised valleys. The preserve's anomalous climate is the product of its hogback ridges and deep gorges, which were carved by glacial melt waters and considered among the best examples of incised meanders in the eastern United States. Adjacent to Shades State Park in west-central Indiana, Pine Hills was named a national natural landmark in 1968 and became the state's first nature preserve the following year. It composes 480 forested acres.

The more than 300-million-year-old sandstone underlying the preserve was formed over millions of years from sediments deposited below an inland sea that once covered western Indiana, along with western Kentucky and most of Illinois. Glaciers later scoured the area flat, but, as they retreated, their melt waters cut deeply into the bedrock of what is now western Indiana. These torrents of water formed incised valleys, with narrow ridges known as backbones in between.

Pine Hills' four ridges rise between 70 and 100 feet above the valleys and drop off sharply. The largest is the Devil's Backbone, which is about 125 feet long, 100 feet high, and 7 feet wide at its narrowest point. The valleys below now harbor Clifty, Indian, and Sugar creeks—all much smaller than their glacial predecessors. Another interesting geologic feature in the preserve is Honeycomb Rock—a sandstone wall embedded with fossilized sea algae that eroded more quickly than the surrounding sandstone, forming tiny holes in the rock.

Covering these rugged outcrops are upland and floodplain forests containing trees from various stages of forest succession. The most notable species are the hemlock, Canada yew, and white pine trees that grew up in the cold climate immediately after the last ice age, when they were the most common trees in what is now Indiana. They remain common in Canada but have mostly died out in Indiana and elsewhere in the region. Not only do these species live on in the shade of the hogback ridges at Pine Hills, but both the white pines and hemlocks also continue to reproduce.

Although logging operations in the 1850s cleared many of the area's hardwoods, the white pines and hemlocks were largely left alone. Later landowners established a plantation of white, scotch, and jack pines, along with Norway spruce, but these trees require a great deal of sunlight to grow and reproduce. For this reason, they are now being shaded out by a succession of beech, maple, yellow tulip, and dogwood trees. Some stands of old-growth oak-hickory forest also exist outside the former plantation. The reserve's varied terrain also has encouraged the growth of a wide array of ferns, wildflowers, and other plants.

As one of central Indiana's largest unfragmented forests, the preserve, and the larger Sugar Creek valley of which it is a part, host significant populations of nesting birds, including the wood thrush, worm-eating warbler, cerulean warbler, and Kentucky warbler.

Pine Hills Nature Preserve. (David Black)

Black-throated green and magnolia warblers—both more commonly found in boreal forests further north—also live there. Many migratory birds also rely on the Pine Hills woodlands, including vireos, tanagers, and other thrushes and warblers. Bald eagles frequent the preserve during the winter.

Now protected from logging and other development by its status as a state nature preserve, Pine Hills remains at risk of fragmentation from the larger Sugar Creek valley ecosystem. Much of the watershed is privately owned, and the area is considered a prime target for residential development due to its natural beauty. Valuable timber species also could be logged on private land. If adjacent lands are developed or cleared, isolating wildlife within the preserve, species diversity and viability could be reduced.

Pine Hills Nature Preserve lies northeast of Shades State Park and can be reached by traveling east on County Road 800S from the park entrance, then turning north onto State Road 234. There are two well-marked trails within the preserve, but rock climbing, rappelling, camping, picnicking, fishing, and hunting are prohibited.

Further Reading

Bloom, Phil. *Hiking Indiana*. Guilford, CT: Globe Pequot, 2000.

Indiana Department of Natural Resources. "Pine Hills Nature Preserve." http://www.in.gov/dnr/naturepreserve/files/NP_Pine_Hills-color.pdf.

The Nature Conservancy. "The Nature Conservancy's Journey with Nature: Pine Hills Nature Preserve." http://www.nature.org/wherewework/northamerica/states/indiana/misc/art22888.html.

PIONEER MOTHERS MEMORIAL FOREST

The mixed hardwoods of Pioneer Mothers Memorial Forest include 88 acres of old-growth woodlands—one of the few tracts of this size remaining in the state—as well as a buffer zone of secondary forest. With its towering 200- and 300-year-old trees, the virgin forest has been designated a state research natural area and a national natural landmark. Located just south of the town of Paoli in Hoosier National Forest, the 258-acre memorial forest is used for comparative research on forest management practices.

The woodland lies atop the Crawford Escarpment, part of the karst topography of southern Indiana. Its sandstone and limestone bedrock formed over millions of years from deposits at the bottom of an ancient inland sea that covered western Indiana, western Kentucky, and much of Illinois. Later tectonic uplifting raised the area between 650 and 830 feet above sea level, and water erosion formed the sinkholes and subterranean streams that exist throughout the forest. Glaciers from the last ice age did not reach this area; instead, its loam and silt-loam soils were formed from weathering of the sandstone, which generally lies atop limestone layers. Thicker colluvial soil deposits exist at the bases of small hills and slopes, nurturing deeper-rooted trees.

Black walnut, white oak, white ash, and yellow poplar (also known as tulip trees) dominate the canopy in the old-growth forest, with many exceeding 50 inches in diameter. Oaks and hickories are other common tree species, particularly in the younger forests surrounding the area. Other trees include beech, sassafras, hard maple, black locust, red cedar, sycamore, black gum, mulberry, green ash, hackberry, red elm, and Kentucky coffee tree. Vegetation is more sparse in the shady understory of the old-growth forest than elsewhere in the forest but includes such shrubs as flowering dogwood, redbud, pawpaw, spice bush, hornbeam, greenbrier, and wahoo. Common wildflowers include hooked crow foot, jack-in-the-pulpit, mayapple, violets, forest phlox, cream-colored avens, wild ginger, eastern bluebell, trillium, and touch-me-nots (also known as impatiens.) Several fern species also grow here. Some of these plants can be found in the secondary forest as well.

Such varied and intact forest habitat provides shelter to numerous migratory and nesting birds, including songbirds, woodpeckers, owls, and raptors. Such sensitive species as yellow-breasted chat, American woodcock, and ruffed grouse all live within the forest, but research has shown that the secondary forest may provide better conditions for them than the virgin research natural area. Lick Creek, an intermittent waterway running along the forest's northern boundary, also provides habitat for birds, amphibians, and mammals.

Joseph Cox purchased the land that now composes the memorial forest in 1816 and left 88 acres undisturbed. Upon the death of his grandson, who also had maintained the property, his heirs sold the land to a lumber company for logging in the early 1940s. Soon, however, community activists began raising funds to buy back the land for its conservation value, and the U.S. Forest Service later provided half the money needed. The Pioneer Mothers Memorial Forest was established in 1944, so named because of a $5,900 donation from the Indiana Pioneer Mothers Club. In addition to protections given to the entire parcel, the agreement established the area as a public forest and deemed that no trees within the 88-acre virgin woodland could ever be felled.

The old-growth research natural area now serves as an important scientific baseline, allowing forest managers and outside researchers to observe the natural processes of an undisturbed ecosystem and compare its evolution with that of the surrounding woodlands. Logging has been allowed elsewhere in the memorial forest, with older trees cut in some areas to allow shade-intolerant hardwoods to reproduce and provide better habitat for certain declining or threatened bird species. The area also is used for educational purposes.

Pioneer Mothers Memorial Forest is open to the public year-round, with trails throughout the area. Hunting, camping, horseback riding, and bicycling all are allowed in the buffer zone, but these activities are prohibited in the old-growth woods. The research natural area is open to hiking, however, and has a short trail through stands of towering trees. The forest can be accessed off Route 37, south of Paoli.

Further Reading
Auten, J.T. "Notes on Old-Growth Forests in Ohio, Indiana, and Illinois." Technical Note No. 49. U.S. Forest Service, Central States Forest Experiment Station. 1941.

"Establishment Record of the Pioneer Mothers Memorial Research Natural Area within the Hoosier National Forest." Unpublished report on file at the Northern Research Station, Rhinelander. August 14, 1943. http://nrs.fs.fed.us/rna/documents/establish ment/in_hoosier_pioneer_mothers_memorial.pdf.

Myers, C.C., P.L. Roth, and G.T. Weaver. *Pioneer Mothers' Memorial Forest Baseline Data*. Department of Forestry, Southern Illinois University at Carbondale Technical Bulletin, no. 1 83 (1983).

WESLEY CHAPEL GULF OF THE LOST RIVER

The 8.3-acre-wide chasm of the Wesley Chapel Gulf of the Lost River is the largest known feature in the vast subterranean caves of the Lost River—which itself is possibly the longest cave system in Indiana. Located in western Orange County, the 455-acre preserve surrounding the gulf lies atop a vast karst landscape formed by erosion of limestone bedrock. The property is jointly owned and managed by the U.S. Forest Service and The Nature Conservancy in an effort to protect the cave system and its unusual inhabitants, which include three species previously unknown to scientists. Wesley Chapel Gulf also is a national natural landmark.

Named for a nearby church, the gulf is a major geological feature of the Lost River, which flows through a complex cave system of twisting, multilevel channels. With at least 347 unexplored pathways, it is believed to be the longest cave system in Indiana. The river's waters occasionally rise to the surface, as they do at a spring two miles west of the gulf, only to filter underground again through cracks, sinkholes, and solution channels in the underlying limestone. Such subterranean pathways have formed over many years as water combined with carbon dioxide in the air, soil, and decomposing vegetation to form a weak acid that slowly dissolves limestone.

Like other gulfs, Wesley Chapel started out as a collapsed sinkhole, but it is so large (far wider than any other known feature of the Lost River) that scientists think more than one such collapse over a large, weakened area of limestone may have been responsible. As rock at the mouth of the chasm broke down, it would have obstructed the flow of water, leading to further erosion and even greater collapse across a widening area. Today, Wesley Chapel Gulf measures 1,075 feet long and averages about 350 feet wide; its steep walls range from 25 feet on the northwest side to 95 feet on the southwest side.

Deep alluvial soil deposits at the base of the gulf also attest to the massive erosion required for its formation, and scientists have estimated that water flow has dissolved about 720,000 cubic yards of limestone from the site. As the surrounding waters continue to erode the gulf's perimeter, it will collapse further and grow over time. After heavy rains, between 4,000 and 5,000 cubic feet of water per second flow through the Lost River's underground channels. Under such conditions, the gulf's floor floods with up to five feet of churning water. Because of the constant threat of flash floods, recreational caving is prohibited.

Due to the fast rate of water flow through the Lost River's underground channels, along with the overall lack of soils to filter out pollution, the watershed is highly susceptible to contamination. Chemicals, fertilizers, pesticides, and herbicides in runoff waters from surrounding farms and homes threaten the health of this fragile ecosystem. Some water also has been diverted from the watershed for irrigation. Water quality affects animals within the gulf and the larger cave system, which have adapted over time to the unusual conditions—including a complete lack of sunlight in most areas. At least 25 species live in the caves, including three that were first discovered here. Among them are cave beetles, blind crickets, blind cavefish, and blind crayfish.

The Wesley Chapel Gulf preserve was a family farm, with most lands cleared for growing crops and grazing livestock, from 1900 until 1996, when The Nature Conservancy and the U.S. Forest Service purchased the land from the family for a significant discount because the family did not want the parcel to be developed. No farming or grazing has occurred on the land since, but the Forest Service does not actively manage the property, and therefore no above-ground habitat restoration has occurred. The conservancy is working to acquire additional lands between Wesley Chapel Gulf and the Orangeville Rise, the second-largest spring in the state, about two miles to the west. By preventing development on lands adjacent to these two preserves, the conservancy aims to protect water quality in the larger Lost River cave system.

Although recreational caving is not allowed within either The Nature Conservancy or the National Forest preserves, both sites are open to the public for hiking on numerous trails. Wesley Chapel Gulf can be accessed off County Road 350 West, southwest of the town of Orleans.

Further Reading

Durbin, James M. et al. "Wesley Chapel Gulf Revisited: Geomorphic Processes Affecting Development of the Alluvial Floor of a Karst Gulf in Orange County, Indiana." *Proceedings of the Indiana Academy of Science*. December 30, 2003.

U.S. Forest Service, Hoosier National Forest, "Wesley Chapel Gulf." http://www.fs.fed.us/r9/hoosier/docs/wesley_chapel.htm.

WESSELMAN WOODS NATURE PRESERVE

Located within the city of Evansville, the Wesselman Woods Nature Preserve protects 197 acres of old-growth lowland forest—nearly 10 percent of Indiana's total remaining virgin forest coverage. Evansville is the only U.S. city with a population of more than 100,000 to have a woodland of such size within its borders. Designated a national natural landmark, Wesselman Woods also is unusual for the density of its trees and the degree to which tree species at the northern edge of their range dominate the canopy.

Like the rest of the city, the forest stands on top of the former floodplain of the Ohio River. In addition to its virgin hardwoods, which compose the vast majority of the forest, the preserve also hosts some younger woodlands, forested wetlands, a seasonal pond, and a reconstructed prairie. Sweet gum and yellow poplar (also known as tulip trees) are the dominant species throughout the preserve, but sugarberry, southern red oak, and cherrybark oak also are common. The forest has never been logged and has seen little disturbance in its history.

Some trees are believed to be more than 300 years old, and, as a result, the preserve hosts the state's largest examples of several species: Biltmore ash, green hawthorn, mockernut hickory, pawpaw, schenck red oak, and sweet gum. The last two state-champion trees rise to 130 feet and 132 feet tall, respectively. In all, the woods host 117 native vascular plant species—a very diverse population considering the preserve's location and moderate elevation changes (just 20 feet across the entire woods). In addition to the age and diversity of its trees, Wesselman Woods' overall tree density—125 per acre—is considered high, and the area covered by the bases of its trees (187 square feet per acre) is the highest known density of any forest in the state.

Based on an October 2008 preliminary sampling, Wesselman Woods also hosts 3 amphibian species, 2 reptile species, 9 mammal species, and 45 species of bird. Common birds in the preserve include woodpeckers, warblers, owls, raptors, and songbirds. Raccoons, squirrels, and white-tailed deer are abundant, and foxes and coyotes occasionally have been spotted. Marbled salamanders, part of a small and declining population in the state, are among the preserve's rarest animals.

The city of Evansville has worked to protect the salamanders and to create habitat for as great a diversity of wildlife as possible. To this end, a small manmade pond, a reconstructed prairie, and a grassy berm all have been added to the preserve. Efforts to control invasive weeds, including Japanese honeysuckle, which outcompetes native vegetation in some areas, involve ongoing invasive removal and reseeding of native plants. A severe overpopulation of native deer within the preserve also has become a threat. City officials have resorted to killing some deer to keep the population under control and to avoid overbrowsing, which can devastate young saplings and prevent vegetation from reproducing.

Wesselman Woods is located at 551 North Boeke Road in downtown Evansville. The preserve is open Tuesday through Sunday. More than six miles of trails wind through the forest, and a nature center with educational exhibits also is on site.

Further Reading

Davis, Mary Byrd. *Eastern Old-Growth Forests: Prospects for Rediscovery and Recovery.* Washington, DC: Island Press, 1996.

Wesselman Nature Society. "Wesselman Woods Nature Preserve." http://wesselmanna turesociety.org/woods/index.php.

WYANDOTTE CAVE

The largest of southern Indiana's limestone caves, Wyandotte Cave encompasses 25 miles of passages on five levels. Located in Crawford County, the cave is protected within Wyandotte Caves State Recreation Area. It is known for its massive stalactite and stalagmite formations, as well as for its bat colonies, which include the federally endangered Indiana bat.

Like the many other caves, sinkholes, and subterranean passageways of south-central Indiana's karst topography, Wyandotte Cave was formed over many years by slightly acidic water flow. Rain mixed with carbon dioxide in the air to form a weak solution of carbonic acid, which dissolved the alkaline limestone bedrock as it worked its way through cracks in the rock. As these crevices grew, an underground watershed formed, eroding deeper into the earth and leaving behind massive caverns linked to numerous passageways.

Although Wyandotte Cave's streams have since dried up, the effects of acidic rainwater continue to play a role in cave evolution. As the carbonic acid solution drips through the roof of a cave, the water evaporates and leaves behind tiny deposits of limestone carbonate. These slowly build up—as stalactites on the roof and stalagmites on the cave floor, where water drips directly below. Among Wyandotte Cave's most impressive features is the Pillar of the Constitution—a furrowed, white calcite column formed from a stalactite that grew into its corresponding stalagmite. The formation is more than 70 feet wide. Other caverns in the cave system harbor helictites (irregular stalactites) and a 175-foot-tall rock pile. A cavern known as Rothrock Cathedral has a circumference of nearly 1,300 feet.

The cave system maintains a fairly constant temperature all year, averaging 52° F due to constant air circulation known as cave breathing due to drafts frequently felt at its entrance. Such conditions make Wyandotte Cave an ideal site for hibernating bats, especially the federally endangered Indiana bat. Scientists have estimated that, historically, more than one million Indiana bats overwintered in Wyandotte Cave, but 150 years of human disturbance from year-round cave tours had reduced their numbers to 28,584 in 2001. The following year, the Indiana Department of Natural Resources ended winter cave tours that had begun in the early 1850s.

By the spring of 2003, there were about 31,217 hibernating bats in the caverns, and their numbers have continued to rise. More than 4,500 Indiana bats also returned to Bat's Lodge, which had been used by tens of thousands of bats in the 1850s but had been abandoned by the animals by the time systematic surveys began in 1981. During hibernation, the bats are highly vulnerable to any disturbance that arouses them from their rest, since this can lead to burning more energy than the bats have stored for a winter without food. Bats that expend too much energy during this time die before spring or are left too weak to migrate to their summer habitat in nearby forests. The few bats that remain in Wyandotte Cave during the summer months are better able to handle disturbances, according to U.S. Fish and Wildlife Service researchers. Indiana bats also face threats from

Wyandotte Cave. (Timothy K Hamilton)

loss of summer habitat as forested areas become scarcer and more fragmented, and from a lack of insects (their primary food source) due to pesticide use and other environmental contaminants.

Other more common bats also use the caverns, both for winter hibernation and, in the case of females, for giving birth and raising young in the summer. These include gray bats, big brown bats, and Eastern pipistrelle bats. The cave hosts an array of insects, including the globally imperiled Wyandotte cave mite and the state-endangered Wyandotte cave springtail. Salamanders commonly live at the mouths of such caves but are more common in the wetter environs of nearby Little Wyandotte Cave, where residual pools of water also host southern cavefish.

Organized tours of Wyandotte Cave are held from May 1 until Labor Day. The Wyandotte Caves State Recreation Area lies off State Highway 62, just outside the town of Wyandotte.

Further Reading

Cope, Edward D. "On the Wyandotte Cave and Its Fauna." *American Naturalist* 6 (1872):109–16.

Jackson, George F. *Wyandotte Caves*. Livingston, PA: 1953.

Lewis, Julian J. The Subterranean Fauna of the Blue River Area. Final Report, The Nature Conservancy, 1998.

Berry Woods, 52

Bluebell Hollow Preserve, 54

Broken Kettle Grasslands Preserve, 55

Decorah Ice Cave, 57

Fred Maytag II Family Preserve, 58

Freda Haffner Preserve, 59

Grand River Grasslands, 61

Hayden Prairie State Preserve, 63

Loess Hills State Forest, 64

Richard W. Pohl Memorial Preserve at Ames High Prairie, 66

Sioux City Prairie, 68

Swamp White Oak Preserve, 70

IOWA

There is a reason that Iowa is ranked last in the amount of remaining intact remnant natural places—the vast and extremely fertile soils left by the last glaciation. In addition to the great changes to the landscape, Iowa is the midwestern state with the fewest ecoregions—only four. Even without most of the state given over to cropland, it appears at first glance to lack the diversity of the other states. But this is not the case. The glaciers left behind the rich loess soils that now feed much of the country and the world, and also created the kettle lakes in the northeastern part of the state. Forests occur primarily along the river ways, with eight percent of Iowa being covered by trees or forests, a small number by most states but more than most would expect. Historically, about 20 percent of the state was forests. Wetlands were once significant though now are greatly reduced due to farming activities such as ditching and channelization. Prairies, however, were the most widespread ecosystem in Iowa, and major efforts are underway to protect the remaining prairies. Restoration efforts are also significant.

The following entries give a broad overview of the ecological diversity in Iowa. More importantly, these natural areas also demonstrate the enormous challenge in protecting and restoring such landscapes in a state dominated by agriculture. Nonetheless, these sites highlight not only the threats to natural systems but also threats to people in the form of degraded water quality and erosion, to name a few. The management approaches being demonstrated on these preserves are significant not just for the preservation of natural areas in a state with so little remaining high-quality habitat but also for their possible widespread application. Patch-burn grazing, for instance, which is used to replicate historical natural and manmade ecological patterns for managing grasslands, may have application in the agricultural industry as a whole. The Iowa entries cover much of the ecological diversity of the state, the challenging circumstances preserve managers face, and the solutions being implemented.

BERRY WOODS

Berry Woods is a mature high oak woodland—a declining forest type in Iowa and throughout the region. Located just south of Des Moines, the 42-acre preserve harbors a wide array of hardwood trees, wildflowers, and fungi. The Nature Conservancy owns and manages the property, which was named a biological state preserve in 1980.

The forest grows atop the fine loess soils deposited across the southern Iowa drift plain by the last glaciers to reach the area more than 500,000 years ago. The Des Moines lobe, the most recent ice sheet to move across Iowa, stopped just north of Berry Woods, leaving its older soils intact. However, melt waters from the lobe's retreat about 12,000 years ago did reach the area, forming numerous streams and rivers that carved through the previous glacial till and leaving behind rolling hills and valleys.

Large, mature white oaks, red oaks, shagbark hickories, and basswoods dominate the forest canopy at Berry Woods, but their distribution varies depending on topography and soil moisture. Oak-hickory woodlands typically occur in drier areas with well-drained soils—mainly atop hills and on southwest-facing slopes. Common plants growing on the floor of such forests include mayapple, bloodroot, and sedges.

Oak-maple-basswood woodlands grow best in moist conditions but still require well-drained soils. This type of oak forest occurs mainly on north- and east-facing slopes and along the upper hillsides of stream or river banks. Typical ground cover plants here include hebatica, wild ginger, and sweet cicely; many fungi also grow in these areas. Berry Woods hosts numerous wildflowers, including spring beauty, Dutchman's-breeches, toothwort, white trout lily, wild geranium, liverleaf, false rue anemone, Indian pipe, ironwood, bellwort, and showy orchids.

The various forest levels—canopy, subcanopy, understory, and forest floor—provide habitat for many bird species, including migrating songbirds, cavity nesters, and ground dwellers. Among the avian species found at Berry Woods are ruby-throated hummingbirds, eastern wood pewees, catbirds, northern orioles, red-headed woodpeckers, black-capped chickadees, cardinals, white-breasted nuthatches, house wrens, and American robins. Common mammals include opossums, eastern chipmunks, and eastern cottontails. Iowa's high oak woodlands frequently host fox snakes, wood turtles, and ornate box turtles. Along waterways or where conditions are particularly shaded and moist, with sufficient debris on the forest floor, salamanders and frogs also can be found.

Iowa's total forested areas—which cover eight percent of the landscape—have increased in recent decades as cattle grazing has declined and pasture land has reverted to woodlands, and as wildfire suppression has encouraged succession of prairies to red cedar forests in the west. However, oak forests such as those at Berry Woods are declining due to a number of factors. Chief among these are fire suppression, forest succession to more shade-tolerant tree species, and overbrowsing by deer. Prior to European settlement, wildfires and those set by Native Americans frequently swept through Iowa's prairies and the edges of its forests, killing off many tree saplings but leaving the fire-tolerant

Berry Woods. (John C. Hildebrand)

oaks behind and aiding in their regrowth. Fire suppression policies since the 1930s have allowed the oak forest canopy to fill in with mature trees, but oak saplings need a great deal of sunlight to grow. Showy orchids, one of the Berry Woods' well-known wildflower species, also require sunny growing areas and have declined where shade is excessive. Maple trees, on the other hand, thrive in the shady understory and are beginning to take over many oak forests. Overpopulation of deer due to the extirpation of native predators also has taken a toll, because intense deer grazing kills young trees.

In addition to its efforts to preserve the native oak forests at Berry Woods, The Nature Conservancy has opened the site to research and teaching for biology classes at nearby Simpson College. The preserve also is open to the public for hiking and wildlife viewing. Located four and a half miles northwest of the town of Indianola, Berry Woods can be reached via County Road B14, off Route 71 between Milford and Spencer.

Further Reading

Iowa State University. "Managing Iowa Habitats: Restoring Iowa Woodlands." University Extension. http://www.extension.iastate.edu/Publications/PM1351I.pdf.

Van Der Linden, Peter J., and Donald R. Farrar. *Forest and Shade Trees of Iowa.* Ames: Iowa State University Press, 1993.

BLUEBELL HOLLOW PRESERVE

Bluebell Hollow Preserve has one of the greatest concentrations of important rare species in the Midwest and on only 100 acres. The preserve is owned by The Nature Conservancy and is only open to the public on special field trips because of the fragile nature of its inhabitants. Bluebell Hollow Preserve is in the Driftless Area ecoregion, so named because the last glacial advance had little impact on the region compared to surrounding areas. In eastern Iowa, where the preserve is located, the land is very different from the rest of Iowa. The topography consists of steep slopes, rock outcrops, and dense forests. These conditions have created unique habitats. Limestone and dolomite rocks are being weathered away, creating karst features, including caves, sinkholes, and springs. The preserve contains boreal microclimates found much further north in the algific talus slopes at Bluebell Hollow. In fact, Bluebell Hollow has more than 27 such slopes.

Algific talus slopes are rare and unique ecosystem because of the very particular conditions required to create and maintain them. Found only in the Driftless Area of Minnesota, Wisconsin, Illinois, and Iowa, algific talus slopes are also only found in regions of karst topography. A slope of talus—or loose, broken rock—covers fractured limestone bedrock from which cold air (algific means cold producing) emits during the summer. The fractures at the top of the slopes allow water to enter the gaps in the rock in the summer, eventually reaching shale, which angles the water and air toward the slope. In winter, the water freezes from cold air drawn into the passages. As the ice slowly thaws in spring and summer, it draws warm air through the passageways. The warm air passes over the ice, is cooled, and exits through the talus on the slopes, as if through vents, bathing the downward side of the slopes with cool air during the growing season. In the winter, the air movement is reverse, because the air inside the passages is warmer than the air outside. This natural bellows maintains a relatively constant temperature of 37° F to 45° F on the slopes in the summer. This exchange has allowed plants and invertebrates that depend on these boreal conditions to thrive. Such organisms are now only found further north, in the northern parts of Minnesota, Wisconsin, and Michigan on into Canada. The organisms were left behind as the last glaciers retreated, being now isolated in these biological islands much further south from their current typical range.

Nature is often more resilient than we expect, recovering relatively quickly when the effects of environmental degradation are removed. Algific talus slopes, however, are truly fragile systems that are extremely susceptible to outside influence. Also, because the populations surrounding and depending upon them are isolated, once they are gone, they cannot recover. Because this system depends upon groundwater, it is vulnerable to contamination from livestock and dairy farming and damage to the surface from vehicles, livestock, or people, which could also affect the entrances to the passages in addition to changing groundwater flow. The algific talus slopes are covered by a typically sparse canopy of black ash (*Fraxinus nigra*), white and yellow birch (*Betula papyrifera/alleghaniensis*), mountain maple (*Acer spicatum*), and other plants. Loss of this overstory would result in desiccation, warming of the soils, and reducing leaf litter required for the rare Iowa

Pleistocene snail (*Discus macclintocki*), for instance. Protection of this unique ecosystem requires all these conditions but, most importantly, protecting the hydrology of the land surrounding and feeding the system—particularly the areas uphill from the sinkholes and the entrance to the underground passages. For this reason, most algific talus slopes are not open to the public.

The sensitive nature of this unique community highlights one of Iowa's more widespread environmental concerns: groundwater contamination from fertilizer and pesticide applications as well as the impact of livestock production. Algific talus slopes also highlight the interaction of geology, topography, ecology, and hydrology.

Further Reading

Anderson, Wayne I. *Iowa's Geological Past: Three Billion Years of Change*. Iowa City: University of Iowa Press, 1998.

Larson, Douglas W., Uta Matthes, and Peter E. Kelly. *Cliff Ecology: Pattern and Process in Cliff Ecosystems*. New York: Cambridge University Press, 2000.

BROKEN KETTLE GRASSLANDS PRESERVE

Broken Kettle Grasslands Preserve, owned and managed by The Nature Conservancy, lies within the loess hills of the Western Corn Belt Plains ecoregion, a region once covered by tall-grass prairie, now over 75 percent used for cropland agriculture and most of the remainder for livestock. The loess hills is a unique area because the glacial drift is over 200 feet deep in some areas. The loess soils of the deeply dissected hills are highly erodible but relatively stable with grass cover. The loess hills extend from northern Iowa into northwestern Missouri. Because of the steep hills in this area of the ecoregion, land is used more for pasture and woodland than cropland, as is typical in the Western Corn Belt Plains. Broken Kettle Grasslands is The Nature Conservancy's largest preserve in Iowa at 3,000 acres, as well as the largest contiguous prairie.

The preserve's many ridge tops provide habitat for a wide variety of organisms because of the dramatic changes in topography in a relatively small space. In the loess hills one finds plants and animals more common further west in the Central Great Plains ecoregion. Typical tall-grass prairie plants such as big bluestem (*Andropogon gerardii*), side-oats grama (*Bouteloua curtipendula*), and lead plant (*Amorpha canescens*) are common. The western kingbird (*Tyrannus verticalis*), the Great Plains toad (*Bufo cognatus*), and the recent discovery at the preserve of the prairie rattlesnake (*Crotalus viridis*), all whose easternmost range is western Iowa, are representative of this once biologically diverse region.

Because of extensive agricultural operations, most of the tall-grass prairie has been changed to cropland or degraded under extensive grazing. Throughout Iowa, streams and groundwater are degraded because of runoff from fertilizers and pesticides used on cropland as well as the impact of concentrated livestock production (primarily hogs and cattle). In this particular narrow strip of the state along the Big Sioux and the Missouri rivers, where the loess hills are located, erosion is an additional problem. The region has one of the highest erosion rates in the county at up to 40 tons per acre per year. The Nature Conservancy and other conservation agencies and groups are attempting to address these problems with creative management techniques.

Prairie ecosystems occurred on a landscape scale, and it is difficult to manage such an ecosystem, with all its intricacies, on fragmented, small tracts. For this reason, Broken Kettle is a center for The Nature Conservancy's efforts in the northern portion of the loess hills. Some neighboring private landowners, for instance, have given their land as a conservation easement, which protects the land from future development as well as providing financial and technical assistance in the management of the natural resources. Where it is contiguous to other tracts of land adjacent to Broken Kettle, the preserve is effectively enlarged. Such efforts have essentially doubled the size of managed and protected land in the area.

Prescribed burns are also an important management tool. Because prairies are fire-dependent ecosystems, fire is critical to removing old vegetation, adding nutrients back to the soil, and suppressing invasive species, as well as controlling the encroachment of fire-intolerant shrubs and trees. The prairies were dominated by millions of American

Broken Kettle Grasslands Preserve. (Craig Hemsath)

bison that had an impact on the grasslands from grazing to wallowing. This disturbance was part of the prairie ecosystem, and patch-burn grazing is becoming a more common practice that attempts to duplicate the natural grazing patterns of bison. Only parts of the prairie are burned every year, encouraging cattle to graze only newly burned areas, mimicking the traditional grazing of the American bison. In fall 2008, just under 30 American bison were reintroduced to Broken Kettle. Their introduction will enhance the prairie ecosystem. It is only on a large scale, however, that such animals can successfully be reintroduced without their presence being counterproductive. In particular, because of the erosive nature of the loess hills, this will be an important test to see how to best manage grazing animals without creating the erosion problems so prevalent in many grazing situations.

The preserve is open to the public and provides an outstanding opportunity to see beautiful vistas of western Iowa's past landscape as well as one of the more comprehensive tall-grass prairies in the Midwest.

Further Reading

Blanco, Humberto, and Rattan Lal. *Principles of Soil Conservation and Management.* New York: Springer Science+Business Media, 2008.

Foré, Stephanie, ed. *Proceedings of the 18th North American Prairie Conference: Promoting Prairie.* Kirksville, MO: Truman State University Press, 2004.

Olson, George, and John Madson. *The Elemental Prairie: Sixty Tallgrass Plants.* Iowa City: University of Iowa Press, 2005.

DECORAH ICE CAVE

The Decorah Ice Cave sits on only three acres of land in the Driftless Area ecoregion of Iowa but stands out in particular as the largest known glacière, or ice cave, east of the Black Hills. This region stands out from the rest of Iowa with its steep slopes and high relief. The limestone bedrock in this region exhibits typical karst features such as sinkholes, caves, and springs, which are atypical for the rest of Iowa. Although most Iowa caves maintain a relatively constant temperature of around 47° F, the Decorah Ice Cave begins to develop ice after the coldest weather has passed in March, freezing to around 10 inches thick on the cave walls in June, only to melt with the onset of cooler weather in September. The cave was discovered in 1860 and gained international attention. It is believed that the downward-sloping interior traps cold winter air, freezing the surrounding rock. The same rock also warms the air, which escapes through crevices in the roof of the cave, drawing more cold air into the cave. As water enters the cave from spring melts, the water freezes to the walls.

Although most caves in the Midwest occur in the karst region of southern Missouri, this small northeastern region of Iowa contains most of the state's caves. Since the caves are carved out by slightly acidic water dissolving the limestone and dolomite rocks, these formations are the most vulnerable to groundwater contamination. Iowa's streams have been heavily impacted by agricultural operations—in particular, by grazing cattle whose waste contaminates nearby streams. By creating vegetated buffers and not allowing cattle into streams, waterways are afforded some protection. Nevertheless, cattle have had a substantial impact on the aquifers in Iowa, affecting not only natural ecosystems but drinking water as well.

The Decorah Ice Cave is a geological state preserve owned and managed by the city of Decorah, located in the Barbara Barnhart VanPeenen Memorial Park north of Decorah and relatively isolated from agricultural activity. A rare springtail of more northern habit has been found only in this cave in Iowa. Nearby, there are algific talus slopes, and the aligific vents are visible. These are extremely rare ecosystems that depend on warm air being cooled as it moves down underground passages, exiting in openings on the lower portions of the slope. Animals and plants found only in the boreal regions have survived in these cool microclimates. From the ice cave to these algific talus slopes, one is reminded of the importance of what lies beneath the surface; what is usually not seen is as important to the ecosystem above ground.

The cave, though difficult to traverse because of the slippery, icy floor, is open to the public. The cave's historical significance and unique properties in conjunction with the surrounding topography call attention to the geology of the region.

Further Reading

Brick, Greg A. *Iowa Underground: A Guide to the State's Subterranean Treasures.* Boulder, CO: Trails Books, 2004.

Iowa DNR Geological Survey. *Groundwater Issues in the Paleozoic Plateau: A Taste of Karst, a Modicum of Geology, and a Whole Lot of Scenery.* Iowa Groundwater Association Field Trip Guidebook No. 1, Iowa Geological and Water Survey Guidebook Series No. 27.

FRED MAYTAG II FAMILY PRESERVE

The 84-acre Fred Maytag II Family Preserve is located in the Interior River Valleys and Hills ecoregion, which is primarily located in Illinois and is found only in the southeast corner of Iowa along the Mississippi River and into central Missouri and Illinois. The ecoregion consists of wide, flat-bottomed valleys; forested slopes; and dissected glacial-till plains. Unlike adjacent ecosystems, less than half of the area is cropland, 30 percent is pasture, and the remainder is forest. However, in the region of the Maytag Preserve, rivers have undergone dramatic changes, having been channelized with numerous dams and locks upstream from St. Louis. The oak-hickory forest, floodplain forest, and tall-grass prairie have almost completely been replaced by agriculture because the deep, silty soils support cropland. This land was once dominated by water, and flooding from rivers and streams created extensive wetlands.

The Maytag Preserve contains one of the few channel fens in Iowa. A fen ecosystem receives nutrients and most of its water from nonprecipitation sources such as upslope sources and groundwater. Water also flows through a fen so it takes on the characteristics of the underlying bedrock. Fens are less acidic than bogs, which typically occur in the northern states of the Midwest and into Canada. Fens appear as watery meadows absorbing excess runoff, thereby reducing flooding, improving water quality, and providing unique habitat.

Fens are found around the world in northern latitudes, but the fens found in the glaciated Midwest, and in a few unglaciated parts of Missouri, make them a globally rare ecosystem. The extensive hydrological changes to U.S. water systems over the past 100 years from draining the land, channelizing streams, and digging ditches has destroyed or altered the environment needed for a fen. Aerial photos of the surrounding agricultural land provide a dramatic testament to the extensive drainage of cropland. The many turtle and amphibian species; the flowers, grasses, and sedges; and the many rare species found in the preserve add to the significance of this as an already unique ecosystem. With a global ranking of importance, the preserve is special in also being open to the public. The main threat to the preserve and other fens' survival comes from changes to the surrounding hydrology as well as invading nonwetland species. The Nature Conservancy is working with surrounding landowners to increase the buffer around the preserve. This preserve, along with Swamp White Oak Preserve, also owned and managed by The Nature Conservancy and about one mile north on the Cedar River, highlights two unique and quite difference water-dependent ecosystems in close proximity. Together they protect important examples of important ecosystems that were once more widespread as well as calling attention to the importance of wetland ecosystems to Iowa's future.

Further Reading
Amon, J. P., C. A. Thompson, Q. J. Carpenter, and J. Miner. "Temperate Zone Fens of the Glaciated Midwestern USA." *Wetlands* 22, no. 2 (2002): 301–17.
Panno, S. V., V. A. Nuzzo, K. Cartwright, B. R. Hensel, and I. G. Krapac. 1999. "Impact of Urban Development on the Chemical Composition of Groundwater in a Fen-wetland Complex." *Wetlands* 19, no. 1 (1999).

FREDA HAFFNER PRESERVE

The 110-acre Freda Haffner Preserve contains a typical glacial feature frequently found in the Des Moines Lobe, which is the extent of the last glaciation into Iowa—a kettle hole. When a giant block of ice breaks off from a retreating glacier, it sometimes forms a depression with glacial drift called a kettle hole. The Freda Heffner

Preserve's kettle hole is in a prairie, so this is a prairie kettle hole. It is one of the largest kettle holes in Iowa as well as one of the best examples because of the very diverse prairie community associated with it. Iowa endangered species such as the northern grasshopper mouse (*Onychomys leucogaster*) and the regal fritillary butterfly (*Speyeria idalia*) are found here in addition to 360 vascular plants and 34 mosses and liverworts. The preserve is a high-quality wet mesic prairie and sedge meadow with dry gravel prairie on the ridge tops. This varied topography in such a small space creates the circumstances for this incredible diversity. The stunning views of the prairie landscape allow one to see the Little Sioux River valley from the top of the kettle hole. This is one of the more popular preserves to visit and serves as an important educational tool about prairie ecosystems for many students and groups.

The preserve is located in the Western Corn Belt ecoregion, which, in general, is nearly level glacial till covered by fertile loess soils. However, the Des Moines lobe ecoregion, an ecoregion within the Western Corn Belt Plains ecoregion, is distinctive in being one of the youngest regions of Iowa. A distinguishing characteristic from the rest of the ecoregion is its lack of loess over the glacial drift. Most of the natural lakes found in Iowa are in the Des Moines lobe, yet many have also been drained for agriculture. The land most altered in Iowa has been the wet prairie of the Des Moines lobe, having been drained for agriculture many years ago.

The region along the Little Sioux River in this ecoregion has been designated by The Nature Conservancy as one of its priority conservation areas because of the potential it has despite the substantial changes to the land over the past 100 years. Over 2,700 acres have been protected in addition to the Freda Haffner Preserve, primarily at the Iowa Department of Natural Resources Waterman Prairie in this conservation area. In early 2008, The Nature Conservancy had raised over $18 million toward restoration efforts throughout the state, with the Little Sioux River Valley being designated as one of six best remaining areas for conservation in Iowa. The goal is to eventually protect over 20,000 acres in the valley.

The area along the valley is not as suitable for agriculture as other areas in the state but has been extensively grazed and hayed. For this reason, more prairie has survived than in areas converted to agricultural crops. Yet massive drainage projects over the decades have dramatically altered the hydrology of the region, and only a small fraction of the wetland ecosystems remain. The preserve is being managed with prescribed burns, and over 50 acres of prairie has been restored. The incredible diversity of organisms, typical and rare at the preserve, illustrates the possibilities and challenges that face this region.

Further Reading

Andersen, Kathy L. "Historic Alteration of Surface Hydrology on the Des Moines Lobe." *Iowa Geology*, no. 25 (2000).

Kemmis, T. J., E. A. Bettis, III, and D. J. Quade. "The Des Moines Lobe in Iowa: A Surging Wisconsinan Glacier." American Quaternary Association, Program and Abstracts, 13th Biennial Meeting, Minneapolis, 1994.

Samson, Fred B., Fritz L. Knopf, E. Benjamin Nelson, and Al Steuter. *Prairie Conservation: Preserving North America's Most Endangered Ecosystem.* Washington DC: Island Press, 1996.

GRAND RIVER GRASSLANDS

The Grand River Grasslands is not a specific site but a priority conservation area consisting of over 70,000 acres. Nearly all of the tens of thousands of square miles of prairie in the United States have vanished. The Western Corn Belt Plains ecoregion was once covered by tall-grass prairie. Now, 75 percent of the ecoregion is in cropland agriculture, and much of the remainder is used for livestock grazing. The Grand River Grasslands is part of a project to save and restore this once vast landscape. Although the study area is located in the Central Irregular Plains ecosystem, it is just south of the Western Corn Belt Plains and shares with it the rich loess deposits from previous glacial advances, the soil of which makes this some of the best farmland in the world.

This project is unique in that it is attempting to restore and conserve an entire landscape on a grand scale. To do this, The Nature Conservancy, Missouri and Iowa state conservation divisions, private landowners, and businesses are working together to make this a reality. The tall-grass prairie ecosystem did not historically exist in fragments or small sites, as is the case with more specialized habitats such as caves or algific talus slopes. The prairies occurred on a landscape not of human scale. To truly preserve such an ecosystem, with all its intricate ecological components of aquatic, land, and air, one must think on a much greater scale.

The anchor for the Grand River Grasslands is the 3,680-acre Dunn Ranch in Missouri owned by The Nature Conservancy. This site, of which 1,000 acres has never been plowed, is discussed in detail in the Missouri section. Other areas are protected with preserves in Missouri and Iowa. Sites in Iowa such as the 1,000-acre Kellerton Bird Conservation Area and 2,000-acre Ringgold Wildlife Area, which contains 1,000 acres of the largest untilled tall-grass prairie site in Iowa (there are larger prairie sites in Iowa but not of tall-grass), were acquired and are being expanded to preserve remnant prairie tracts, critical habitat, and, most importantly, functionally link all the protected land, private and public, to provide corridors for native species in Iowa. From Dunn Ranch to Pawnee Prairie in Missouri, to Ringgold Wildlife Area across the Iowa border and Kellerton Wildlife area further north, these major preserves serve as anchors in the Grand River Grasslands conservation area. Traditionally, these preserves would be functionally managed and conceptually treated as separate sites. Nature does not function as distinct units but as a continuum with what we distinguish as a type of habitat or ecosystem blending into another. Natural areas are being managed more and more as ecosystems. By having a long-range, holistic approach to conservation in the Grand River Grasslands, private and public preserve managers are taking a more integrated approach. This mindset has been very fruitful.

The large-scale approach has encouraged more private landowners to become involved in protecting and restoring habitat. The creation of a conservation area enables more information to be disseminated to the public as well as making conservation personal. Typically, adjacent private landowners view a preserve as something separate from their own land, neither functionally nor ecologically linked. By presenting the picture of the outdoors as interconnected, people begin to understand that nature knows no boundaries. This increased awareness is encouraged by a stepped-up effort to involve private landowners through projects such as the Conservation Reserve Program in Iowa, which makes money and expert guidance available to landowners who wish to put farmed land into temporary grassland. This is part of the statewide State Acres for Wildlife Enhancement program, which targets other conservation areas in addition to the Grand River Grasslands. It is only through these partnerships with private landowners that such large-scale conservation programs will work.

This landscape-scale approach also helps to disseminate new conservation practices. For instance, the tall-grass prairie is a fire-resistant ecosystem adapted to frequent fires set by nature and Native Americans. However, with tens of millions of buffalo in addition to other large herbivores, grazing was also a significant ecological process. Studies are being done in patch-burn grazing, where different patches are burned each year. Cattle prefer grazing the fresh new growth and leave the older burned patches alone for the most part. This allows legumes (pea-family plants) and flowering plants more light, thereby increasing their diversity. After three years or more, the same patch is burned again. New systems such as this work within established economic realities. The involvement of people in a larger conservation effort while offering conservation alternatives that maintain people's livelihood is a much more powerful approach to conservation. If people have a reason to conserve that directly impacts them, and if their small conservation efforts are part of a much larger effort, they will be more willing to make changes because they can see and are part of the bigger picture, which is the interconnectedness of ecosystems.

There are a number of preserves, public and private, within the Grand River Grasslands in Iowa and Missouri that are open to the public.

Further Reading

Knapp, Alan K., John M. Briggs, David C. Hartnett, and Scott L. Collins. *Grassland Dynamics: Long-Term Ecological Research in Tallgrass Prairie*. Long-Term Ecological Research Network Series, 1. New York: Oxford University Press, 1998.

Regen, Elise, Lois Wright Morton, James Miller, and David Engle. *Grand River Grasslands: Survey of Landowners and Community Leaders*. Iowa State University, University Extension Sociology Technical Report 1025. Ames: Iowa State University, 2008.

Shirley, Shirley. *Restoring the Tallgrass Prairie: An Illustrated Manual for Iowa and the Upper Midwest*. Iowa City: University of Iowa Press, 1994.

HAYDEN PRAIRIE STATE PRESERVE

Hayden Prairie State Preserve encompasses one of the largest tall-grass prairies in Iowa, where less than one percent of these native grasslands remains intact. With 242 acres of wet, mesic, and dry prairie habitat, Hayden Prairie hosts more than 200 plant species, including two that are federally endangered. Located in northern Howard County, the preserve is a national natural landmark that became the state's first prairie preserve in 1945, when it was named for botanist Ada Hayden, one of the first Iowans to publicly advocate prairie preservation.

The preserve's varied grassland habitats are the product of the hilly, loess-covered landscape of the state's northeastern Iowan surface landform. Here, during an intensely cold period between 21,000 and 16,000 years ago, at the height of the last ice age, deposits from previous glaciers were frozen into tundra and permafrost. The freezing and thawing of such conditions moved, loosened, and eroded the rocky landscape into its current form, with glacial boulders scattered across rolling topography.

The rocky, hilly nature of this area also likely saved Hayden Prairie from conversion to farmland—the fate of the vast majority of Iowa's tall-grass prairies. Prized for their fertile black soils, these grasslands were quickly converted to farmland when European settlers began arriving in the 1850s. In general, those grasslands that remain today were either too steep or too rocky to plow. They are now fragments in a landscape of crops and grazing lands, but the largest, like Hayden Prairie, remain ecologically diverse and productive.

Slight differences in elevation and soil moisture throughout the preserve support subtly different grassland communities, though their borders are ill defined and often run into one another. On hills and rises where soils hold low to intermediate levels of water, dry and mesic prairie species dominate. Among these are the quintessential prairie grasses—big bluestem, Indian grass, and prairie dropseed—as well as such wildflowers as heart-leaved alexander, Maximilian sunflower, and wood lily.

On lower slopes and in areas where standing water occasionally accumulates, such species as prairie cordgrass, blue-joint, bog reedgrass, big bluestem, mat muhly, and various sedges are the most common inhabitants. In slight depressions where water collects more frequently, sedges, rushes, cattails, and wetland wildflowers often grow. The increasingly rare Henslow's sparrow, which has been sighted at Hayden Prairie, prefers such lowland prairie habitat.

In all, the preserve harbors more than 200 plant species, including prairie bush clover and the western prairie fringed orchid, both of which are on the federal endangered species list. Other wildflowers in the preserve include Michigan lily, rattlesnake master, bastard toadflax, prairie blazing star, leadplant, and wild rose.

Such flowering plants support more than 20 butterflies, including the wild indigo duskywing, pearl crescent, and eastern-tailed blue. The regal fritillary, a federal species of special concern, and the Powesheik skipperling, a candidate for listing as an endangered species, also are found at Hayden Prairie. Common birds in the preserve include bobo-links, dickcessels, northern harriers, meadowlarks, pheasants, and upland sandpipers. Deer and rabbits also are common.

Like the rest of Iowa's remaining grassland inhabitants, Hayden Prairie's flora and fauna risk a loss of genetic diversity due to their isolation in a fragmented habitat. Prairie flowers and grasses also are under threat from invasive species, including reed canary grass, Canada thistle, white sweet clover, and yellow sweet clover, all of which grow rapidly and will outcompete native vegetation if left unchecked. Aspens and other tree species have begun to shade out sun-loving prairie grasses and wildflowers at the prairie's edges. In the past, frequent wildfires and those intentionally set by Native Americans kept the prairies open, killing off invasive plants and young trees while helping the native grasses reproduce. During the 20th century, however, fire suppression has led to an invasion of woody species in grassland habitats. In an effort to halt woodland encroachment, the Iowa Department of Natural Resources conducts an ongoing weed and tree eradication program with the help of volunteers.

Hayden Prairie State Preserve is open to the public for hiking and wildlife viewing. It has several walking paths along old firebreaks, though these are sometimes obscured or overgrown by the tall grasses. The preserve is located off County Road A23, five miles west of the town of Lime Springs.

Further Reading

Herzberg, Ruth, and John Pearson. *The Guide to Iowa's State Preserves*. Iowa City, IA: University of Iowa Press, 2001.

Corcoran Hill, Elizabeth, and Kate Corcoran. *Hiking Iowa*. Guilford, CT: Globe Pequot, 2005.

Jones, Stephen R., and Ruth Carol Cushman. *A Field Guide to the North American Prairie*. Boston, MA: Houghton Mifflin Harcourt, 2004.

Minnesota Department of Natural Resources. "Prairie Grasslands Description." http://www.dnr.state.mn.us/snas/prairie_description.html.

LOESS HILLS STATE FOREST

Loess Hills State Forest is located on the western edge of the loess hills, the wind-blown glacial deposits that form a distinct range along western Iowa and Missouri. The state forest is comprised of four units of 11,266 acres. The Little Sioux Unit is recognized as a national natural landmark representing the best example of loess topography in the United States. Loess is wind-blown, fine-grained, silty sediment. In the United States, loess is the result of glacial activity. Ancient glaciers ground rocks almost o a powder. After the glaciers retreated and these deposits dried, the highly erodible soils were carried by westerly winds and deposited on either side of the Mississippi and the Missouri rivers. Because the deposits come from ice age winds, scientists are able to determine past climates and wind directions by the patterns of deposits seen today. From aerial photos, the demarcation of these deposits is striking, particularly along the Loess Hills State Forest sites. Human settlement patterns are also clearly visible from the air, with highways and agricultural fields further marking the edge of the distinct flat land adjacent to the loess hills with its more forested and deeply dissected ridges.

This region has the greatest accumulation of loess in the United States, where the depth can be as great as 200 feet or more, creating some of the most dramatic representations of this unique topography. Only in Shaanxi, China, along the Yellow River, is loess found as deep and extensive, making this narrow region in Iowa globally significant. The loess hills in China have been much more greatly altered by natural and human activity than the loess hills of Iowa.

The rich soils of the loess hills and the dramatic terrain support a variety of plant communities and wildlife in a relatively small area. Once black bear (*Ursus americanus*), elk (*Cervus canadensis*), buffalo (*Bison bison*), antelope (*Antilocapra americana*), and gray wolves (*Canis lupus*) roamed this region, but now it is home to much smaller animals. The woods were historically more sparse, open, and parklike. In addition to hunting, fire suppression and agriculture have changed the landscape that once supported the larger mammals. These changes have also reduced the prairies and oak savannas as well as the associated animals who depend on this habitat, such as the greater prairie chicken (*Tympanuchus cupido*), prairie rattlesnake (*Crotalus viridis*), and plains pocket mouse (*Perognathus flavescens*). Coincidently, animals that thrive alongside humans and in a more forested environment, such as white-tailed deer, raccoon, and pheasants, for example, have flourished. Environmental organizations and government agencies such as the Iowa Department of Forestry are looking at ways to reverse this trend. For instance, 600 acres of the Loess Hills State Forest has been planted with oaks, walnuts, ash, and poplars as well as 250 acres of native grasses in attempts to restore the historical landscape.

The forests are being managed according to the Iowa Department of Natural Resources (DNR) Forest Ecosystem Management Guide, which attempts to mange woodlands to benefit wood production, wildlife, water quality, recreation, and the protection of plant and animal communities. This approach highlights the strengths and difficulties many government agencies are facing. While trying to preserve natural communities and the natural systems they depend upon, such as soil and water, public managers also face pressures from agriculture, the timber industry, and manufacturing. Although it is important to balance all these concerns, agencies historically gave preference to individual natural resources. The shift has been toward a more holistic approach, and the DNR's efforts at the loess hills reflect this. For instance, oak savannas are in many ways a transitional forest ecosystem between the hardwoods forests of the east to the grasslands and prairies to the west. These boundaries are not distinct. The DNR is managing the savannas and prairies collectively through the use of prescribed burns and other methods. More than 2,500 acres are burned annually, and other areas are burned on a rotational basis. Tests are also being conducted using various management techniques such as rotational grazing, burning, and shrub removal.

Loess soils have unique properties. They can form steep angles and are stable when dry but extremely erodible and susceptible to collapse because of a lack of clay particles that bind wet soils. The historical savannas and prairies maintained the integrity of the loess hills for the most part. But dense forests with little understory and extensive grazing have exposed these highly erodible soils to the forces of running water. The loess hills are structurally fragile with as high as 40 tons per acre being lost to erosion every year. This is one of the highest erosion rates in the United States. Not only is valuable agricultural land being lost, but local streams are being silted over, which changes the water quality and necessitates frequent dredging operations to maintain ditch and stream channels.

The loess hills present some of the most dramatic landscapes to be seen in Iowa, highlighting the interconnections of geology and living ecosystems and the effects that human activity has had on the land. Through the research and management activities at the Loess Hills State Park, we are better understanding the nature of this unique environment and how to we can balance human activities with the needs of this distinct natural system.

Further Reading

Johnson, Paul S. "Thinking about Oak Forests as Responsive Ecosystems." In *Upland Oak Ecology Symposium: History, Current Conditions, and Sustainability,* edited by Martin A. Spetich. Gen. Tech. Rep. SRS–73. Asheville, NC: U.S. Department of Agriculture, 2004.

Mutel, Cornelia F. *The Emerald Horizon: The History of Nature in Iowa.* Iowa City: University of Iowa Press, 2007.

Mutel, Cornelia F. *Fragile Giants: A Natural History of the Loess Hills.* Iowa City: University of Iowa Press, 1989.

RICHARD W. POHL MEMORIAL PRESERVE AT AMES HIGH PRAIRIE

Encompassing 27 acres of tall-grass prairie, woodlands, and a stream, the Richard W. Pohl Memorial Preserve at Ames High Prairie is in the middle of Ames, a city with a population of about 55,000. Located next to Ames High School, the preserve originally was to be a school parking lot, but community activists argued for its preservation as an educational asset instead. Now managed and leased by The Nature Conservancy, owned by the high school, and protected as a state preserve, the prairie hosts more than 200 plant and bird species in an urban environment.

The soils below Ames High Prairie were left behind by the last glacier to enter the state, beginning about 15,000 years ago. Known as the Des Moines lobe, its southern limit was the present-day city of the same name. When it melted about 12,000 years ago, this glacial lobe left behind sand and gravel deposited by melt water streams, as well as poorly drained clay and peat from more stagnant glacial lakes in depressions. Thus was formed a series of relatively dry, well-drained uplands interspersed with low wetlands and riparian areas.

Ames High Prairie's grasslands occur atop the well-drained soils of low hills and ridges, while its young woodlands grow in the depressions in between and along Squaw Creek, a Skunk River tributary that runs through the property. The preserve's tall-grass prairie "islands" are under constant threat of encroachment by the successional forest, whose trees shade out the sun-loving prairie vegetation.

Despite the small, fragmented nature of the preserve's grassland openings, they host more than 100 plant species. Big bluestem and Indian grass dominate, growing to heights of up to nine feet and up to six feet, respectively. Other common grasses in the prairie include blue-eyed grass, side-oats grama, prairie dropseed, and little bluestem. Among the preserve's many wildflowers are purple coneflower, pale coneflower, alum root, cream wild indigo, downy gentian, giant Saint-John's-wort, lead plant, prairie dandelion, prairie Indian plantain, purple prairie clover, rough blazing star, silky aster, sky-blue aster, thimbleweed, and white wild indigo. Within the preserve's woodlands, elm, hackberry, black locust, and honey locust are the dominant tree species, while poison ivy and Tartarian honeysuckle occupy the understory.

Preserve at Ames High Prairie. (Marisa Landrigan)

The regal fritillary and duskywing rare butterflies that depend on prairie wildflowers; both species frequent Ames High Prairie, as do monarch butterflies. More than 100 species of prairie and woodland birds also use the preserve, including mourning doves, brown thrashers, American goldfinches, song sparrows, American robins, white-breasted nuthatches, and cardinals. White-throated sparrows, common yellowthroats, Swainson's thrushes, and least flycatchers migrate through the preserve in spring and fall. Other residents include raccoons and eastern cottontails.

In an effort to maintain the preserve's prairie remnants, The Nature Conservancy, together with the high school and local volunteers, has an ongoing program to remove saplings and other woodland vegetation from the edges of the grasslands. Another threat to the preserve—the loss of biodiversity due to its isolation from other prairie habitats—is one that has no effective remedy.

Ames High Prairie is open to the public for educational purposes and is used as an outdoor classroom both by the high school and nearby Iowa State University. It is open year-round for hiking and wildlife observation and can be accessed off 20th Street, just west of Ames High School.

Further Reading

Herzberg, Ruth, and John Pearson. *The Guide to Iowa's State Preserves.* Iowa City: University of Iowa Press, 2001.

Jones, Stephen R., and Ruth Carol Cushman. *A Field Guide to the North American Prairie.* Boston, MA: Houghton Mifflin Harcourt, 2004.

SIOUX CITY PRAIRIE

At 157 acres, Sioux City Prairie is one of the country's largest urban native grasslands. It hosts typical Iowa tall-grass prairie species as well as many plants and animals normally found in the Great Plains further west. Located within the boundaries of Sioux City, which has a population of about 82,000, part of the prairie was slated for development before The Nature Conservancy acquired the land and made it a nature preserve in 1983.

The unusually thick silt soils of the loess hills are the basis for Sioux City Prairie's grasslands and its rugged, well-drained landscape. Only one location on earth, in China, has deeper or larger loess deposits. Iowa's fine loess (wind-blown silt) soils were formed by glaciers grinding across the landscape further north during the last ice age. During seasonal melting, floodwaters carried this glacial till south along the Missouri River. As the loose silt became desiccated during later droughts, particularly between 28,000 and 12,000 years ago, winds swept it out of the river valley and redeposited it elsewhere. For this reason, Iowa's deepest loess deposits today are found along the leeward sides of hills and ridges.

With its relatively steep terrain, the preserve hosts dry and mesic (intermediate moisture level) tall-grass prairie on higher ground, and woodlands in its valleys. Within the grasslands, such common prairie vegetation as big bluestem, Indian grass, and side-oats grama grow alongside skeleton weed and scarlet gaura—plants that are far more common in the western Great Plains. Prairie moonwort, an extremely rare fern that is also a Great Plains inhabitant, grows in Sioux City Prairie as well.

Many butterflies live and feed within the preserve's grasslands, including Ottoe skippers, Pawnee skippers, and Olympia marblewings—all rare. The preserve also supports a population of regal fritillary butterflies, a federal species of special concern. Numerous birds frequent Iowa's western grasslands, including migrating raptors, the upland sandpiper, and the rare Bell's vireo.

With less than one percent of the state's native tall-grass prairies remaining, Sioux City Prairie provides critical habitat despite its small size. However, its plants and animals risk a loss of biodiversity due to their isolation from other prairie fragments. This is an issue that has no effective remedy in an urban setting, but much larger prairie tracts nearby—including the 7,000-acre Broken Kettle Grasslands—provide greater diversity in the larger Loess Hills region. The Nature Conservancy has set a goal of preserving more than 100,000 acres in the area.

Invasive plants, wildfire suppression, and the local extinction of such native grazing species as bison and elk also threaten Sioux City Prairie's wildlife. Prior to European settlement in the 1850s, grazing and fires kept invasive species in check while helping the native prairie vegetation, which has evolved to regenerate rapidly after such events. The elimination of these natural processes has allowed trees to encroach on the edges of the grasslands, shading out the sun-loving grasses and wildflowers. Nonnative weeds also have taken hold, including leafy spurge. In an effort to control these invaders within the preserve, The Nature Conservancy has released flea beetles, which eat leafy spurge. The organization also conducts regular, controlled fires with help from biology students at Briar Cliff University.

Sioux City Prairie is an educational resource for both university and local high school students. It also is open to the public. Adjacent to Briar Cliff University, it can be accessed off College Road, where a university lot provides parking at the preserve's northeast corner.

Further Reading

Jones, Stephen R., and Ruth Carol Cushman. *A Field Guide to the North American Prairie*. Boston, MA: Houghton Mifflin Harcourt, 2004.

LandScope America. "Iowa Conservation Summary." http://www.landscope.org/iowa/overview/.

The Nature Conservancy in Iowa. "The Loess Hills." http://www.nature.org/wherewework/northamerica/states/iowa/preserves/art19446.html.

SWAMP WHITE OAK PRESERVE

Swamp white oak savanna is a globally rare ecosystem, an even rarer variant of oak savanna habitat. The combination of open oak woodland and wetland results in an extremely diverse floodplain community ecosystem, of which Swamp White Oak Preserve is one of the most well-preserved examples. The preserve lies in the Interior River Valleys and Hills ecoregion, which is located on the wide, flat-bottomed valleys of the glaciated areas along the Illinois, Iowa, and Missouri border. It is a transitional area between the forested Ozarks to the south and the plains and croplands to the north.

The Nature Conservancy, owner of the 372-acre preserve, is working to preserve habitat along the Cedar River on which the preserve is located. The preserve is also an important conservation site for The Nature Conservancy's Upper Mississippi River Program, which has identified the lower Cedar River as a priority area in the upper Mississippi watershed. The preserve is part of long-term goals of conserving and restoring 5,000 acres of swamp white oak floodplain. By so designating the preserve's importance, techniques used in the restoration and preservation of this unique habitat are given special consideration. For instance, various organizations such as the Iowa Soybean Association, Iowa Department of Natural Resources, University of Iowa, the Natural Resource Conservation Service, and the Environmental Protection Agency, among others, are partnering with The Nature Conservancy in scientific monitoring of the river and various management techniques for their effectiveness.

Swamp white oak (*Quercus bicolor*) is the dominant tree in this habitat. It is one of a limited number of oak trees that withstands periodic flooding characteristic of the preserve. The varied habitat of the preserve is home to more than 320 plant species, a variety of amphibians, and reptiles such as the smallmouth salamander (*Ambystoma texanum*) and the venomous massasauga rattlesnake (*Sistrurus catenatus catenatus*) as well as many resident and migratory birds including the red-shouldered hawk (*Buteo lineatus*).

The sandy floodplains, which are the result of the last glaciation, which ended around 12,000 years ago, have provided the aquatic and terrestrial conditions for the scattered trees and diverse grass, sedge, and forb understory. Conversely, because so few remnants of this savanna type exist, we have few sites as reference for the composition and structure. As a result, it has been difficult to develop proper restoration and management strategies. Often, lowland savannas are managed in much the same way that the more often studied upland savannas are. There are so few lowland savanna remnants because most of the arable land has been drained and converted to agriculture, used for grazing, invaded by exotic species, and encroached by woody species as a result of decades of fire-suppression. The detrimental effects on the lowland savannas have been even greater than that of the uplands.

The Swamp White Oak Preserve was managed from the start similar to the way upland savannas are managed: with prescribed fires and mechanical thinning of undesirable species to reduce the canopy; opening the understory to light; reducing the number of seedlings of shade-tolerant or non–fire-adapted species; and increasing oak seedlings, thereby regenerating the oak species. Controlling reed canary grass, a typical wetland invader, was also made a priority. Management of the preserve, however, was through practice of these techniques without integrating research—that is, without using the scientific method, such as collecting baseline data (data on the habitat composition before management), replication, and monitoring to evaluate the results of using upland savanna techniques on the lowland savanna. The strategy has been to increase the size and relative abundance of oak species, a strategy used in upland oak savannas. New research has suggested that restoration goals should include a mix of tree sizes and species in this more diverse habitat. Increased sedimentation and storm water runoff from agricultural fields is an important concern as well, particularly in a farmland-rich breadbasket state such as Iowa. Sedimentation may have been an important factor in the increase in reed canary grass populations. The excess nutrients may be feeding the invasion of this species, and understanding its effects may be just as important as using fire as a management tool for control of the grass; that is, reduction of sedimentation may reduce the vigor of reed canary grass.

Many lessons can be learned in the process of managing a globally rare community; not just about a unique ecosystem but also the challenges facing those who wish to understand and protect it.

The Fred Maytag II Family Preserve, which contains a rare fen ecosystem, is only about one mile to the south of Swamp White Oak Preserve, illustrating the diverse and high-quality water-dependent ecosystems still found in Iowa and this region.

Further Reading

Brudvig, L. A., and H. Asbjornsen. "Oak Regeneration before and after Initial Restoration Efforts in a Tallgrass Oak Savanna." *American Midland Naturalist* 153 (2005): 180–86.

Dettman, Connie L., and Catherine M. Mabry. "Lessons Learned about Research and Management: A Case Study from a Midwest Lowland Savanna, U.S.A." *Restoration Ecology* 16, no. 4 (December 2008): 532–41.

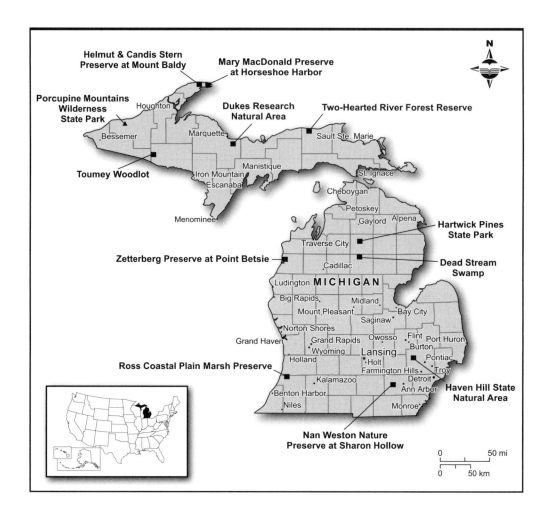

MICHIGAN

Being bordered on three sides by four of the great lakes—Lake Superior, Lake Michigan, Lake Huron, and Lake Erie—Michigan has many unique characteristics. The state is well-forested, with just over half of the state in forest. The Upper Peninsula and northern part of the state contains boreal forests, which transition to eastern deciduous forests in the south. Of course, lake and shoreline habitat are significant features in the natural places of Michigan, with many unique ecosystems particular to these environments. The variety of habitat is by no means limited to the great lakes, though they have a great influence upon natural communities. Wetlands, fens, prairies, bogs, and forest communities are well represented in Michigan in addition to the shoreline habitats. Notwithstanding the many wild places in Michigan, urban pressures are ever increasing and encroaching upon natural areas.

Michigan is relatively untouched compared to the Corn Belt states and heavily populated Ohio. However, logging, agriculture, and urbanization seem even more significant because of abundant natural beauty. Shaped by the last glaciation and continually being shaped by people today, Michigan has many efforts underway to protect and preserve the beauty of its natural places.

DEAD STREAM SWAMP

Located in Missaukee and Roscommon counties, the 11,680-acre Dead Stream Swamp National Natural Landmark is part of a larger 30,000-acre bog forest that is one of the nation's largest northern white cedar swamps. An example of the climax in bog forest maturation, it is also the largest semiwilderness area in the Lower Peninsula.

The swamp's tributaries, including Dead Stream and Cole Creek, flow from the northwestern corner of Houghton Lake and serve as the headwaters of the Muskegon River. The waters average just a few feet deep; they flow across thick mats of peat averaging 3 to 7 feet deep but sometimes reaching a thickness of 16 feet.

The underlying peat—an accumulation of partly decomposed plant matter that builds up below the surface of a bog—supports a network of mosses, shrubs, and sedges in the low, poorly drained flats that comprise the majority of Dead Stream Swamp. The highly acidic, sometimes abiotic conditions created by the peat are similar to those found more commonly in lake bed deposits in the Upper Peninsula. This environment fosters the growth of acid-loving sphagnum-heath mats, a combination of small evergreen shrubs and mosses that eventually breaks down to form the underlying peat.

The Dead Stream Swamp Landmark area also includes about 800 acres of deciduous upland forest on the low, sandy ridges that rise periodically from the bog. Here, white cedar and red, white, and jack pines are the dominant tree species; hemlock, balsam fir, aspen, paper birch, and other species also grow here. The presence of pine trees in particular prompted a great deal of logging in the Dead Stream Swamp in the early 20th century, leading to the construction of a railroad to carry logs to the Muskegon River. Logging continues to threaten white cedar swamps throughout the nation, but logging is prohibited in the Dead Stream Swamp area, which is managed by the Michigan Department of Natural Resources.

Bear Lake, a 60-acre pond surrounded by an extensive sphagnum-heath mat, is another dominant feature of the landmark area. In some areas of the swamp, wild rice grows, attracting such bird species as wood ducks, Canada geese, black ducks, mallards, goldeneyes, and buffleheads. In early spring, scaup, mergansers, and loons converge just

Dead Stream Swamp. (Brandon Schalk)

before the breakup of ice on the swamp's surface. Bald eagles and ospreys also are common. In addition, the Dead Stream Swamp hosts muskrats, mink, river otters, deer, and a significant population of black bears. The existence of such varied animal species—as well as an abundance of fish, including bluegills and pike—lures many hunters and fishers to the Dead Stream Swamp region, but most visitors remain in the 2,100-acre Dead Stream Flooding just above the Reedsburg Dam, which joins with the larger Dead Stream Swamp.

Access to the swamp is limited due to a lack of roads and marked trails through the area. However, it can be reached via boat ramps at the Reedsburg Dam State Forest Campground at the southern end of the Dead Stream Flooding. Motorized boats are prohibited in the Dead Stream Swamp, but all of its 30,000 acres can be reached by paddling a short distance upstream from the flooding through shallow, slow-flowing waters.

Further Reading

Michigan Department of Natural Resources. "Landowner's Guide: Bogs and Fens." http://www.michigandnr.com/publications/pdfs/huntingwildlifehabitat/Landowners_Guide/Habitat_Mgmt/Wetland/Bogs_Fens.htm.

Michigan Department of Natural Resources. "Landowner's Guide: Swamps." http://www.michigandnr.com/publications/pdfs/huntingwildlifehabitat/Landowners_Guide/Habitat_Mgmt/Wetland/Swamps.htm.

Prince, Hugh. "Wetlands of the American Midwest: A Historical Geography of Changing Attitudes." University of Chicago Research Papers, January 1998.

U.S. Geological Survey, Northern Prairie Wildlife Research Center. "Regional Landscape Ecosystems of Michigan, Minnesota, and Wisconsin: Sub-section VII.2.2. Grayling Outwash Plain." http://www.npwrc.usgs.gov/resource/habitat/rlandscp/s7-2-2.htm.

DUKES RESEARCH NATURAL AREA

In the Upper Peninsula's Hiawatha National Forest, the Dukes Research Natural Area (RNA) covers 233 acres of northern hardwood forest meant to act as a control plot for the larger, 5,000-acre Dukes Experimental Forest. Although logging continues in the experimental forest and in the national forest as a whole, the RNA has been left to grow with little human interference since it was set aside in 1974. No logging has occurred within its boundaries for more than 90 years, making it essentially an old-growth forest. Thus, the area provides a comparison for the various and evolving timber-cutting methods within the larger forest and in similar forests throughout the region.

Due to its location near Lake Superior, about 15 miles southeast of the town of Marquette, the RNA receives much higher levels of precipitation than sites elsewhere on the peninsula. Lake-effect snowfall averages 140 inches annually, and reaches 300 inches in some years; average annual rainfall is nearly 34 inches, evenly distributed throughout the year. The entire Dukes Forest is on top of moraine deposits left behind by the Green Bay lobe of a massive glacier as it retreated during the last ice age. Much of its soils—composed mainly of sandy loams with some Linwood muck—drain poorly, resulting in significant wetlands within the forest. Here, white cedar, spruce, and hardwood conifers thrive.

Although the area is overwhelmingly flat, with elevations ranging from 1,070 to 1,100 feet, better drainage exists on slightly higher ground, supporting eastern hemlock (*Tsuga canadensis*), yellow birch (*Betula alleghaniensis*), red maple (*Acer rubrum*), black ash (*Fraxinus nigra*), and American elm (*Ulmus americana*) trees. In intermediate mesic zones, sugar maples (*Acer saccharum*) predominate. Common shrubs in the area include chokeberry (*Aronia melanocarpa*), bush honeysuckle (*Diervilla lonicera*), leatherwood (*Dirca palustris*), winterberry (*Ilex verticillata*), fly honeysuckle (*Lonicera canadensis*), bramble (*Rubus* sp.), autumn willow (*Salix serissima*), beaked hazel (*Corylus cornuta*), common mountain holly (*Nemopanthus mucronata*), and red-berried elder (*Sambucus pubens*).

The Dukes Research Natural Area also provides a home to white-tailed deer (*Odocoileus virginianus*), deer mice (*Peromyscus* sp.), red-backed voles (*Clethrionomys* sp.), least chipmunks (*Eutamais* sp.), eastern chipmunks (*Tamias striatus*), red squirrels (*Tamiasciurus hudsonicus*), gray squirrels (*Sciurus carolinensis*), flying squirrels (*Glaucomys* sp.), short-tailed shrews (*Blarina* sp.), American common shrews (*Sorex cinereus*), snowshoe rabbits (*Lepus americanus*), black bears (*Ursus americanus*), porcupines (*Erethizon dorsatum*), ruffed grouse (*Bonasa umbellus*), and woodcocks (*Scolopax minor*).

Research in the Dukes Experimental Forest began in 1926, the year the land was donated to the U.S. Forest Service by the Cleveland Cliffs Iron Company. Since 1974, the research natural area has provided a control area for the environmental costs and benefits of various timber-cutting cycles, logging methods, and timber restocking and regeneration programs. Such studies have become the basis for management of northern hardwood forests throughout the Great Lakes region. They also provide learning opportunities for landowners interested in managing properties containing northern hardwoods. Environmental groups, however, have complained of a lack of public input prior to sales of timber from areas adjacent to the RNA—including plans in 2005 to log part of the experimental forest between the main access road and the RNA.

There are no roads within the RNA, but it can be accessed via roads through the Dukes Experimental Forest, which lies off Michigan Route 94. Hunting and other human interference is prohibited, but exceptions have been made for local Native American tribes, which are permitted to gather wild plants under strict guidelines for religious or ceremonial use.

Further Reading
"Establishment Report for the Dukes Research Natural Area within the Hiawatha National Forest." Unpublished report, Northern Research Station, Rhinelander. http://www.nrs.fs.fed.us/rna/documents/establishment/mi_hiawatha_dukes.pdf.

Kraft, L. S., T. R. Crow, D. S. Buckley, and E. A. Nauertz. "Effects of Harvesting and Deer Browsing on Attributes of Understory Plants in Northern Hardwood Forests, Upper Michigan, USA." *Forest Ecology and Management*. Digital—October 11, 2004.

Michigan Department of Natural Resources. "Landowner's Guide." http://www.michigandnr.com/publications/pdfs/huntingwildlifehabitat/Landowners_Guide/Introduction/TOC.htm.

Seymour, Robert. S., Jim Guldin, Dave Marshall, and Brian Palik. "Large-scale, Long-term Silvicultural Experiments in the United States: Historical Overview and Contemporary Examples." *Allgemeine Forst Und Jagdseitung* 177, no. 6/7 (2006): 104–12.

Woods, Kerry D. "Intermediate Disturbance in a Late-Successional Hemlock–Northern Hardwood Forest." *Journal of Ecology* 92 (2004): 464–76.

Woods, Kerry D. "Long-term Change and Spatial Pattern in a Late-Successional Hemlock–Northern Hardwood Forest." *Journal of Ecology* 88 (2000): 267–82.

HARTWICK PINES STATE PARK

The 50-acre grove of virgin white pines that gives Hartwick Pines State Park its name is the largest forest of its kind remaining in Michigan's northern Lower Peninsula. White pines once covered the northern part of the state but were heavily logged beginning in the 1840s. Although many of Hartwick Pines' mature trees now are dying, the forest continues to support a diverse array of animals, including large mammals. The state's largest white pine also grows here, measuring 158 feet tall.

The sandy soils of Hartwick Pines are typical of the region's white pine forests and of dry mesic northern forests in general. A type of glacial till, they settled out of ancient glacial lakes or were carried by melt waters across the central Great Lakes region at the end of the last ice age. White pine–dominated forests typically grew up after wildfires, which helped with seed germination and cleared other vegetation, making way for the sun-loving pines.

Many of the white pines in the old-growth forest are more than 200 years old, and they are beginning to die out due to decades of fire suppression that allowed the canopy to fill in, shading out pine saplings and providing habitat for aspen, birch, maple, and other successional species instead. These trees, along with jack pine and oak, are more common elsewhere in the park, where secondary forests have grown up after the former pine forests were cleared.

Still, the dead and dying trees provide a rich habitat for woodpeckers, chipmunks, woodland mice, bats, and salamanders, as well as insects, fungi, and other smaller organisms that rely on dead trees. Birds commonly residing in the forest include hairy, downy, and pileated woodpeckers; red- and white-breasted nuthatches; and northern flickers. Songbirds that live within or frequent the old-growth woods include solitary vireos; blackburnian, black-throated green, and pine warblers; and scarlet tanagers. Wild turkeys frequently roost in the branches of white pines, while the blue racer, a type of snake, prefers the cool, shaded forest floor. Mammals found within Hartwick Pines include red and black squirrels, white-tailed deer, bobcats, coyotes, and black bear.

Typical plants growing in the understory of mature white pine forests include bracken fern, blueberry, bush honeysuckle, wintergreen, chokecherry, and hazelnut. Among the flowering plants inhabiting the forest floor are wild columbine, wild sarsaparilla, big-leaved aster, blue-bead lily, trailing arbutus, whorled loosestrife, Canada mayflower, star flower, and fringed polygala.

Prior to intensive logging between 1840 and 1930, white pines dominated the forests of northern Michigan, including the Upper Peninsula and the northern Lower Peninsula, and the white pine remains the official state tree. Despite their adaptation to sunny conditions, most of these trees did not regenerate due to the practice of slash burning after logging. These fires, intentionally set to clear the forest of leftover debris, burned abnormally hot due to the high volume of flammable brush; most scorched the ground deeply, destroying organic soils and killing even the fire-tolerant pine seed.

Today, Hartwick Pines' forests are protected from human disturbance, but the virgin pines have grown to such an extent that they now provide habitat for shade-loving tree species rather than their own. Since the 1930s, the suppression of small wildfires that help with white pine regrowth have aided this forest succession. Eventually, these towering white pines will all die off, giving way to hardwood forests instead.

Hartwick Pines' virgin forest lies within the 9,672-acre Hartwick Pines State Park, east of Interstate 75 and just north of the town of Grayling. It is open to the public year-round. The Old Growth Forest Foot Trail winds through the white pines, and the Michigan Forest Visitor Center and Logging Museum in the park has extensive information about the area's original forests.

Further Reading

Abrams, Marc D. "Eastern White Pine Versatility in the Presettlement Forest." *BioScience* 51, no. 11 (November 2001):.

Sargent, M.S., and K.S. Carter, eds. *Managing Michigan Wildlife: A Landowners Guide. Dry Mesic Conifers (White Pine)*. East Lansing: Michigan United Conservation Clubs, 1999.

Cohen, J.G. *Natural Community Abstract for Dry-Mesic Northern Forest*. Lansing: Michigan Natural Features Inventory, 2002.http://web4.msue.msu.edu/mnfi/abstracts/ecology/Dry-mesic_northern_forest.pdf.

HAVEN HILL STATE NATURAL AREA

Within just 721 acres, the Haven Hill State Natural Area contains all of southern Michigan's main forest types: tamarack and cedar swamp forest, beech-maple forest, oak-hickory forest, and mixed hardwood forest. Located in the state-managed Highland Recreation Area, Haven Hill protects a wide array of natural habitats in heavily populated southeastern Michigan. Left virtually undisturbed for more than 75 years, it is an anomaly of old-growth forest just 35 miles northwest of Detroit.

Like much of the surrounding region, Haven Hill was formed by the Wisconsin glacier, the Saginaw and Huron-Erie lobes of which converged on the site about 30,000 years ago. When the glacier retreated after the last ice age, it left behind massive glacial deposits known as moraine, forming low-lying hills and ridges. (At 1,132 feet, Haven Hill is Oakland County's highest natural hill.) Melt waters deposited additional sand and gravel over low-lying areas, forming outwash plains, low-lying wetlands, and numerous small ponds.

Ford Motor Company founder Edsel Ford purchased the land in 1923 and used it to build an estate and small farm, but he left much of the property in its natural state. One exception was the creation of Haven Hill Lake, which Ford formed by damming a small stream that previously had run through a marshland. After Ford's death, his family sold the land to the state of Michigan in 1946. Since then, the state Department of Natural Resources has worked to restore historical buildings but has otherwise left the property untouched. Haven Hill provides a home to numerous birds, reptiles, amphibians, and mammals as well as an abundance of wildflowers, shrubs, and trees.

Lowland conifers, primarily tamarack with smaller numbers of northern white cedar, dominate the Haven Hill area's lowest elevations, thriving in the peat mats that have formed through the partial decomposition of plant matter in wetlands. Tamaracks, common to southern Michigan, prefer full sunlight and the acidic soils of bogs, where peat mats formed by sphagnum moss and sedges can be several feet thick. Ferns, orchids, and such shrubs as bog rosemary and leatherleaf also grow here. Birds common to tamarack bogs include white-throated sparrows, ovenbirds, red-eyed vireos, Nashville warblers, and common yellowthroats. Northern white cedar swamplands, more often found in northern Michigan, occur in more alkaline soil conditions, where water flows through calcium-rich soil deposits.

Haven Hill's hardwood species have established on higher ground surrounding the lowland swamp forests. Beeches and maples prefer the moist but well-drained soils just above the swamps; this forest type also may include birch, basswood, white pine, and hemlock. The area's oak-hickory forests grow best in the sandy, well-drained soils of the highest elevations. Such forests are common to southern Michigan and may also include yellow poplar, elm, maple, and other hardwoods. At Haven Hill, as in many other parts of the state, different types of hardwood forests often blend into one another.

Historically, Michigan's hardwood forests have been valued for logging, but the Haven Hill State Natural Area is protected and has not seen significant logging during the past century. More vulnerable today are the lowland conifers of Haven Hill's swamps, which are susceptible to insect damage, fluctuations in water levels, and uprooting of trees by the wind (windthrow). All of these dangers have threatened the area at one time or another as tracts of land were drained (or, in the case of Haven Hill Lake, inundated) to make way for residential development.

The most recent major disturbance came in the form of a utility corridor built along Michigan Route 59, which runs along Haven Hill's northern boundary. The project cleared land within a mile of the highway, raising fears that the changes could result in more windthrow of lowland conifers, since the surrounding hardwoods that protected them have now largely been cleared. A restoration plan proposed by University of Michigan researchers notes that such clear-cuts also create ready habitat for invasive, nonnative plants as well as the destruction of any new native plant growth by the area's many deer. The plan calls for the control and monitoring of nonnative species, planting of additional native plant species where appropriate, and ongoing monitoring of changes to the Haven Hill Natural Area. To this end, volunteer work projects have been organized to remove invasive species from both the natural area and the surrounding corridor.

Haven Hill State Natural Area is easily accessible. Schools, universities, and international organizations use its educational facilities, and visitors can engage in bird-watching, viewing of wildflowers, hiking, fishing, and historical tours of some of Edsel Ford's original estate buildings.

Further Reading

Bay, Jas. W. *Glacial History of the Streams of Southeastern Michigan*. Bulletin No. 12. Bloomfield Hills, MI: Cranbrook Institute of Science, 1938.

Bonnicksen, Thomas M. *America's Ancient Forests: From the Ice Age to the Age of Discovery*. New York: John Wiley, 2000.

Michigan Department of Natural Resources. "Landowner's Guide." http://www.michigandnr.com/publications/pdfs/huntingwildlifehabitat/Landowners_Guide/Introduction/TOC.htm.

Randall, Carolyn. "Forest Types in Michigan." In *Forest Types in Michigan*. East Lansing: Michigan State University Pesticide Safety Education, 2000. http://www.pested.msu.edu/Resources/bulletins/pdf/Category2/Chap5.pdf.

Stanley, Geo M. *Geology of the Cranbrook Area*. Bulletin No. 6. Bloomfield Hills, MI: Cranbrook Institute of Science, 1936.

Thompson, Paul Woodward. "Vegetation of Haven Hill, Michigan." *American Midland Naturalist* 50, no. 1 (July 1953): 218–23.

Helmut & Candis Stern Preserve at Mount Baldy

Overlooking Lake Superior from near the tip of the Keweenaw Peninsula, Mount Baldy, also known as Lookout Mountain, hosts a unique mix of plant species specially adapted to the harsh conditions of the northern bald community at its peak. Protected within The Nature Conservancy's 1,531-acre Helmut & Candis Stern Preserve, the mountain's rocky ridge line rises to just 730 feet but hosts alpine species typically found at much higher elevations, as well as western prairie plants and stunted stands of white cedar and ground juniper. All have evolved to cope with the strong winds and cold temperatures of Lake Superior winters.

The Helmut & Candis Stern Preserve encompasses all of Mount Baldy, including lower slopes covered with a mix of conifers and northern hardwoods. Species typical of such forests include jack, red, and white pines; hemlocks; balsam fir; aspens; northern pin oaks; hickories; maples; and beech. However, it is the mountain's northern bald habitat, a mix of treeless openings interspersed with wind-twisted cedar and juniper, that interested The Nature Conservancy when it created a preserve there in 2005.

Northern balds exist exclusively on Precambrian bedrock escarpments of such volcanic materials as basalts or basaltic conglomerates. They consist of exposed rock and thin, slightly acidic soils that absorb little moisture and support only sparse vegetation. Such formations can be found on nearby Isle Royale and also extend from the northeastern tip of the Keweenaw Peninsula southwest into much of the western Upper Peninsula. However, Keweenaw's northern balds, formed on conglomerate bedrock, appear to host more varied plant species than the basalt northern balds to the southwest.

In a typical northern bald environment, such hardy shrubs as bearberry (*Arctostaphylos uva-ursi*), common juniper (*Juniperus communis*), staghorn sumac (*Rhus typhina*), and low sweet blueberry (*Vaccinium angustifolium*) dominate. Other common vegetation includes poverty grass (*Danthonia spicata*), wild strawberry (*Fragaria virginiana*), western smartweed (*Polygonum douglasii*), prairie cinquefoil (*Potentilla arguta*), three-toothed cinquefoil (*P. tridentata*), early saxifrage (*Saxifraga virginiensis*), ground cedar (*Diphasiastrum tristachyum*), and sand violet (*Viola adunca*). Such vegetation is uniquely suited to northern bald habitats, where heavy snow, ice, and extreme winds distort and damage larger flora into what is known as krummholz growth. Northern bald ridge lines typically support only grasses, shrubs, and other low-lying vegetation, while dwarfed trees occur at slightly lower elevations or in pockets with more protection from the wind.

Ferns also thrive in some areas, particularly on southern slopes, taking advantage of the relative shelter and the moisture from frequent fog off Lake Superior. Mount Baldy's southern face drops in a 230-foot cliff from the ridge line—another feature typical of northern bald escarpments—and in many areas has eroded into talus slopes. Rare flora found in such environments include the threatened small blue-eyed Mary (*Collinsia parviflora*) and prairie buttercup (*Ranunculus rhomboideus*), as well as the northern gooseberry (*Ribes oxyacanthoides*), listed by the state as a species of special concern. The rare redstem ceanothus (*Ceanothus sanguineus*), also listed as threatened, lives almost exclusively on the southern talus slopes of northern bald habitats.

Various raptors depend on the northern bald environments, including the threatened merlin (*Falco columbarius*), a small falcon that makes its home in northern forests and prairies. Many other birds pass over the area during spring and fall migrations.

Due to the harsh conditions on Mount Baldy, its plant communities are slow to recover from damage and are therefore highly susceptible to trampling and other human interference. As a result, The Nature Conservancy has made a concerted effort to educate visitors about staying on the trail that ascends to the top of the mountain. Such invasive plant species as spotted knapweed (*Centaurea maculosa*), oxeye daisy (*Chrysanthemum leucanthemum*), Canada bluegrass (*Poa compressa*), and sheep sorrel (*Rumex acetosella*) also have caused problems, outcompeting native plants for space. To control invasives, the conservancy is working to remove them and also to maintain healthy forests on Mount Baldy's lower slopes as a way of limiting the nonnative plant encroachment.

The Helmut & Candis Stern Preserve is located along the Eagle Harbor Shortcut Road off U.S. Route 41. From a gravel parking lot about 1,000 feet off the road, visitors must walk one and a half miles to The Nature Conservancy property boundary and the start of the Nicole Bloom Memorial Trail that leads steeply to the top of Mount Baldy. The mountain also can be viewed from a turnoff along Brockway Mountain Drive, between the towns of Eagle Harbor and Copper Harbor. Hiking, skiing, snowshoeing, and environmental education and research all are allowed within the preserve.

Further Reading

Albert, D. A., P. Comer, D. Cuthrell, D. Hyde, W. MacKinnon, M. Penskar, and M. Rabe. "The Great Lakes Bedrock Lakeshores of Michigan." Lansing: Michigan Natural Features Inventory, 1997.

Bornhorst, T. J., and W. I. Rose. "Self-guided Geological Field Trip to the Keweenaw Peninsula, Michigan." *Proceedings of the Institute on Lake Superior Geology* 40, Part 2 (1994):.

Broll, Gabriele, and Beate Keplin. "Mountain Ecosystems: Studies in Treeline Ecology." 2005.

Dorr, John Adam, and Donald F. Eschman. *Geology of Michigan*. Ann Arbor: University of Michigan Press, 1970.

Faber-Langendoen, D., ed. *Plant Communities of the Midwest: Classification in an Ecological Context*. Arlington, VA: Association for Biodiversity Information, 2001.

Given, D. R., and J. H. Soper. 1981. "The Arctic-Alpine Element of the Vascular Flora at Lake Superior." National Museums of Canada, Publication in Botany 10 (1981): 1–70.

LaBerge, G. L. *Geology of the Lake Superior Region*. Phoenix, AZ: Geoscience Press,1994.

Michigan State University Extension, Michigan Natural Features Inventory. "Michigan's Natural Communities: Northern Bald." http://web4.msue.msu.edu/mnfi/communities/community.cfm?id=10695.

MARY MACDONALD PRESERVE AT HORSESHOE HARBOR

A t the northernmost tip of the Upper Peninsula, the 1,433-acre Mary MacDonald Preserve at Horseshoe Harbor encompasses critical bedrock lakeshore and bedrock glade habitat on the shores of Lake Superior. It also protects 11 threatened or rare species found within the preserve. With strong winds off the lake and exposed rock outcroppings underlying much of the area, the preserve is primarily a landscape of sparse, hardy vegetation. However, rock ridges along the shore protect a boreal forest of conifers and hardwoods further inland.

Thrust upward by a Precambrian rift in the middle of the North American continent some 600 million years ago, the Mary MacDonald Preserve lies atop the basalt and volcanic conglomerate bedrock of the Keweenaw Peninsula. This base supports the volcanic bedrock lakeshore habitat, which is defined by an extreme scarcity of soils; those that have formed exist only in cracks and gaps in the bedrock. High winds also blow frequently across the preserve—especially in the harsh, cold winter months. As a result, vegetation is scarce, with only moss and lichens surviving in many areas.

Further from the lake, hardy herbs and woody shrubs grow in moist depressions and cracks between the rocks. In this intermediate zone, such herbaceous species as harebell (*Campanula rotundifolia*), wild strawberry (*Fragaria virginiana*), three-toothed cinquefoil (*Potentilla tridentata*), downy oatgrass (*Trisetum spicatum*), yarrow (*Achillea millefolium*), hair grass (*Deschampsia cespitosa*), butterwort (*Pinguicula vulgaris*), fescue (*Festuca saximontana*), and dwarf Canadian primrose (*Primula mistassinica*) exist along with such shrubs as the threatened bog-bilberry (*Vaccinium uliginosum*) and low sweet blueberry (*Vaccinium angustifolium*), and bearberry (*Arctostaphylos uva-ursi*), common juniper (*Juniperus communis*), creeping juniper (*J. horizontalis*), and dwarf raspberry (*Rubus pubescens*).

Beyond the lakeshore, along the preserve's cliffs and ridges, volcanic bedrock glade habitat supports many of the same plant species, along with scattered, wind-blown trees that rarely grow larger than shrubs. The most common include balsam fir (*Abies balsamea*), northern white cedar (*Thuja occidentalis*), paper birch (*Betula papyrifera*),quaking aspen (*Populus tremuloides*), white pine (*Pinus strobus*), and white spruce (*Picea glauca*). Growing on steep terrain, in thin soils that promote shallow root systems, these trees are particularly prone to uprooting by the wind. However, they also provide a barrier that shelters a more diverse boreal forest habitat from the fierce elements of Lake Superior's shore.

In the boreal forest, slower-growing conifers and hardwood trees thrive in the damp conditions fostered by heavy precipitation and fog. Here grow many of the same trees that exist in the volcanic bedrock glade. In this more protected area, however, they reach much larger proportions and are joined by such species as red oak and red, white, and jack pines. Soils remain thin in the boreal forest, so shallow roots are the norm as they are in the bedrock glade, leaving trees subject to high rates of windthrow even here. The dense forest canopy lets in little sunlight, thus leaving a sparse understory.

The varied habitats in the preserve provide a home to such notable animals as the black bear and snowshoe hare; they also shelter peregrine falcons, snowshoe hares, ruffed grouse, golden-crowned kinglets, black-throated green warblers, and yellow-rumped warblers. The preserve's coastal location provides critical feeding and resting grounds for a host of migrating birds each spring.

To protect this Keweenaw Peninsula ecosystem, The Nature Conservancy established the preserve in 1982, when local resident Mary MacDonald donated 535 acres for conservation. The conservancy has purchased additional lands in the intervening years to bring the preserve to its current size and protect a larger swath of this fragile ecosystem.

The thin soils, lichens, and mosses of the bedrock lakeshore and glade communities are especially prone to damage by foot traffic and off-road vehicles, and all vegetation is slow to recover in the harsh climate. In similar habitats elsewhere in the region, shoreline development and logging of the boreal forest are also major threats. Such activities are banned at the Mary MacDonald Preserve, however. The Nature Conservancy also prohibits bicycles, and it encourages hikers to stay on marked trails and respect the fragility of this environment.

The Mary MacDonald Preserve is open to the public year-round, from dawn until dusk. It can be reached from the town of Copper Harbor by taking U.S. Route 41 until the pavement ends, then continuing down a narrow dirt road for another two miles.

Further Reading

Dorr, John Adam, and Donald F. Eschman. *Geology of Michigan*. Ann Arbor: University of Michigan Press, 1970.

Kost, M. A., D. A. Albert, J. G. Cohen, B. S. Slaughter, R. K. Schillo, C. R. Weber, and K. A. Chapman. "Natural Communities of Michigan: Classification and Description." Michigan Natural Features Inventory, Report No. 2007–21, Lansing, MI, 2007.

NAN WESTON NATURE PRESERVE AT SHARON HOLLOW

The Nan Weston Nature Preserve at Sharon Hollow protects the headwaters and upper floodplain of the River Raisin—as well as one of the state's few remaining high-quality southern mesic forests. Administered by The Nature Conservancy, the 249-acre preserve is just outside the town of Manchester, between the cities of Jackson and Ann Arbor in southeastern Michigan. The southern mesic (intermediate moisture-level) forest here is the only such habitat left in the upper River Raisin watershed. Along with floodplain forests in swampy areas of the Nan Weston Nature Preserve, this environment is rare or nonexistent further downstream, as the river winds through mainly agricultural land.

Beech and sugar maples dominate southern mesic forests, which once covered much of southern Michigan and much of the southern Great Lakes region. Such trees thrive in southern Michigan's well-drained soils—mainly silty loam, loam, or sandy loam deposited by three glacial lobes that joined here to form the Jackson interlobate between 13,000 and 16,000 years ago. At the Nan Weston Nature Preserve, silver maple, red ash, and white oak also grow in the mesic habitat, which occurs along the banks of the river and its tributaries, as well as on other areas of slightly higher ground within its territory. In lower-lying, swampy areas in the floodplain, black ash, American elm, and yellow birch are the dominant tree species. Small kettle lakes are common throughout the area.

Although the floodplain forest in and near Sharon Hollow is young, with little old growth due to previous logging, it nonetheless provides critical shelter to several rare and endangered species. Among them are the federally endangered Indiana bat (*Myotis sodalist*), the locally rare blue ash tree (*Fraxinus quadrangulata*), and the locally rare herbs goldenseal (*Hydrastis canadensis*) and American ginseng (*Panax quinquefolius*). An abundance of wildflowers also grow throughout the preserve, blooming beginning in early May and continuing throughout the summer.

Migratory songbirds rest and feed in the Nan Weston Nature Preserve in both spring and fall, and many bird species live in the area year-round. Among those commonly seen in the preserve are the barred owl; sandhill crane; chestnut-sided, wood, and cerulean warblers; dickcessel; arcadian flycatcher; and northern oriole. The distinctive mating vocalizations of male northern spring peepers (*Pseudacris crucifer*), one of several frog species in the preserve's wetlands, can be heard beginning in late April.

Numbers of white-tailed deer—another common forest resident—have exploded within the area due to the elimination of such natural predators as wolves and cougars, both of which were locally extinct by the beginning of the 20th century. Overbrowsing by deer has taken a major toll on plant reproduction, prompting The Nature Conservancy to allow regulated deer hunting within the preserve.

Other threats to the preserve—and the River Raisin watershed in general—include increased residential and commercial development, the continued effects of past logging, and disturbance by agriculture. As the area developed, many natural wetlands were drained, and today runoff of fertilizers and pesticides from farms and increased erosion from tillage of the land threaten the health of the river, its tributaries, and the forests they support. Such development also has fragmented remaining forests in the area, leading to concerns that pockets of threatened and endangered species are losing genetic diversity due to their isolation from one another. The Nature Conservancy is working to determine how many additional populations of Indiana bats might exist in the area and whether they can survive in the preserve long term.

With its relatively healthy forest ecosystem, the preserve is an important buffer to runoff from surrounding homes, businesses, and farms. Its soils filter out pollutants before they can reach streams, rivers, and, eventually, the Great Lakes. The preserve also remains relatively free of invasive plant species, though some—especially garlic mustard—threaten to encroach on the forest from adjacent areas.

The Nature Conservancy purchased 22 acres in Sharon Hollow in 1983, but the preserve was greatly expanded in 1992, when the family of local bird-watcher Nan Weston made a donation allowing the conservancy to expand the property to its current size. The Nan Weston Nature Preserve is open year-round, from dawn until dusk, for hiking, cross-country skiing, and bird-watching. It is located off of Michigan Route 52, south of Interstate 94, on Easudes Road outside the town of Manchester.

Further Reading

Dodge, K. E. "River Raisin Assessment." Michigan Department of Natural Resources, Fisheries Special Report #23, 1998.

Kost, M. A., D. A. Albert, J. G. Cohen, B. S. Slaughter, R. K. Schillo, C. R. Weber, and K. A. Chapman. "Natural Communities of Michigan: Classification and Description." Michigan Natural Features Inventory, Report No. 2007–21, Lansing, MI, 2007. http://web4.msue.msu.edu/mnfi/abstracts/ecology/Mesic_southern_forest.pdf.

Michigan Department of Environmental Quality Staff Report. A Biological Survey of the River Raisin Watershed, Jackson, Hillsdale, Lenawee, Monroe, and Washtenaw Counties, Michigan, June, August, and September 2000. MI/DEQ/SWQ-01/116, 2002.

Seelbach, P. W., M. J. Wiley, J. C. Kotanchik, and M. E. Baker. A Landscape-Based Ecological Classification System for River Valley Segments in Lower Michigan (MI-VSEC version 1.0). MDNR Fisheries Research Report 2036, 1997.

U.S. Geological Society, Northern Prairie Wildlife Research Center. "Regional Landscape Ecosystems of Michigan, Minnesota, and Wisconsin: Sub-Section VI.1.3. Jackson Interlobate." http://www.npwrc.usgs.gov/resource/habitat/rlandscp/s6-1-3.htm.

PORCUPINE MOUNTAINS WILDERNESS STATE PARK

Porcupine Mountains Wilderness State Park, in Michigan's western Upper Peninsula, contains what is considered by the state to be the largest tract of virgin northern hardwood forest in North America. Designated as a national natural landmark, the park's approximately 60,000 acres on the southern shores of Lake Superior include 35,000 acres of primary forest that has never been logged. Also within its boundaries are previously logged forests of successional aspen and birch, an exposed basalt rock escarpment supporting northern bald habitat, and various types of wetlands. With topography ranging from 601 feet at the lakeshore to 1,958 feet at Summit Peak, the Porcupine Mountains are two billion years old—part of one of the world's oldest mountain chains.

Rising sharply from Lake Superior, the mountains are Precambrian bedrock made up of basalts, basaltic conglomerates, and shale. (The shale, rich in copper, was the source of copper mining in the area through the mid-1900s.) Most of this underlying rock is covered with loam and clay soils deposited by glaciers at the end of the last ice age. The bedrock is exposed, however, along a 12-mile-long ridge line separating the lake from the Big Carp River Valley and Lake of the Clouds. This outcropping supports northern bald habitat, with hardy shrubs, grasses, and other low-lying vegetation clinging to cracks in the rock. Among the most common are bearberry (*Arctostaphylos uva-ursi*), common juniper (*Juniperus communis*), and low sweet blueberry (*Vaccinium angustifolium*). Dwarfed pines also grow in some spots along the escarpment.

Mature eastern hemlock and sugar maples dominate the virgin northern hardwood forest at the center of the park, forming a closed canopy that lets in little sunlight and limits growth of plants in the understory. Yellow birch, red maple, basswood, green ash, and northern red oak also grow in the forest. Along many of the park's boundaries, including its one and a half miles of Lake Superior shoreline, aspen and birch have replaced logged forests. Within the flood plains of the Big Carp and Little Carp rivers, wetland forests of white cedar, tamarack, and black ash are common. Thick mats of peat often underlie such lowland conifer forest. Also growing in the park are the rare western monkey flower, small blue-eyed Mary, ram's head lady's slipper, Hooker's fairy-bells, slender cliff brake, and male fern—all of which are rare, threatened, or endangered species.

Such varied vegetation and environments support numerous locally rare and endangered animals as well, including the gray wolf, wood turtle, peregrine falcon, merlin, and bald eagle. More common bird species include the barred owl, pileated woodpecker, northern parula, Swainson's thrush, hermit thrush, common merganser, wood duck, great blue heron, American bittern, and various warbler species. Black bears, fishers, varying hares, red foxes, coyotes, bobcats, porcupines, striped skunks, and small numbers of moose also have made the Porcupine Mountains their home. Reptilian and amphibian species in the park include yellow-spotted salamanders, wood frogs, wood turtles, northern ring-necked snakes, and red-bellied snakes. Notable insects include horntails, giant ichneumon wasps, dragonflies, and stoneflies.

Michigan's largest state park and one of the largest wilderness areas in the Midwest, the Porkies, as they are known locally, were established as a state park in 1945 to preserve this ecosystem by preventing further logging in the area. However, continued disturbances from copper mining as well as proposals for a road through the park in the 1960s prompted the state legislature to establish Porcupine Mountains State Park as an official wilderness area in the early 1970s. Under the designation, such activities, as well as the use of bicycles and off-road vehicles, are prohibited.

Open year-round, the park encompasses about 90 miles of hiking trails and numerous backcountry campsites. In winter, it is open to cross-country skiing, with 26 miles of groomed trails. Most of the park is open to hunting, and fishing also is allowed in Mirror Lake, Lake of the Clouds, and area rivers. Porcupine Mountains Wilderness State Park straddles Ontonagon and Gogebic counties, along Lake Superior, and can be reached via Michigan Route 107 west of Silver City.

Further Reading

Adams, Charles Christopher, et al. *An Ecological Survey in Northern Michigan.* University of Michigan University Museum. [City]: Wynkoop Hallenbeck Crawford, 1906.

Neumann, David, and Georgia Peterson. "Northern Hardwood Forest Management." Michigan State University Extension Bulletin. E2769. August 2001. http://forestry.msu.edu/extension/extdocs/E2769.pdf.

Frelich, Lee E., and Craig G. Lorimer. "Natural Disturbance Regimes in Hemlock-Hardwood Forests of the Upper Great Lakes Region." *Ecological Monographs* 61, no. 2 (June 1991): pp. 145–64.

Sargent, M.S., and K.S. Carter, eds. 1999. *Managing Michigan Wildlife: A Landowners Guide.* East Lansing: Michigan United Conservation Clubs, 1999.

U.S. Geological Survey, Northern Prairie Wildlife Research Center. "Regional Landscape Ecosystems of Michigan, Minnesota, and Wisconsin: Subsection IX.8. Lake Superior Lake Plain." http://www.npwrc.usgs.gov/resource/habitat/rlandscp/sub9-8.htm.

ROSS COASTAL PLAIN MARSH PRESERVE

The 1,449-acre Ross Coastal Plain Marsh Preserve hosts ancient sand dunes interspersed with seasonally flooded wetlands known as coastal plain marshes. Located in the southwest corner of the state not far from Lake Michigan, these marshes support plants and animals normally found along the coasts of the Atlantic Ocean and the Gulf of Mexico. Such habitat—rare in the Great Lakes region—prompted The Nature Conservancy to establish the preserve on donated land in 1988. Northern hardwood forests exist within the preserve's boundaries as well.

Also known as a dune and swale complex, the preserve's series of parallel sand dunes and low, seasonally flooded meadows formed about 4,000 years ago along the shores of an ancient body of water, Lake Nipissing, that preceded the current Great Lakes. Created by the melting of massive glaciers at the end of the last ice age, Lake Nipissing's water levels were between 25 and 30 feet higher than those of today's Lake Michigan. As with more recent dunes along Lake Michigan, Lake Nipissing's dunes were formed from sand deposited in its bays by rivers and swept along the shore by winds and lake currents. As the lake receded, it formed successive dunes separated by depressions. Today these low points host the coastal plain marshes for which the preserve is known.

Forty-two coastal plain marshes have been identified in Michigan, mainly in its southwest corner; the Ross Coastal Plain Marsh Preserve contains three of them. The sandy soils of such marshes are highly acidic and low in nutrients. They typically flood in spring and dry up almost completely by late summer. Such conditions provide ideal habitat for various grasses, rushes, and sedges at the edges of depressions, which dry up first, and floating aquatic plants closer to the middle, where water lingers later in the season.

In the deepest parts of coastal plain marshes, common plants include water shield (*brasenia schreberi*), yellow pond lily (*nuphar advena*), sweet-scented water lily (*nymphaea odorata*), and bulrush (*scripus subterminalis*). On slightly higher ground are found tall beak-rush (*eleocharis macrostachya*), spike-rush (*e. robbinsii*), sedge (*fimbristylis autumnalis*), and umbrella grass (*fuirena squarrosa*). The margins of the marshes contain the most diverse flora, including such species as bushy aster (*aster dumosus*), blue-joint grass (*calamagrostis canadensis*), sedges (*carex scoparia*), coastal plain flat-topped goldenrod (*euthamia remota*), swamp dewberry (*rubus hispidus*), and sphagnum moss (*sphagnum subsecundum*). The fourth and final ring of vegetation, in the shrub and tree zone that generally experiences only limited flooding, includes black chokeberry (*aronia prunifolia*), buttonbush (*cephalanthus occidentalis*), dogwoods (*cornus* spp.), and smooth highbush blueberry (*vaccinium corymbosum*).

Among the flora found in the Ross Coastal Plain Marsh Preserve are eight rare or endangered species, including globe-fruited seedbox, meadow beauty, appressed bog clubmoss, and netted nut-rush. Meadow beauty, a small herb that produces beautiful pink-purple flowers containing bright yellow stamens, is common.

On the high ground of wooded dunes grow northern hardwood forests of sugar maple, beech, ash, basswood, yellow birch, and other species. As one of the largest contiguous woodlands in southern Michigan, the preserve provides shelter to many migrating birds, particularly in early fall. Among these are the hooded and blackburnian warbler. Also common to coastal plain marshes are several locally rare and endangered bird species, including the northern goshawk, red-shouldered hawk, piping plover, merlin, bald eagle, and osprey.

Beavers and white-tailed deer have a major impact on the health of the preserve ecosystem. The former builds dams throughout the dune and swale complex, flooding formerly dry areas and vice versa. Such changes can drastically impact the types of vegetation in various areas over time. Deer have had a largely negative impact on the preserve in recent years, as their numbers have ballooned due to the elimination of many local predatory species, including gray wolves and cougars. Overbrowsing by the large deer population threatens many plant species and has prompted The Nature Conservancy to allow limited hunting in the preserve.

The Ross Coastal Plain Marsh Preserve is open for walking and bird-watching year-round, from dawn until dusk. Just north of the town of Watervliet, off Interstate 94, it can be accessed off road CR-376, three miles west of Michigan Route M-140.

Further Reading

Brodowicz, W. W. "Report on the Coastal Plain Flora of the Great Lakes Region." Michigan Natural Features Inventory, 1989.

Chapman, K. A. *Community Characterization Abstract: Coastal Plain Marsh*. Minneapolis, MN: Midwest Regional Office of The Nature Conservancy, 1990.

Dorr, John Adam, and Donald F. Eschman. *Geology of Michigan*. Ann Arbor: University of Michigan Press, 1970.

Kost, M.A., D.A. Albert, J.G. Cohen, B.S. Slaughter, R.K. Schillo, C.R. Weber, and K.A. Chapman. "Natural Communities of Michigan: Classification and Description." Michigan Natural Features Inventory, Report No. 2007–21, Lansing, MI, 2007.

Toumey Woodlot

The Toumey Woodlot is an old-growth beech-maple forest (also known as northern hardwood forest) covering 24 acres on the campus of Michigan State University. Designated a national natural landmark in 1976, the woodlot's central 13.5 acres have never been logged and therefore contain an extremely rare example of undisturbed northern hardwood forest in the Lower Peninsula. Younger forest growth encompassing 10.5 acres provides a buffer around the virgin hardwoods. Surrounded by pasture, open fields, and the university campus, the Toumey Woodlot has been a fragment for more than a century.

Beech-maple forests require mesic (intermediate moisture) conditions and typically grow on the well-drained, loamy soils left behind by glaciers in the Great Lakes region. Because such conditions characterize much of Michigan's landscape, beech-maple forests historically covered significant portions of the state. However, the value of hardwood trees for timber made them subject to intense logging throughout the state's early history. The slow-growing nature of such trees makes it difficult for forests to regenerate after such major disturbances. Although sugar maple and American beech species dominate the Toumey Woodlot—and old-growth northern hardwood forests in general—basswood, black cherry, white ash, and red oak also grow within the canopy. American elms formerly grew here as well, but they have been nearly wiped out by Dutch elm disease.

Such trees create a closed canopy that promotes relatively little growth in the understory, because little sunlight filters through to the ground. However, many shade-loving plants make their home in northern hardwood forests, including such shrubs as mountain maple (*A. spicatum*), alternate-leaved dogwood (*Cornus alternifolia*), beaked hazelnut (*Corylus cornuta*), leatherwood (*Dirca palustris*), prickly gooseberry (*Ribes cynosbati*), and red elderberry (*Sambucus pubescens*). Closest to the ground grow red baneberry (*A. rubra*), maidenhair fern (*Adiantum pedatum*), wild leek (*Allium tricoccum*), wild sarsaparilla (*Aralia nudicaulis*), jack-in-the-pulpit (*Arisaema triphyllum*), rattlesnake fern (*Botrychium virginianum*), blue cohosh (*Caulophyllum thalictroides*), bunchberry (*Cornus canadensis*), spinulose woodfern (*Dryopteris spinulosa*), fragrant bedstraw (*Galium triflorum*), large-flowered bellwort (*Uvularia grandiflora*), common trillium (*Trillium chloropetalum*), and American ginseng (*Panax quinquefolius*), which is on Michigan's list of threatened plant species. Morel mushrooms often grow here as well.

Beech-maple forests also support a wide array of songbirds and, sometimes, the state threatened red-shouldered hawk. They can provide shelter for many migrating birds, including the black-throated blue warbler (*Dendroica caerulescens*), black-throated green warbler (*Dendroica virens*), scarlet tanager (*Piranga olivacea*), and ovenbird (*Seiurus aurocapillus*). However, many birds that nest or feed in beech-maple forests require large, contiguous tracts of forested land and are therefore more common in forests of the Upper Peninsula than in smaller, isolated tracts like the Toumey Woodlot.

The woodlot, along with the rest of the state's hardwood stands, is susceptible to various insect pests and diseases. Forest tent caterpillars, in particular, feed on many hardwood species and can completely defoliate maple-beech forests. More typically, however, forests experience smaller, less-damaging cycles of tent caterpillars about every 10 years. Such diseases as nectria canker, eutypella canker, and sapstreak disease also can cause tree damage. So far, however, the woodlot has remained largely unscathed by these natural threats. Instead, its isolated nature within an urbanized area creates the greatest danger to the genetic diversity of its species.

Michigan State University's forestry department has used the woodlot for study since the university purchased it from the estate of Frank Bennett in 1939. The Bennett family had owned the land since 1852 and left it relatively undisturbed. The Toumey Woodlot is on the university campus, in the city of East Lansing.

Further Reading

Dickmann, Donald, and Larry A. Leefers. *The Forests of Michigan*. Ann Arbor: University of Michigan Press, 2003.

Favour, P. "Evaluation of Toumey Woodlot, Ingham County, Michigan for Eligibility for Registered Natural Landmark Designation." Manuscript, Michigan State University Office of Campus Park & Planning, East Lansing, 1975.

Medley, K. "Floristic Analysis of Toumey Woodlot: A Natural Area Ppreserve, Michigan State University." Manuscript, Michigan State University Department of Botany and Plant Pathology, Beal-Darlington Herbarium, East Lansing, 1983.

Schneider, G. "A Twenty-Year Ecological Investigation in a Relatively Undisturbed Sugar Maple-Beech Stand in Southern Michigan." *Agricultural Experiment Station Research Bulletin* 15 (1966).

Two-Hearted River Forest Reserve

Located in the heart of Michigan's largest swath of protected land, the Two-Hearted River Forest Reserve encompasses 23,338 acres of forest surrounding the Two-Hearted River's main branch, in the northeastern Upper Peninsula. Immortalized in Ernest Hemmingway's short story, "Big Two-Hearted River," the waterway is considered one of the nation's best trout-fishing locations and holds a state natural river designation. The river is in pristine condition, and the surrounding ecosystem is one of the state's last major undeveloped areas, providing habitat for numerous endangered species.

The Northern Great Lakes Forest Project, of which the reserve is a part, connects two and a half million acres of undeveloped land—from Tahquamenon Falls State Park in the eastern Upper Peninsula all the way to Ottawa National Forest and the Porcupine Mountains Wilderness State Park in the west. It is part of the largest contiguous conservation corridor in the Midwest. All of the 271,338 acres of connecting lands are in private hands, including the Two-Hearted River Forest Reserve, which is owned and managed by The Nature Conservancy. With the help of various foundations and the state government, the conservancy also purchased a working conservation easement on the remaining 248,000 acres, now owned by the Forestland Group, LLC under a special agreement with the state.

Unlike the conservancy's many preserves elsewhere in the nation, the Two-Hearted River Forest Reserve is open to hunting and—importantly on a Class I trout stream—fishing. The conservancy also allows carefully planned, sustainable timber harvesting under the state's Commercial Forest Act. Under the conservancy's working conservation easement, similar provisions exist throughout the Northern Great Lakes Forest Project lands. The idea behind allowing more varied uses of this massive swath of land is to make its protection economically viable, and even desirable, to the residents of nearby towns and to the state, which continues to collect taxes on these properties.

Although no major settlements or farms have ever been established within the Two-Hearted River watershed, its valuable timber resources—especially its white pines—attracted extensive logging during the late 1800s. By the early 1900s, virgin pine stands had been exhausted, and loggers turned instead to the hardwood trees. Today, thanks to reforestation efforts begun in the 1930s by the Civilian Conservation Corps and continuing to the present, much of the forest has returned, although wildfires and deer browsing have prevented regeneration in some areas.

Near the Two-Hearted River's headwaters, its tributaries, including the upper waters of its north and west branches, mainly run through conifer swamps. Further downstream in the reserve, however, the river enters an area of sandy and loamy soils that support northern hardwood and pine forests. Among the more common tree species here are alder, spruce, balsam, white pine, red pine, birch, and various hardwoods including maples. The river valley also deepens as it moves through the reserve toward Lake Superior, giving rise to different kinds of trees in the sandy river bottom than those that grow on the banks above.

Along with the surrounding protected areas, the Two-Hearted River Forest Reserve supports an extraordinarily diverse array of native wildlife—including many threatened and endangered species that are extinct elsewhere in the state. Gray wolves, bald eagles, common loons, and ospreys are among the rare animal species found within the watershed. Moose have been sighted in the area as well. More common animals include deer, black bear, coyote, fox, grouse, woodcock, beaver, snowshoe hare, porcupine, red squirrel, and various birds, including sandhill cranes and the black-backed woodpecker.

In the river, brook trout are the most abundant fish, but rainbow trout and menominee also are common. All these fish require the cold, clear waters and sandy bottom of a healthy northern river such as the Two-Hearted.

The Two-Hearted River Forest Reserve is open to the public year-round for hiking, bird-watching, fishing, and nonmotorized boating and canoeing. Hunting also is permitted in season. The reserve, north of the town of Newberry, can be accessed off County Road 407, just north of Pine Stump Junction. A small dirt road named Dawson Trail leads to a footpath into the reserve.

Further Reading

Michigan Department of Natural Resources. "Two-Hearted River Natural River Plan." December 1973. http://www.michigan.gov/documents/Two_Hearted_River_Plan_22961_7.pdf.

Michigan Department of Natural Resources, Eastern Upper Peninsula Eco-region. "Two-Hearted Headwaters Management Summary." http://209.85.173.132/search?q=cache:-DHPfO2WYmAJ:www.michigandnr.com/Publications/PDFS/ForestsLandWater/Ecosystem/EUP/final-MAsummaries/31_Two_Hearted_Headwaters_MA_summary.doc+michigan+two-hearted+river+forest+preserve&cd=3&hl=en&ct=clnk&gl=us&client=firefox-a.

ZETTERBERG PRESERVE AT POINT BETSIE

The Zetterberg Preserve at Point Betsie hosts an ever-shifting ecosystem of sand dunes, interdunal wetlands, and boreal forest on the shores of Lake Michigan. Located in Benzie County just south of Sleeping Bear Dunes National Lakeshore, this 100-acre dune complex provides habitat for rare and threatened plant species, as well as a wide array of migratory birds. The Nature Conservancy established the preserve in 1988, when Steve and Connie Zetterberg donated 71 acres of virgin sand dunes owned by their family for generations.

A wooded dune and swale complex is at the heart of the Point Betsie environment, formed over thousands of years with the retreat of large glacial lakes that preceded Lake Michigan. The process continues today in the same way, as rivers and streams deposit sand at their mouths in the lake, and winds and lake currents move the sands along the shore. The result is a series of parallel dunes, with depressions in between that have formed into wetlands. Younger dunes closest to the shore host sparse, shallow-rooted vegetation and are still being shifted by the wind. Further inland, older dunes are more stable and, in the case of the Zetterberg Preserve, host boreal forests of mainly evergreen trees.

The shifting dunes closest to the preserve's shoreline host the state and federally threatened Pitcher's thistle (*Cirsium pitcheri*); on the leeward sides of these same dunes grows the state threatened fascicled broomrape (*Orobanche fasciculata*), which is more rare in Michigan than the Pitcher's thistle. More common vegetation in this area includes marram grass (*Ammophila breviligulata*), dune grass (*Calamovilfa longifolia*), autumn willow (*Salix serissima*), sand dune willow (*S. cordata*), bearberry (*Arctostaphylos uva-ursi*), and balsam poplar (*Populus balsamifera*). These open dunes also provide critical habitat for the state threatened Huron locust (*Trimerotropis huroniana*).

Boreal forest on the preserve's inland dunes includes balsam fir (*Abies balsamea*), paper birch (*Betula papyrifera*), red oak (*Quercus rubra* L.), and creeping juniper (*Juniperus horizontalis*). White spruce (*Picea glauca*) and northern white cedar (*Thuja occidentalis*) are other common trees found in boreal forests.

In the low-lying swales between the preserve's dunes, standing water levels fluctuate seasonally, forming wetlands that harbor such plant species as sweet gale (*Myrica gale*), shrubby cinquefoil (*Potentilla fruticosa*), blue-joint grass (*Calamagrostis canadensis*), Kalm's lobelia (*Lobelia kalmii*), false asphodel (*Tofieldia glutinosa*), grass of Parnassus (*Parnassia glauca*), and various rushes. The edges of typical interdunal wetlands host shrubs requiring slightly drier conditions, including black chokeberry (*Aronia prunifolia*), red-osier dogwood (*Cornus stolonifera*), and bog birch (*Betula pumila*).

The Zetterberg Preserve's varied vegetation—especially its seasonal pond habitat—provides sanctuary to numerous migrating birds, including the semipalmated plover. Cedar waxwings make their home among trees and shrubs in the preserve, while spotted sandpipers and killdeer congregate along the sandy beach.

Invasive weeds—especially baby's breath (*Gypsophila paniculata*)—pose the most serious threat to the dune habitat. Baby's breath has deep roots that stabilize the normally shifting sand dunes and outcompete the threatened Pitcher's thistle. It also quickly covers the dunes, threatening the existence of the Huron locust, which requires pristine, sparsely vegetated coastal sand dunes for its survival. To halt the aggressive spread of baby's breath at the preserve, The Nature Conservancy has established a program to eradicate as much of the plant as possible.

The Zetterberg Preserve is open to the public year-round for hiking and bird-watching. It can be accessed off Michigan Route 22, about four and a half miles north of the town of Frankfort.

Further Reading

Albert, D.A., and P.J. Comer. *Natural Community Abstract for Wooded Dune and Swale Complex*. Lansing: Michigan Natural Features Inventory, 1999.

Cohen, J.G. 2007. *Natural Community Abstract for Boreal Forest*. Lansing: Michigan Natural Features Inventory, 2007.

Comer, P.J., and D.A. Albert. A Survey of Wooded Dune and Swale Complexes in Michigan. Report to Michigan DNR, Land and Water Management Division, Coastal Zone Management Program, 1993.

Dorr, John Adam, and Donald F. Eschman. *Geology of Michigan*. Ann Arbor: University of Michigan Press, 1970.

Hutchins, Brian. *Michigan's West Coast: Explore the Shore Guide: A Journey to 500 Public Parks and Points of Access Along the Lake Michigan Shoreline*. Roscommon, MI: Abri-LLC, 2005.

MINNESOTA

Minnesota is famous for its more than 11,842 lakes (there are many more unnamed that are smaller than 10 acres). However, the state is rich in a diversity of natural environments. The boreal forests of the northern part of the state have in many ways defined the state—evergreen forests, peat bogs, and numerous wetlands and rivers. But, like much of the Midwest, this region was shaped by the last glaciation, which left behind not only the many lakes but also a land rich for farming. Prairie once extended along the entire western part of the state in a large arc extending through much of southern Minnesota, where the land is extensively farmed. The southeastern corner of the state is part of the Driftless Area, a region where the last glacial advances had little effect on the landscape.

Prairie, northern boreal forests, and southern hardwood forests meet in Minnesota. Despite nearly 60 percent of the population living in the metropolitan area of the Twin Cities of Minneapolis and St. Paul, the low population density has not meant that natural areas in the rest of the state have remained untouched. Much of the arable land is cultivated, and the vast forests have been logged intensively in the past 150 years. Only the least-populated northern part of the state, with its harsh climatic extremes and difficult-to-drain wetlands, has remained relatively intact. The following entries highlight a variety of natural areas demonstrating the diverse ecosystems of Minnesota. Many ecological patterns in Minnesota are best seen from the air, and readers are encouraged to use online mapping Web sites when reading the entries.

ANCIENT RIVER WARREN CHANNEL

Glacial melt waters formed the Ancient River Warren Channel about 11,000 years ago, when they breached a moraine wall near present-day Browns Valley, on the Minnesota–South Dakota border. Now designated a national natural landmark, the channel was carved through the 975-foot-high moraine wall when the massive postglacial Lake Agassiz rose above this level. The resulting torrent of water through Browns

97

Valley and into southern Minnesota created a wide valley—as wide as five miles across in some places—that today holds the much smaller Minnesota River.

Lake Agassiz, which preceded the current Great Lakes, covered an area from what is now northern Saskatchewan and Manitoba to eastern North Dakota and northwestern Minnesota. Its surface area was larger than that of all the current Great Lakes combined, and, as glaciers melted at the end of the last ice age, the lake rose rapidly. Drainage to the north was blocked by various ice dams, so Lake Agassiz eventually breached the glacial moraine at Browns Valley, which represents the north-south continental divide. It flowed through this gap and into present-day Minnesota from about 11,000 years ago until about 9,500 years ago, cutting the moraine down by more than 800 feet—to a level of between 100 and 125 feet—across a one-and-a-half-mile swath.

As Lake Agassiz receded, the River Warren dried up, leaving behind Big Stone Lake, which now drains south into the Minnesota River and eventually to the Gulf of Mexico. North of the moraine, Lake Traverse serves as the headwaters of the north-flowing Bois de Sioux and Red River of the North watersheds, which make their way toward Canada's Hudson Bay. The moraine wall remains a significant point along the continental divide, but the River Warren Channel, also known as the Traverse River Gap, continues to serve as an overflow point; both Big Stone Lake and Lake Traverse have periodically breached the moraine in modern times, whenever either reached flood stage. In the 1930s, the U.S. Army Corps of Engineers stopped most future overflows with a series of dams, dikes, and culverts.

The moraine wall at the center of this complicated dual watershed was formed as a series of glaciers deposited vast quantities of sediments on top of Precambrian bedrock. Today, such deposits, also known as glacial till, reach depths of more than 300 feet at the wall. Along much of the valley that now contains the Minnesota River, however, they were scraped away completely by the torrent of the Warren River, leaving behind only exposed bedrock.

Big Stone Lake now hosts perch, panfish, walleye, northern pike, sunfish, and black crappies; the first two fish species breed in the lake naturally, and the others are stocked by the Minnesota Department of Natural Resources (DNR) for recreational fishing. Downstream, the upper Minnesota River hosts natural populations of such fish as walleye, panfish, sheepshead, buffalo, quillback, suckers, and carp. The DNR also stocks channel catfish, northern pike, crappies, and smallmouth bass in the river. The broad Ancient River Warren Channel also harbors wooded hills on its banks and important wetlands lower in the valley. Wild rice is a common plant in the wetlands. Such habitat provides a home and migratory stopover for many species of songbirds and waterfowl; it also hosts a wide range other animals.

Three-quarters of the land in this watershed has been converted to agriculture, mainly for growing soybeans, corn, and other grains, but also for raising livestock. An estimated 80 percent of wetlands in the channel have been drained for agriculture, animal feedlots, and other development. Agricultural pesticides, herbicides, manure, and fertilizers now run into the watershed, along with eroded sediments from farmland tillage. Pollution of surface waters is considered a moderate to severe problem by the state Pollution Control Agency, resulting in high concentrations and loads of suspended sediments and nutrients linked to artificial drainage ditches and a reduction in wetlands that normally would filter out many of these pollutants. Such conditions have led to eutrophication—a reduction in dissolved oxygen due to high nutrient levels that promote algal blooms—in many areas of the watershed. High levels of sediment in the water also decrease aquatic plant photosynthesis and harm other aquatic life.

By the 1980s, Big Stone Lake was in a hypereutrophic state—the most severe form of eutrophication. To reverse these effects, the state launched the Big Stone Lake Restoration Project in 1985, with the goal of managing lake levels and the surrounding feedlots, grazing lands, croplands, and remaining wetlands. In addition, the federal Conservation Reserve Program offers annual payments to farmers who plant some of their land with native grasses and trees to reduce erosion. By 1994, eight percent of agricultural land in the Upper Minnesota River watershed was enrolled in this program, but those numbers have increased greatly since. Nutrients and algal blooms also have been reduced.

Although the portion of the Ancient River Warren Channel carved through the Browns Valley area is a mixture of public and private lands not always open to the public, Big Stone Lake and the Minnesota River are accessible via several state parks, including Big Stone Lake State Park, which offers camping, bird-watching, fishing, hunting, hiking, swimming, and boating. It is located off Minnesota Route 7, seven miles northwest of the town of Ortonville.

Further Reading

Bray, Edmund. *Billions of Years in Minnesota: The Geological Story of the State*. St. Paul: Science Museum of Minnesota, 1980.

Ojakangas, Richard W., and Charles L. Matsch. *Minnesota's Geology*. Minneapolis: University of Minnesota Press,1982.

Tester, John. *Minnesota's Natural Heritage*. Minneapolis: University of Minnesota Press, 1995.

Waters, T. F. *The Streams and Rivers of Minnesota*. Minneapolis: University of Minnesota Press,1977.

BIG BOG STATE RECREATION AREA

Big Bog State Recreation Area covers 9,459 acres in the vast peatlands in north-central Minnesota. Located in Beltrami County just north of Upper Red Lake and east of the 87,580-acre Red Lake Peatlands State Natural Area (82,783 acres of which is owned by the state), this state-owned land is part of what is known locally as the Big Bog. This vast 585-square-mile area—of which 170,000 acres (265 square miles) is protected—is the largest peat bog and natural wilderness in the United States outside of Alaska (a bog is a wetland that receives all its water from precipitation rather than groundwater). The area has been designated a nNational natural landmark by the National Park Service because of its geological features and plant communities. Although there are other bogs in the state and the country, none provides the diversity of plants and ecosystems that are usually lacking in the harsh conditions of this type of ecosystem as in the Big Bog. The Big Bog State Recreation Area allows visitors an opportunity to discover this unusual ecosystem.

The recreational area has a southern unit, which contains campgrounds and a day use area on Red Lake, and an over 9,000-acre peatland northern unit, which has an interpretive center and miles of boardwalk for experiencing the peatlands up close. The Big Bog Recreation Area was created in part for economic reasons. Walleye fishing in Upper Red Lake had been an important source of income from tourism and commercial fishing in one of the most sparsely populated and economically depressed areas of Minnesota. When the walleye population crashed in the 1990s, many tourism operators went out of business. There was a grassroots effort from the Upper Red Lake Area Association to create a more sustainable tourist attraction for the area, and, in 2005, Big Bog State Recreation Area was opened.

Bogs are little understood in part because they are found primarily in the northernmost areas of the world where permafrost, or permanently frozen subsoil, is common, thus making it difficult to study groundwater and subsurface drainage that is critical to the formation of peatlands, a particular type of bog. The Minnesota peatlands, however, are free of permafrost. The peatlands are part of the once-vast Glacial Lake Agassiz, which was located in Canada and extended into northern Minnesota. This glacial lakebed is a virtually level landscape with poor drainage. The peatlands surrounding the Red Lake area, nonetheless, contain a diversity of landforms often resembling typical land features such as channels and islands. These landforms include water tracks formed by the movement of surface water and teardrop islands, circular islands, and ovoid islands. These features are formed by movement and variations in the surface and subsurface water. Uniquely, all these features are found in the Big Bog, and together these landforms create what is known as the patterned peatlands because of the repeating patterns created in the landscape. The Red Lake Peatlands, as a result, is the largest and most diversely continuous patterned peatland in the lower United States.

Peat is a type of soil in which plant material is still visible. Peatlands form because low oxygen, cold temperatures, and a short growing season prevent the normal decomposition of decaying plants. The Red Lake Patterned Peatlands are the result of the gradual accumulation of thousands of years of plants. The diversity of features in the patterned peatlands and lack of permafrost are of international interest in better understanding bog ecosystems. In fact, recent years have seen increased interest in the preservation and protection of bogs. For these reasons, the patterned peatlands provides an opportunity to better understand these unusual ecosystems.

Boreal or northern hardwood forests and conifer and hardwood swamp forest are scattered throughout the Big Bog State Recreation Area. Carnivorous plants are commonly associated with the wet acidic soils of bogs, and the rare English sundew (*Drosera anglica*) is found here. Rare animals such as the northern bog lemming (*Synaptomys borealis*) the sandhill crane (*Grus canadensis*) also inhabit this patterned peatland. Three new species of butterflies were recently discovered within the recreation area.

Big Bog State Recreation Area offers the opportunity to explore one of the most inaccessible and least understood ecosystems in the United States. With cooperation from the Upper Red Lake Area Association and the federal government, the Big Bog is being managed with minimal impact for a sustainable future as a natural, cultural, and economic resource.

Further Reading

Tester, John R. *Minnesota's Natural Heritage: An Ecological Perspective*. Minneapolis: University of Minnesota Press, 1995.

Wright, H. E. Jr., Barbara A. Coffin, and Norman E. Aaseng, eds. *The Patterned Peatlands of Minnesota*. Minneapolis: University of Minnesota Press, 1992.

CEDAR CREEK ECOSYSTEM SCIENCE RESERVE—ALLISON SAVANNA

Just 20 miles north of the Minneapolis–St. Paul metropolitan area, the Helen Allison Savanna Scientific and Natural Area encompasses one of the few remaining oak savannas in the Midwest. The Nature Conservancy owns and manages the 86-acre preserve, which lies at the southern end of the 5,460-acre Cedar Creek Ecosystem Science Reserve. North America's three largest ecosystems—western prairies, northern evergreen forests, and leafy eastern forests—all converge in this nine-square-mile area. The Allison Savanna Scientific and Natural Area protects 54 acres of oak savanna, along with smaller areas of sand dunes, wet meadows (also known as marshes), and willow-aspen thickets.

The Allison Savanna sits on the Anoka Sandplain, a flat, sandy outwash that formed from glacial melt water deposits along the Mississippi River about 16,000 years ago. Conifers, mainly consisting of spruce, first covered the area between 1,000 and 1,500 years after the glaciers retreated. As the climate warmed, the spruce were eventually replaced by birch trees, which gave way in turn to oak savanna. This habitat consists primarily of sun-loving prairie grasses and forbs (broad-leaved wildflowers native to western prairies), with scattered trees, including northern pin oak, bur oak, American hazelnut, chokecherry, and quaking aspen. Common vegetation includes such grasses as big bluestem, little bluestem, Indian grass, porcupine grass, and switchgrass as well as such wildflowers as Indian paintbrush, lupine, coreopsis, hoary puccoon, leadplant, silky prairie clover, goldenrod, and aster. Rhombic-petaled evening primrose—a state species of special concern—also grows here. Tussocks, sedges, and marsh ferns prefer the moist conditions of the marshes.

Cedar Creek Ecosystem Science Reserve. (Kathleen McCarthy)

As transition zones between western tall-grass prairies and eastern woodlands, oak sa-vannas host a wide variety of insects, birds, and other animals. The sand dunes that exist on higher ground in the Allison Savanna area, along with marshes that have formed in the seasonally flooded depressions between dunes, provide additional wildlife habitat.

Ninety-two bird species have been observed in the Allison Savanna, including seven woodpecker species, numerous sparrows and warblers, eastern bluebirds, kinglets, brown thrashers, wild turkeys, and eastern towhees. Rare sandhill cranes, red-winged blackbirds, and common yellowthroats are found in marshy areas. Such predatory birds as ospreys, Cooper's hawks, red-shouldered hawks, and red-tailed hawks also are occasionally seen. Reptiles and amphibians that frequent the savanna and its wetlands include eastern tiger salamanders, spring peepers, gray tree frogs, wood frogs, gopher snakes, and the rare Bland-ing's turtle. White-tailed deer, grasshoppers, and numerous rodent species also thrive here.

Oak savannas once covered 10 percent of the state of Minnesota, but today just 65,000 acres of this habitat remain in all of the Midwest—two-tenths of a percent of what existed before European settlement. For centuries, grazing by native ungulates—mainly bison and elk—along with natural fires and those intentionally set by Native Americans, maintained this habitat, which evolved to depend on such disturbances. Oak trees and other prairie vegetation are tolerant of, and in some cases dependant on, fire, which kills off most young woodland plant species. For this reason, when European settlers began suppressing fires, forests encroached upon many savannas. Mass killings of bison eliminated natural grazing cycles, on which many prairie plant species depend for seed germination and reproduction. Much savanna habitat also was converted to farmland or, later, taken over by residential and commercial development. Rapid suburban sprawl has been a more recent threat.

In 1962, two years after The Nature Conservancy acquired the Allison Savanna with the help of a major donation from local activist Helen Allison Irvine, the conservancy began controlled burning of about one-third of the property each year on a rotating schedule. The University of Minnesota, which owns and manages the larger Cedar Creek Ecosystem Science Reserve, has also conducted conservation projects, including hand seeding various prairie plant species. The state of Minnesota designated the Allison Savanna an official scientific and natural area in 1979.

The Allison Savanna and the larger Cedar Creek reserve are sites of much scientific research on ecology and on the benefits these ecosystems provide to the health of the planet and human development. They are open to the public year-round for walking, bird-watching, and other passive recreation. The Allison Savanna is accessible from Minneapolis and St. Paul by traveling north on Minnesota Route 65. The preserve is near the town of Bethel, off County Road 15.

Further Reading

Anderson, R.C. "Overview of Midwestern Oak Savanna." *Transactions of the Wisconsin Academy of Sciences, Arts and Letters* 86 (1998): 1–18.

Faber-Langendoen, D., and M.A. Davis. "Effects of Fire Frequency on Tree Canopy Cover at Allison Savanna, Eastcentral Minnesota, USA." *Natural Areas Journal* 15 (1995): 319–28.

Haarstad, J., and B. Delaney. "The Habitats of Cedar Creek. Cedar Creek Natural History Area, University of Minnesota. Saint Paul, Minn." 1998. http://www.cedar creek.umn.edu/habitats/.

U.S. Geological Survey, Northern Prairie Wildlife Research Center. "Regional Landscape Ecosystems in Michigan, Minnesota, and Wisconsin: Subsection III.3. Anoka Sand Plain." http://www.npwrc.usgs.gov/resource/habitat/rlandscp/sub3–3.htm.

ITASCA WILDERNESS SANCTUARY SCIENTIFIC AND NATURAL AREA

The Itasca Wilderness Sanctuary Scientific and Natural Area harbors a coniferous forest of virgin red and white pines as well as small bogs and kettle lakes near the headwaters of the Mississippi River. Also known as knob and kettle terrain, this landscape represents the largest of Minnesota's three biomes. The 1,580-acre sanctuary, located in Itasca State Park, provides habitat for rare flora and fauna as well as a site for scientific research.

Coarse, glacially deposited soils characterize the Itasca moraine. Mainly composed of sands and sandy loams, along with some crushed-limestone deposits, this glacial till covers the underlying Precambrian rock at a depth of 200 to more than 600 feet. Such well-drained soils—along with a short growing season and significant precipitation during that time—nourish Minnesota's coniferous forests, which cover two-fifths of the state, primarily the north-central and northeastern regions. These woodlands can include white pine, red pine, jack pine, black spruce, fir, and upland white cedar tree species.

White and red pines dominate the Itasca Wilderness Sanctuary's old-growth coniferous forests, though other trees are found here as well, including balsam fir, maples, and American elm. Most of the sanctuary's pines are between 100 and 300 years old; the state's largest red pine resides here, and the state's largest white pine grows just outside the sanctuary border. Below the coniferous forest canopy grow such shrubs as beaked hazel, dogwood, honeysuckle, and mountain maple. The accumulation of pine needles on the forest floor promotes acidic soil conditions where such herbaceous ground plants as clintonia, rose twisted-stalk, wintergreen, and pyrola thrive.

Within the coniferous forest, bogs and the area's two small kettle lakes—Bohall and Beaver lakes—have formed in moraine depressions carved by successive glacial advances. (The sanctuary also borders the much larger Lake Itasca.) Water collects seasonally in the bogs—mainly during the summer growing season, when 40 percent of precipitation occurs—providing habitat for wetland plants such as wild rice. Highly acidic and low in nutrients, the Itasca Wilderness Sanctuary's bogs are favorable to such species as sphagnum mosses, sedges, rushes, pondweed, and acid-loving shrubs, including leatherleaf and various heathers. The tall white bog orchid, tall northern bog orchid, small northern bog orchid, and large round-leaved orchid also favor the sanctuary's wetland areas.

This knob and kettle combination of coniferous forest interspersed with wetlands hosts a wide array of animals. Gray wolves, black bears, beaver, porcupine, deer, chipmunks, squirrels, and hognose snakes all live within the sanctuary. Bird species are numerous and include bald eagles, sharp-tailed grouse, sandhill cranes, upland sandpipers, common terns, yellow rails, red-necked grebes, trumpeter swans, and common loons, along with several types of heron, cormorant, hummingbird, woodpecker, nuthatch, tanager, finch, and warbler species. This ecosystem also is one of the state's most important habitats for red-shouldered hawks.

The largest threats to Minnesota's coniferous forest communities come from development of private forest lands and the resulting fragmentation of remaining forests into small, isolated parcels. Overall, however, the north-central and northeastern portions of the state remain relatively undeveloped, with numerous locally and federally protected forests in close proximity to one another.

The Itasca Wilderness Sanctuary was set aside for research, interpretation, and preservation by the state in 1938, becoming the first of Minnesota's scientific and natural area properties. It is open to the public year-round via the surrounding 32,000-acre Itasca State Park. No bicycles or motorized vehicles are allowed in the sanctuary, and there are only two short walking trails within its boundaries. However, a road open to cars and bicycles skirts its western and southern edges. Itasca State Park is 30 miles south of the town of Bemidji, off U.S. Highway 71.

Itasca Wilderness Sanctuary Scientific and Natural Area. (Christopher Franklin)

Further Reading

Minnesota Department of Natural Resources. "Scientific and Natural Areas." http://www.dnr.state.mn.us/snas/index.html.

Minnesota Department of Natural Resources, Division of Ecological Services. "Tomorrow's Habitat for the Wild and Rare: An Action Plan for Minnesota Wildlife, Comprehensive Wildlife Conservation Strategy." 2006. http://files.dnr.state.mn.us/assistance/nrplanning/bigpicture/cwcs/profiles/pine_moraine_outwash_plains.pdf.

Ojakangas, Richard W., and Charles L. Matsch. Minnesota's Geology. Minneapolis: University of Minnesota Press, 1982.

Smith, William K., and Thomas M. Hinckley, eds. *Ecophysiology of Coniferous Forests*. Academic Press, 1996.

KEELEY CREEK RESEARCH NATURAL AREA

J ust south of Minnesota's border with Canada, the Keeley Creek Research Natural Area preserves 640 acres of pine forest and peat bogs characteristic of the northern coniferous forest biome. Lying within Superior National Forest, in the state's largely undeveloped northeast corner, Keeley Creek's pristine forests provide habitat to a wide array of wildlife. Its peat bogs also store immense amounts of carbon and methane, making them a major factor in global climate change. The creek for which the area is named runs through its northwest corner.

Established as a research natural area in 1942, the Keeley Creek area sits atop the Tower-Ely glacial drift and bedrock complex, a thin base of soils left behind by the retreat of successive glaciers. As massive glacial lakes began to shrink about 9,000 years ago, the area's cool, moist climate prevented the lake bottoms from completely drying out, and, as a result, dead vegetation decomposed slowly, and never completely. The resulting buildup of partly decayed plant matter, mainly sphagnum mosses, has formed peat mats many feet thick over seven million acres of northern Minnesota—a larger area than in any other state but Alaska.

Saturated with water either year-round or most of the year, Keeley Creek's peat bogs occupy lowland areas where poorly drained soils are made acidic by the decomposing sphagnum mosses. Black spruce trees grow up from the peat and dominate the area's lowland forest community, which also hosts tamaracks and balsam firs. Common shrub species in this type of conifer bog include low sweet blueberry, bog laurel, cotton grasses, pitcher plants, cranberry, and round-leaved sundew.

On the much drier, sandy soils of the Keeley Creek area's higher elevations, jack pine forests grow. Balsam fir and quaking aspen are secondary tree species in the pine forest.

Common bird species in the area include spruce grouse, ruffed grouse, yellow-bellied flycatcher, palm warbler, Connecticut warbler, northern waterthrush, and Lincoln's sparrow. Also occupying such forests are great horned owls, bald eagles, and many hawks, finches, sparrows, and warblers, including the endangered Kirtland's warbler. Mammals in the Keeley Creek area include wolves, black bear, coyote, fox, bobcat, moose, white-tailed deer, snowshoe hares, and beavers.

Like all of the Great Lakes region's coniferous forests (also known as boreal forests), the Keeley Creek Research Natural Area is rapidly changing due to a lack of major wildfires as well as a rapidly warming climate. Pine forests and peat bogs alike are highly dependent on wildfires, yet fire suppression efforts have prevented any major wildfires since about 1870. Jack pines and black spruce both require fire to germinate their seeds; young trees of both species also do best in the full sunlight created after a forest canopy is cleared by fire. Without fire, mature stands of jack pines such as those in the Keeley Creek area are eventually overtaken by more shade-tolerant species.

Global warming also is speeding up the demise of Minnesota's coniferous forests. Hardwood tree species more common to areas further south have been steadily encroaching on the cold-loving conifers. Jack pines in particular grow best in cold climates with harsh winters, but milder winters in northern Minnesota during recent decades have given an advantage to hardwoods, especially red maples. Climate change also has resulted in wetter summers over the past 20 years, further reducing the wildfires that normally would kill young hardwoods and help conifers reproduce. As a result, scientists at the University of Minnesota predict that the state's northern coniferous forests—including those of Keeley Creek—will change dramatically over the next 50 years.

As temperatures rise, the peat bogs could add to the problem. Peatlands cover 14 percent of the state but hold 37 percent of its stored carbon—more than any other ecosystem. Scientists have expressed fears that warmer temperatures will speed up plant decomposition in the peat mats, releasing the greenhouse gases carbon and methane at much higher rates and, in turn, further speeding global warming. To prevent such a cycle, Minnesota's government is considering various peat bog protection and restoration initiatives, including preventing drainage of these areas for development and restoring peat bogs that have previously been drained.

The Keeley Creek Research Natural Area is off Minnesota Route 1, south of the town of Ely in Superior National Forest. Like the rest of the forest, it is open to the public, but, due to the swampy nature of its terrain and a lack of trails or lakes, it is difficult to access. Most visitors to the area travel instead to nearby lakes, including those of the Boundary Waters Canoe Area, to see similar habitat by kayak or canoe.

Further Reading

Ahlgren, C. E. "Some Effects of Fire on Reproduction and Growth of Vegetation in Northeastern Minnesota." *Ecology* 41 (1960): 431–45.

Ahlgren, C. E. "Vegetational Development Following Burning in the Northern Coniferous Forest of Minnesota." *Proc., Soc. of Am For.* (1959).

LeBarron, Russel K., and Clare Hendee. "Establishment Record of the Keeley Creek and Lac La Croix Research Natural Areas within the Superior National Forest." Unpublished report on file at the Northern Research Station, Rhinelander, 1942. http://nrs. fs.fed.us/rna/documents/establishment/mn_superior_keeley_creek_lac_lacroix.pdf.

U.S. Forest Service. "Kuchler Type: Conifer Bog." http://www.fs.fed.us/database/feis/ kuchlers/k094/all.html.

U.S. Forest Service. "Kuchler Type: Great Lakes Pine Forest." http://www.fs.fed.us/data base/feis/kuchlers/k095/all.html.

MOE WOODS PRESERVE

Located in the transition zone from western prairie grasslands to eastern deciduous forests, the Moe Woods Preserve hosts oak savanna and maple-basswood forest habitat. The Nature Conservancy manages the preserve, which is split into two separate parcels in southwestern Minnesota—120 acres in Pope County and 48 acres in Kandiyohi County. The deciduous hardwood forest in and between the two properties is a large remnant of this habitat type that is surrounded by oak savanna and prairie.

Underlying the prairie-forest transition zone are the deposits of successive glaciers, including moraine soil and rock deposited by movement of the glaciers themselves, as well as finer sediments deposited by glacial melt waters. In general, the irregular topography of this region, along with its many lakes and wetlands, prevented the advance of wildfires from the nearby prairies and allowed fire-intolerant hardwood forests to grow instead. Wildfires remained crucial, however, to the development of oak savannas, which consist of fire-tolerant oak species scattered among fields of fire-dependant prairie vegetation. In general, deciduous forests grew at or to the southeast of a natural line of moraine hills and ridges built up at the edge of the area's most recent glacier, while oak savannas and, further west, prairies, developed on the other side of the dividing line.

Oak savannas consist mainly of sun-loving prairie grasses and forbs (broad-leaved wildflowers native to western prairies), with scattered trees. Northern pin oak and bur oak are the most common tree species, but hardwood forest transition species including American hazelnut, chokecherry, and quaking aspen trees also can grow on the savanna, especially at its forested edges. Common oak savanna vegetation includes such grasses as big bluestem, little bluestem, Indian grass, porcupine grass, and switchgrass, as well as such wildflowers as Indian paintbrush, lupine, coreopsis, hoary puccoon, leadplant, silky prairie clover, goldenrod, and aster.

The maple-basswood forest at the heart of the Moe Woods Preserve is a mesic, or intermediate moisture-level, habitat, in contrast with the drier surrounding savanna. It is dominated almost entirely by basswood trees; the sugar maples that usually are the majority tree species in such forests are virtually absent. American elms also are common in the forest, as are ironwood trees, found mainly in the shady understory. Smaller numbers of oak, black cherry, and green ash trees grow throughout the forest. Vegetation on the forest floor is generally sparse because little sunlight filters through the thick canopy. Many wildflowers bloom briefly in spring, before tree leaves fully develop, and then the flowers die as the canopy fills in. Among them are showy orchid, yellow lady's slipper, trout lilies, Dutchman's-breeches, spring beauty, toothwort, and false rue anemone. Red baneberry, mayapples, bloodroot, jack-in-the-pulpit, wild ginger, hepatica, and trilliums are more tolerant of shade and therefore can continue to grow and bear fruit through the summer. Ferns and wild leeks are other common ground plants.

Common animals in Minnesota's deciduous forests include deer, skunks, opossums, mice, shrews, garter snakes, gray tree frogs, turkeys, and numerous songbirds, including vireos and warblers.

Like much of Minnesota's forested land, all of the Moe Woods has been logged or grazed in the past. Meanwhile, much of the area's former oak savannas have been converted to farmland. As a result, both habitat types cover only a fraction of their pre–European-settlement ranges, and deciduous forests in particular have become highly fragmented, isolating many forest-dwelling species from populations elsewhere.

The Moe Woods, purchased by The Nature Conservancy from a local family in 1971, is now protected from all logging or development, and the conservancy has engaged nearby landowners in preserving the area as well—a crucial move because the southern portion of the preserve is completely surrounded by private land. In all, 15 landowners have pledged not to develop or otherwise damage forested lands surrounding the Moe Woods preserve, registering an additional 406 acres with the conservancy.

The southern Moe Woods Preserve is not accessible to the public because it is entirely encircled by private property. The northern portion, in Pope County, is west of the town of Brooten and can be accessed via a circuitous route of trails off County Highway 8. However, because there are no trails, and some of its boundaries are unmarked, The Nature Conservancy recommends visiting only with a topographical map, compass, and knowledge of how to use them.

Further Reading

Minnesota Department of Natural Resources. "Oak Savanna Subsection." http://www.dnr.state.mn.us/ecs/222Me/index.html.

Minnesota Department of Natural Resources. "Southern Mesic Maple-Basswood Forest." Mesic Hardwood Forest System—Southern Floristic Region. http://files.dnr.state.mn.us/natural_resources/npc/mesic_hardwood/mhs39.pdf.

Peterson, D. W., P. B. Reich, and K. J. Wrage. "Plant Functional Group Responses to Fire Frequency and Tree Canopy Cover Gradients in Oak Savannas and Woodland." *Journal of Vegetation Science* 18 (2007): 3–12.

Reich, P. B., D. A. Peterson, K. Wrage, and D. Wedin. "Fire and Vegetation Effects on Productivity and Nitrogen Cycling across a Forest-Grassland Continuum. *Ecology* 82 (2001): 1703–19.

U.S. Geological Survey, Northern Prairie Wildlife Research Center. "Regional Landscape Ecosystems of Michigan, Minnesota, and Wisconsin: Subsection III.1. Hardwood Hills." http://www.npwrc.usgs.gov/resource/habitat/rlandscp/sub3–1.htm.

PIGEON RIVER CLIFFS PRESERVE

Encompassing the headwaters of the Pigeon River in far northeastern Minnesota, the Pigeon River Cliffs Preserve hosts a largely pristine watershed as well as unusual communities of plant species native to alpine and arctic regions. The 100-acre preserve lies along a one-mile stretch of the watershed where South Fowl Lake flows into the Pigeon River, which marks the state's easternmost border with Canada. The preserve is owned and managed by The Nature Conservancy.

The Pigeon River is the largest waterway to enter Lake Superior from Minnesota, draining a 628-square-mile area before reaching its terminus just past the town of Grand Portage. Of all of Lake Superior's major tributaries, it is one of just a few that remain free of commercial or industrial development along its banks. Logging has taken place along the river on both sides of the border, but much of the surrounding lands have not been disturbed during the past 50 years.

The Rove slate hills that define the area's underlying geology were formed almost two billion years ago, in the Precambrian Era, when most of what is now Minnesota was part of an ancient sea bed. After it dried up, the sea left behind a thick layer of mud and sand deposits that later hardened into slates, shales, and sandstones known as the Rove Formation. This relatively soft bedrock layer erodes easily, so when waterways formed in the area after the retreat of the last glaciers about 10,000 years ago, they carved several gorges, including the one through which the Pigeon River now runs. Downstream from the preserve, large waterfalls formed over intrusions of harder igneous rock—mainly basalts formed by a volcanic rift about one billion years ago—that it could not erode. Such rock "dikes" are absent at the Pigeon River Cliffs Preserve, however, so here the river flows downstream at a leisurely pace.

The riverbed is covered with sand, gravel, and stones—moraine sediments deposited by retreating glaciers. Such conditions combined with clear, cold waters make ideal habitat for native brook trout, lake trout, and steelhead (a trout species that lives in Lake Superior for much of its life but travels upstream to spawn). Northern pike, smallmouth bass, walleye, yellow perch, and white suckers also live in the watershed.

Common land animals in the preserve include moose, wolves, black bear, bobcats, lynx, pine martens, and fishers. Among the bird species that make the preserve's coniferous forests their home are the spruce grouse, northern goshawk, raven, boreal chickadee, gray jay, red crossbill, and white-winged crossbill. Bald eagles are common, and numerous warbler, sparrow, raptor, and waterfowl species also use the preserve either as a migratory stopover or as a seasonal home.

Supporting this diverse array of wildlife is the coniferous forest biome that defines northeastern Minnesota. Here, cold-weather-loving evergreens such as black spruce, tamarack, balsam fir, red pine, white pine, and jack pine are the primary tree species. The first three thrive best in lowland peat bogs, and the rest prefer drier soils on slightly raised land.

The Pigeon River Cliffs also host plants that are native to alpine habitats of the Rocky Mountains and the White Mountains of New Hampshire and some arctic plants found near northern Canada's Hudson Bay. Both groups include hardy mosses, lichens, and low-growing shrubs and herbs accustomed to rocky outcroppings and harsh winter climates. Notable among the preserve's alpine and arctic plant species are sticky locoweed and alpine milk vetch, both of which are listed as state endangered species.

Such plants are highly sensitive to damage, even from footsteps, since they regenerate very slowly. For this reason, The Nature Conservancy encourages preserve visitors to stay on trails; bicycles and off-road vehicles are prohibited. The Pigeon River Cliffs Preserve is open year-round, and the 65-mile-long Border Route Hiking Trail crosses the property. A limited amount of public hunting is allowed in the preserve, which can be accessed via South Fowl Road, about 15 miles north of the town of Hovland off County Road 16.

Increased residential development—particularly in areas with lake or river views, such as those along the Pigeon River Cliffs—is another major threat to the watershed and surrounding forests. In addition to purchasing the preserve lands in 2002, The Nature Conservancy acquired 750 acres on the Canadian side of the river, farther downstream near Middle Falls. The conservancy is working with the Ontario Ministry of Natural Resources, the Grand Portage Ojibwe tribe, and the Ontario Park Service to secure further protections along both banks of the river.

Further Reading
Bray, Edmund C. *Billions of Years in Minnesota*. St. Paul, MN: North Central, 1977.
Minnesota Department of Natural Resources. "Natural History—Minnesota's Geology."
    http://www.dnr.state.mn.us/snas/naturalhistory.html.
Ver Steeg, Karl. "Some Features to the Tributaries to Lake Superior in Northeastern
    Minnesota." *Ohio Journal of Science* 48, no. 2 (March 1948).

PINE POINT RESEARCH NATURAL AREA

In the Chippewa National Forest in northeastern Minnesota, Pine Point Research Natural Area is an example of the state's coniferous forest biome, harboring pine-covered uplands interspersed with wet marshlands. Like other research natural areas, Pine Point has been set aside as a permanently protected area within the larger forest, to be maintained in its natural state for research purposes and as a control area for the impact of various forest uses elsewhere. Established in 1932, Pine Point encompasses 1,239 acres, including 24-acre Leech Lake and 95 acres of aspen-birch forest.

The Itasca moraine upon which Pine Point sits is a mixture of coarse, glacially deposited debris (moraine) and sandy, loamy, or calcareous soils later deposited by glacial melt waters in outwash plains and till plains. These deposits cover the underlying Precambrian bedrock at depths of between 200 and more than 600 feet. Red pine and jack pine—the most numerous tree species at Pine Point—thrive on the well-drained soils in upland areas of the outwash and till plains. In the poorly drained depressions between these uplands where organic muck has accumulated, sedge meadows dominate.

Red pine woodlands are by far the dominant habitat within Pine Point's coniferous forest, covering 550 acres in all. Jack pine forests also are common, however. Both species established themselves following major wildfires in the 1690s, 1830s, and 1890s, but they are now part of a mature forest that has not experienced a major burn since. Northern conifers rely on fire to reproduce, and young trees cannot grow in the shady interior of a mature forest. For this reason, the pines of Pine Point now are at risk of being overtaken by more shade-tolerant trees. Aspen and birch trees also grow within the forest but are not part of this succession.

Ground cover in coniferous forests tends to be sparse due to the lack of sunlight, but numerous shade-tolerant shrubs and other plants can be found in the understory. At Pine Point, common shrub species include serviceberry (*Amelanchier* spp.), round-leaved dogwood (*Cornus rugosa*), beaked hazelnut (*Corylus cornuta*), American hazelnut (*Corylus americana*), bush honeysuckle (*Diervilla lonicera*), and chokecherry (*Prunus virginiana*). Common herbaceous plant species include wood anemone (*Anemone quinquefolia*), wild sarsaparilla (*Aralia nudicaulis*), big-leaved aster (*Aster macrophyllus*), thick-leaved wild strawberry (*Fragaria virginiana*), Canada mayflower (*Maianthemum canadense*), and early meadow rue (*Thalictrum dioicum*).

In addition to its forests, Pine Point also encompasses 493 acres of sedge meadows, the dominant habitat in marshy lowlands. Here, sedges, grasses, rushes, and forbs (broad-leaved, flowering plants) grow in the poorly drained muck. Common plant species in such wetlands include hummock sedge (*Carex stricta*), lake sedge (*Carex lacustris*), Canada blue-joint grass (*Calamagrostis canadensis*), fowl bluegrass (*Poa palustris*), woolgrass (*Scirpus cyperinus*), marsh milkweed (*Asclepias incarnata*), arrow-leaved tearthumb (*Polygonum sagittatum*), water pepper (*Polygonum hydropiper*), common bugleweed (*Lycopus americanus*), blue vervain (*Verbena hastata*), swamp aster (*Aster lucidulus*), redstem aster (*Aster puniceus*), sawtooth sunflower (*Helianthus grosseserratus*), giant goldenrod (*Solidago gigantea*), and joe-pye weed (*Eupatorium maculatum*).

Much of the waters from these wetlands, which fluctuate seasonally, drains very slowly into Leech Lake. Such watersheds also are common on the end moraines and outwash plains of the area.

Pine Point's varied habitats provide food, shelter, and homes to many animal species, including black bear (*Ursus americanus*), white-tailed deer (*Odocoileus virginianus*), snowshoe hare (*Lepus americanus*), North American porcupine (*Erethizon dorsatum*), ruffed grouse (*Bonasa umbellus*), and bald eagle (*Haliaeetus leucocephalus*). Songbird and water fowl species also are abundant.

Along with the rest of the Chippewa National Forest, the Pine Point Research Natural Area is open to the public. It contains no roads or marked trails, however, and in general is used for scientific research and educational purposes. Research natural area lands can be used for "non-manipulative research, observation, and study," but all such projects must be approved by the U.S. Forest Service. Surrounding forest areas, which provide better recreational opportunities, host habitat similar to Pine Point, but, unlike Pine Point, much of it is open to logging and other extractive uses.

Further Reading

Boe, Janet. "Minnesota County Biological Survey, Cass County Biological Survey." 1992–1995. Biological Report No. 59. Minnesota Department of Natural Resources, 1998.

Kurmis, Vilis. "Forest Vegetation of Pine Point Natural Area, Chippewa National Forest, Minnesota. University of Minnesota, College of Forestry." Report to the North Central Forest Experiment Station. 1972.

Kurmis, Vilis, and D. Ness. "The 1969 Inventory of Red and Jack Pine Covertypes in Pine Point Natural Area, Chippewa National Forest. University of Minnesota, School of Forestry. Report to the North Central Forest Experiment Station. 1969.

Walley, J.M. 1932. "Establishment Record of the Pine Point Research Natural Area within the Chippewa National Forest." Unpublished report on file at the Northern Research Station, Rhinelander.http://www.nrs.fs.fed.us/rna/documents/establishment/mn_chippewa_pine_point.pdf.

RED ROCK PRAIRIE

The native tall-grass prairie of Red Rock Prairie Preserve is a remnant of the vast grasslands that once covered 18 million acres in western Minnesota—one-third of the state. The Nature Conservancy initially established the 611-acre preserve to protect the state-endangered and federally threatened native prairie bush clover, which was found on the site in the early 1980s. However, the conservancy has worked to restore the entire parcel, which also includes wet sedge meadows at the base of slopes. The preserve is part of just 150,000 acres of prairie habitat remaining in the state.

The Sioux quartzite bedrock underlying Red Rock Prairie juts above the soil in various outcrops that hindered tilling and therefore precluded farming. Today, two other tall-grass prairie preserves, Jeffers Petroglyphs State Historic Site and Rock Ridge Prairie Scientific and Natural Area, lie along this same exposed quartzite ridge in southwestern Minnesota. The mesic (moderate moisture) soils upon which tall-grass prairies grow ranges from sandy to silty and is rich in nutrients. Such soils also proved highly productive for agriculture, prompting early European settlers to transform Minnesota's vast grasslands into farmland. Even at Red Rock Prairie, 250 acres had been converted to crop fields and pasture, and native plants survived only in rocky areas until a recent restoration effort.

In addition to the grayish-silver prairie bush clover, other rare plants found around the preserve's rock outcrops include tumblegrass, buffalo grass, and mousetail. More common vegetation includes the dominant big bluestem, Indian grass, and prairie dropseed, as well as heart-leaved alexander, Maximilian sunflower, wood lily, gray-headed coneflower, and round-headed bush clover. Among other typical tall-grass prairie species are yarrow, autumn bentgrass, prairie wild onion, Great Plains goldenrod, and various asters and clovers.

Red Rock Prairie also harbors sedge meadows in low-lying areas. Here, water accumulates seasonally and maintains high moisture levels throughout the growing season, nurturing such plants as cordgrass, bird-foot violet, phlox, and coreopsis. Other common wet prairie species include blue-joint, bog reedgrass, bulrushes, spike-rushes, mat muhly, and the various sedges that give this habitat its name.

Numerous birds make their homes in the preserve, including the long-legged upland sandpiper, which migrates from Argentina's grasslands, known as pampas, to nest at Red Rock Prairie. Short-eared owls and golden plovers also are found in the preserve, and many other avian species have been sighted in the area, including ring-necked pheasant, rock pigeon, mourning dove, eastern bluebird, yellow-rumped warbler, American goldfinch, and various types of sparrows and swallows. Red Rock Prairie hosts two butterflies listed as species of special concern: the regal fritillary and Powesheik skipperling. Mammals that frequent the preserve include coyotes, deer, jackrabbits, and various rodents.

Like Minnesota's other remaining grasslands, Red Rock Prairie faces threats from invasive weeds, including smooth brome and Kentucky bluegrass. At the same time, suppression of wildfires—once common occurrences in prairie landscapes—and the elimination of bison and other large ungulates from the area have hindered the reproduction of native plants. Prairie grasses and wildflowers evolved to sprout and reproduce quickly after fire and grazing, while invasive plants typically do not survive such damage.

To restore the preserve's natural conditions, The Nature Conservancy conducts regular controlled burns to enhance native vegetation while keeping invasives under control. The conservancy also restored areas that had been converted to farm uses, planting native grasses and removing all farm structures.

The Red Rock Prairie Preserve is open to the public year-round and can be accessed off Highway 45, a gravel road about 20 miles northeast of the town of Windom, in Cottonwood County. Similar prairie habitat can be found at nearby Jeffers Petroglyphs State Historic Site and Rock Ridge Prairie Scientific and Natural Area.

Further Reading

Knapp, Alan K., John M. Briggs, David C. Hartnett, and Scott L. Collins. *Grassland Dynamics: Long-term Ecological Research in Tallgrass Prairie*. New York: Oxford University Press, 1998.

Minnesota Department of Natural Resources. "Prairie Grasslands Description." http://www.dnr.state.mn.us/snas/prairie_description.html.

U.S. Geological Survey, Northern Prairie Wildlife Research Center. "Wetland Plants and Plant Communities of Minnesota and Wisconsin. III.A. Sedge Meadows." http://www.npwrc.usgs.gov/resource/plants/mnplant/sedge.htm.

SAND LAKE/SEVEN BEAVERS PROJECT COMPLEX

Encompassing the headwaters of the St. Louis River, the 55,800-acre Sand Lake/Seven Beavers Project Complex is a vast, unbroken lowland conifer ecosystem that is one of the largest of its kind in the state. Jointly protected and managed by the Minnesota Department of Natural Resources, St. Louis and Lake counties, the U.S. Forest Service, and The Nature Conservancy, the complex includes nearly 45,000 acres with no roads and is the only significant peatlands in northeastern Minnesota.

The Sand Lake/Seven Beavers Preserve consists of 7,465 acres of scattered parcels acquired by The Nature Conservancy to join previously unconnected public lands. Thus, the preserve lands are within the larger project complex and are the only private lands in the complex.

The St. Louis River releases more water into Lake Superior than any other U.S. watershed. For this reason, the lakes, streams, and wetlands of the Sand Lake/Seven Beavers area are considered crucial to the health of the larger riparian ecosystem. The 4,924-acre Sand Lake Peatland Scientific and Natural Area, in particular, is a crucial component of the watershed's overall health. As the only large peat bog complex in the northeast part of the state, the area is unusual in both its size and location. It has formed on an outwash plain created by deposits from glacial melt waters, rather than atop a former lakebed like other peatlands in the state. Another remarkable aspect of the Sand Lake peatland is its continued outward growth while the sizes of other peat bogs in the state seem to have stabilized.

Minnesota's peat bogs have formed in low-lying areas in coniferous forests, where stagnant pools of water atop poorly drained soils create a low-oxygen environment. Under such conditions, vegetation decomposes slowly and only partially, consolidating over time into mats of peat that can be many feet thick. Such conditions are at the heart of not only the Sand Lake Peatland Scientific Natural Area, but also the larger lowland conifer forest ecosystem within the rest of the Sand Lake/Seven Beavers complex.

Tamarack, black spruce, and white cedar trees grow from the peat mats, dominating the forest canopy. Such shrubs as bog rosemary, bog birch, water horsetail, small cranberry, leatherleaf, marsh cinquefoil, Labrador tea, white beak rush, Hudson Bay bulrush, tufted bulrush, and numerous sedges grow lower to the ground. Carnivorous pitcher plants and the rare Michaux's sedge also are found in the area.

Among the many bird species that make the Sand Lake/Seven Beavers Project Complex their year-round home are the spruce grouse, northern goshawk, boreal chickadee, gray jay, white-winged crossbill, and red crossbill. Various raptors, warblers, sparrows, and waterfowl also migrate through the area or nest there temporarily. Among other birds common to lowland conifer ecosystems are Connecticut warblers, rusty blackbirds, and olive-sided flycatchers.

Mammals that frequent the preserve and the larger project complex include moose, gray wolves, black bear, pine martens, fishers, lynx, and bobcats. Two butterfly species, disa alpine and bog copper, rely on lowland conifer habitat that includes cranberry shrubs, such as that found in the complex.

The Nature Conservancy and the various public agencies that control these lands coordinate their management and conservation efforts within the project complex. Together, the groups prioritized restoration needs in a 2005 ecosystem analysis document, and the conservancy hired the Blandin Paper Company to conduct forest management planning and ecological classifications on its properties.

The poor soils and wet conditions of the Sand Lake/Seven Beavers area have largely protected the land from agriculture and other development, but the slow-growing plants in such ecosystems remain highly vulnerable to damage. The use of even one off-road vehicle in peat bogs and lowland coniferous forests can alter water drainage patterns and hinder the recovery of damaged plants for many years. For this reason, the Sand Lake/Seven Beavers Preserve and the surrounding public lands are intended for habitat protection rather than for recreational use.

However, the entire complex, including the preserve, is open to the public. The Nature Conservancy recommends visiting in winter, when the boggy terrain is frozen, rendering travel easier and protecting the peat mats from damage. Hiking, cross-country skiing, snowshoeing, and hunting all are allowed in the area, but, with few roads or marked trails, use of a map and compass is essential for extensive exploration.

The Sand Lake/Seven Beavers Project Complex can be reached via County Road 2, 35 miles north of the town of Two Harbors. There is a public access point at Greenwood Lake, off an old logging road. Here a trail travels for one mile through conservancy preserve land, then through five miles of old logging roads through a mix of conservancy, national forest, state forest, and Lake County lands.

Further Reading

Fedora, Mark. "Ecosystem Analysis of the Sand Lake/Seven Beavers Project Area, in the Upper St. Louis Watershed, Minnesota." U.S. Forest Service and The Nature Conservancy. May 12, 2005. http://www.nature.org/wherewework/northamerica/states/minnesota/files/slsb_ecosystem_analysis.pdf.

Minnesota Department of Natural Resources. "Habitats: Forest-Lowland Coniferous." http://files.dnr.state.mn.us/assistance/nrplanning/bigpicture/cwcs/habitats/02.pdf.

Wright, H. E. Jr., Barbara Coffin, and Norman E. Aaseng, eds. *The Patterned Peatlands of Minnesota.* Minneapolis: University of Minnesota Press, 1992.

WALLACE C. DAYTON CONSERVATION & WILDLIFE AREA

The Wallace C. Dayton Conservation & Wildlife Area protects the tall-grass aspen parkland biome—a transitional landscape between Minnesota's dry, windy western prairies and its damp, cold northeastern coniferous forests. Here, the constant competition between diverse ecosystems has created a mosaic of interspersed deciduous forest, grasslands, and fens. Owned and managed by The Nature Conservancy, the preserve is a patchwork of properties totaling 14,576 acres that connects much larger state wildlife management areas in northwest Minnesota. In this way, the conservancy has linked previously fragmented habitat and opened migration routes for wolves, bears, elk, and other mammals.

The area's rocky, poorly drained soils were formed from lake bed deposits beneath Lake Agassiz, an ancient glacial lake that began receding from the area about 10,000 years ago. It left behind vast, flat plains composed of varied soils originally deposited by glacial melt waters and the glaciers themselves. Unlike the soils of the plains to the west and southwest, those of the tall-grass aspen parkland proved unsuitable for farming; thus, large portions of this ecosystem remained intact even after European settlement.

Tall-grass aspen parkland vegetation has evolved to withstand a harsh climate that includes hot summers, cold winters, heavy rains, strong winds, and frequent wildfires. Here, wind and heat cause the soil and plants to lose more water through evaporation than the land receives in annual precipitation. Such conditions have produced a wide variety of plant communities that are constantly competing for dominance.

Groves of trembling aspen and balsam poplar trees, which rely on the area's heavy rains, are far better at retaining moisture than the open grasslands. They are constantly expanding, threatening to shade out tall-grass prairie species that require full sunlight. At the same time, wildfires have long halted the advance of these deciduous forests by killing off young trees while helping prairie vegetation reproduce and regenerate. Grazing by native bison, elk, moose, and deer also serves a similar purpose.

Interspersed throughout this landscape are fens, wet meadows that have formed in low areas where partly decomposed plant material builds up over many years to form peat mats. Fens are different from bogs, which also are based on peat mats, in that they rely on standing water from both precipitation and from ground water seeping up through mineral soils. Due to minerals from ground water, fens are less acidic than bogs, which rest atop a layer of poorly drained muck that traps the acids formed by peat.

The varied conditions of tall-grass aspen park land support a wide variety of grasses, shrubs, sedges, and wildflowers that often overlap at the edges of different habitats. Among the most common are big bluestem grass, cordgrass, and tufted hairgrass. As many as 36 rare or threatened plant species have been found in the preserve, including small white lady's slipper, yellow lady's slipper, several types of willow, and the western fringed prairie orchid, a federally threatened species.

The preserve and surrounding wildlife management areas still harbor most of the animal species native to the region prior to European settlement. These include such large mammals as gray wolves, black bears, moose, and elk; bison, however, are locally extinct. The preserve also is home to significant populations of many grassland and plains bird species that are in decline in the western Great Plains, among them sandhill cranes, sharp-tailed grouse, horned grebes, yellow rails, sharp-tailed sparrows, marbled godwits, and Wilson's phalaropes.

In its efforts to preserve the larger tall-grass aspen parkland biome, The Nature Conservancy is working with the U.S. Fish and Wildlife Service, the Minnesota Department of Natural Resources, other local agencies, and surrounding private landowners. It also has acquired lands across the Canadian border in southeastern Manitoba to further broaden wildlife corridors in this shared ecosystem. The conservancy's Dayton preserve currently connects the Caribou and Roseau River wildlife management areas, but the conservancy also is working with area residents and farmers to promote sustainable agriculture, biological diversity, and conservation easements on adjacent lands. In addition, the conservancy conducts controlled fires to mimic the natural wildfires that have been largely suppressed during the past 200 years.

The Wallace C. Dayton Conservation & Wildlife Area, located near the town of Karlstad, is largely inaccessible due to its remoteness and distribution between and around various public lands. However, hiking and bird-watching are allowed on the properties, and the conservancy is considering controlled hunting, grazing, and other land uses as well.

Further Reading

Jones, Stephen R., and Ruth Carol Cushman. *A Field Guide to the North American Prairie*. Boston, MA: Houghton Mifflin Harcourt, 2004.

Minnesota Department of Natural Resources. "Minnesota's Biomes: Tallgrass Aspen Parkland." http://www.dnr.state.mn.us/biomes/tallgrass.html.

Snetsinger, Susan, and Steve Ventura. "Land Cover Change in the Great Lakes Region from Mid-nineteenth Century to Present." U.S. Department of Agriculture, North Central Research Station. http://www.ncrs.fs.fed.us/gla/reports/LandCoverChange.htm.

Tester, John. *Minnesota's Natural Heritage: An Ecological Perspective*. Minneapolis: University of Minnesota Press, 1995.

WEAVER DUNES SCIENTIFIC AND NATURAL AREA

The Weaver Dunes Scientific and Natural Area represents an anomaly along Minnesota's Mississippi River floodplain: a 300-foot-high terrace of sand dunes that supports sand prairie and oak savanna habitat similar to that normally found in the western part of the state. It also provides critical habitat for the state endangered Blanding's turtle. Owned by The Nature Conservancy, the preserve protects 592 acres of the 10-mile-long, 3-mile-wide dune complex, located near the confluence of the Zumbro and the Mississippi rivers. The state-owned Kellogg-Weaver Dunes Scientific and Natural Area, located just north of the conservancy property, comprises another 697 acres of this same ecosystem. The area also includes floodplain forests.

The dunes sit atop the Paleozoic Plateau, a series of bluffs and deeply carved river valleys that is unique in the state. Initially formed by deposits from glacial melt waters, the bluffs were covered over time by loess (extremely fine, windblown silt) of varying depths. Over the past 10,000 years, wind and the action of rivers past and present have deeply eroded the sedimentary rock underlying the plateau. Within this small strip of land, widely different vegetation has grown depending on a particular area's slope and aspect, and therefore its likelihood of burning, flooding, or eroding away.

In the windiest, most exposed areas, blowouts of bare sand, with only occasional sparse vegetation, are common. Tall-grass prairie and bur oak savannas exist mainly along the dunes' dry upper slopes and ridge lines. The former, made up primarily of such grasses as little bluestem and junegrass, has grown up mainly along broad ridge tops or on south- or southwest-facing slopes—areas prone to the spread of fire. Wildfires are crucial to the health and reproduction of tall-grass prairies, and they also kill off most young trees, keeping the prairies open. Oak savannas, which include scattered pin oak, bur oak, and jack pine among the prairie flora, occur mainly at the edges of the prairie, in steeper areas or on slopes that receive less sunlight and burn less often.

A local population of about 5,000 endangered Blanding's turtles depends on the Weaver Dunes prairies for nesting. In June each year, the females travel from their breeding grounds in nearby wetlands to the sand prairies, where they lay their eggs. Hatchlings travel the same route in reverse when they emerge in late August. Along the way, the turtles must cross roads and highways, and many die along the way each year. Still, the American Museum of Natural History considers the Weaver Dunes the nation's most important habitat for Blanding's turtles due to the large size and diversity of the turtle population there.

Three rare butterflies also breed in the Weaver Dunes sand prairies: the federally endangered Karner blue butterfly, the threatened Ottoe skipper, and the regal fritillary, a species of special concern. The timber rattlesnake, gopher snake, plains pocket mouse, and loggerhead shrike—all threatened species or species of special concern—make their homes on the bluffs. Other notable species include milk snakes and numerous birds, including Henslow's sparrows, prothonotary warblers, red-shouldered hawks, Louisiana waterthrushes, western meadowlarks, Bells vireo, bald eagles, and peregrine falcons. The dunes also support many rare and threatened plants, including sea-beach needlegrass, purple sand grass, beach heather, sand milkweed, wild indigo, goat's rue, and cliff golden-rod. Area rivers host a wide array of aquatic animals, among them paddlefish, shovelnose sturgeon, pallid shiners, American eels, pirate perch, skipjack herrings, and several snails from the Pleistocene Era.

In the valleys below the dry sand prairies and savannas grow hardwood forests domi-nated by cottonwood, black walnut, red oak, basswood, and black oak. Although such forests are most common in the floodplains of the Mississippi and Zumbro rivers and their larger tributaries, they also grow on the moist slopes of the plateau.

Logging of floodplain forests and farming on the prairies beginning in the 1800s re-moved native plants that had held the fine soils in place and greatly altered the Weaver Dunes ecosystem. Such development promoted massive erosion much greater than that induced by wind and water alone. More recent soil conservation efforts have greatly re-duced erosion, but high-sediment and chemical runoff remain a major threat to aquatic life in particular. High quantities of sediments from further upstream in the Zumbro watershed also are filling in crucial Mississippi backwater habitat.

Both The Nature Conservancy and the Minnesota Department of Natural Resources, which acquired their respective properties in the Weaver Dunes area in 1980 and 1982, respectively, have worked to increase awareness about soil conservation and runoff in the area. Conservancy volunteers have removed nonnative plant species, spread native seed in the prairies and savannas, and conducted controlled burns to mimic naturally occurring wildfires.

The Weaver Dunes Scientific and Natural Area, located in Wabasha County near the town of Kellogg, is open to the public. It can be accessed from Township Road 141, off Highway 61.

Further Reading

Minnesota Department of Natural Resources. "Eastern Broadleaf Forest: The Blufflands Subsection." http://www.dnr.state.mn.us/ecs/222Lc/index.html.

The Nature Conservancy, Upper Mississippi River Program. "Weaver Dunes/Zumbro River: Managing Water for Habitat." http://www.nature.org/wherewework/greatrivers/namerica/art21313.html.

Grand River Grasslands–
Dunn Ranch and Pawnee Prairie

Maryville
Albany
Kirksville
St. Joseph
Chillicothe
Macon
Marceline
Hannibal
Moberly
Platte City
Bowling Green
Excelsior Springs
Mexico
Marshall
Kansas City
Boonville
Columbia
Warrensburg
Sedalia
Fulton
Jefferson City
MISSOURI

Tucker Prairie
Pickle Springs
Florissant
St. Louis
Victoria Glade
Sullivan
Festus
Onondaga Cave

Taberville Prairie
Bennett Spring
Savanna
Nevada
Rolla

Grasshopper
Hollow

Lebanon

Shelton L. Cook
Meadow
Springfield
Jackson
Cape Girardeau
Carthage
Ozark
Joplin
Shut-in
Mountain Fens
Monett
Aurora
West Plains
Chilton
Creek
Sikeston
Poplar Bluff
Branson
Big Oak Tree
State Park
Tumbling Creek Cave
Kennett
Hayti

0   50 mi
0   50 km

Missouri

Missouri's natural places are interesting for a number of reasons. Though much of the state has a more "southern" feel compared to the other states in the Midwest volume, Missouri contains habitat in common with much of the Midwest, even the more northerly states. There are prairies along the Iowa border, Mississippi riparian habitat, and deciduous forests like those in the east. Glacial advances did not reach the southern part of Missouri, but they did shape the northern and central parts of the state. Algific talus slopes, a unique habitat, provide a cool, moist environment capable of sustaining boreal forest organisms in some of their southernmost occurrences. The high limestone content of the soils of the southern part of the state makes possible the characteristic karst topography, which includes sinkholes, losing streams, and, most notably, caves. With over 6,000 discovered caves, the importance of the connection between what is above ground and what is below is striking in Missouri. Many of the natural places in the karst landscape are affected by human activities many miles away, because the porous landscape easily absorbs runoff from cattle farming, pesticides, fertilizers, and toxins that have been dumped. These challenges are being met by many innovative approaches and are revealing many connections between human and natural systems that might be easily overlooked. The Missouri Department of Conservation is especially active in the state in educating the public, preserving natural places, and forming partnerships for conservation.

Bennett Spring Savanna

This 920-acre preserve is a high-quality savanna, a rare and disappearing ecosystem because, across the Midwest, undergrowth is gradually filling in the open park-like habitat of this oak- and hickory-dominated type of ecosystem. After more than a century of fire suppression, shrubs and fire-intolerant trees have had a chance to grow and thrive in conditions in which they historically would not have been able to.

Bennett Spring Savanna, however, has much the same composition of trees as were recorded in the earliest survey of the area in 1846. Such historical records are critical to assessing the conditions of natural places. In addition, they help to direct current and future management strategies. The preserve is open to the public and owned by The Nature Conservancy, which manages the savanna through prescribed fires to maintain the ecosystem much as it was 150 years ago. Because of the quality of this site, The Nature Conservancy uses Bennett Spring Savanna as its cornerstone in efforts to restore 15,000 acres for 10 miles along the Niangua River in the Ozark Highlands ecoregion.

Besides being one of the few virtually untouched savannas left in Missouri, the preserve protects the recharge area feeding Bennett Springs, which is a regionally important fishing destination. Bennett Springs is also an example of the changes that have been made to conservation policy in Missouri. Prior to the 1970s, the state park system had an emphasis on recreation and a passive preservation policy. As early as 1974, oak savannas were recognized as distinct ecosystems in Missouri. In 1983, Bennett Spring Savanna was the second site purchased from private landowners by The Nature Conservancy. Combined with Bennett Spring State Park, Bennett Spring Savanna is a benchmark

Bennett Spring Savanna. (Larry Nolan)

for scientific research into restoration of Missouri oak savannas. The preserve has been monitored by The Nature Conservancy since 1987, and data have been collected regarding the restoration and maintenance of degraded and high-quality tracts of oak savanna under different prescribed burn programs. The information collected over the decades is invaluable to preserve managers looking over Missouri oak savannas in a full range of environmental conditions. The presettlement landscape of Missouri was fire dependent, and forests were much more open with a sparse understory and were more extensive than many of the forests of today.

Oak savannas have declined throughout the country because of invasion by non-native species, understory plants, and competition from bottomland and fire-intolerant species such as Eastern red cedar. The primary cause of this decline is the suppression of fire. By doing prescribed burns, controlling where and when fires take place in the savannas, managers are attempting to maintain the health of the savannas. The difference that fire makes can be seen in the improvement of degraded sites in which rare species populations increase and the invasive species decrease. The importance of baseline information is critical to knowing what is working, because without knowledge of the composition of a site before restoration efforts are made and the changes as a result of restoration, it is impossible to know whether the results are positive. In some sense, Bennett Spring Savanna is even more important to this endangered ecosystem type than the site itself.

Further Reading

Hartman, George, ed. *Proceedings of SRM 2002: Savanna/Woodland Symposium.* Columbia: Conservation Commission of the State of Missouri, 2004.

Schroeder, W. A. *Presettlement Prairie of Missouri.* Natural History Series, No. 2, Missouri Department of Conservation, 1981.

BIG OAK TREE STATE PARK

This state park is the only known tract of virtually virgin wet mesic bottomland forest remaining in the northern part of the Mississippi Valley Alluvial Plain ecoregion. This primarily riverine ecoregion extends from the Gulf of Mexico to the southeastern corner of Missouri. This flat, alluvial plain was historically covered by wetlands and bottomland deciduous forests. Being connected to the Gulf of Mexico, the ecoregion in Missouri is the northern limit for many coastal plains species. Cropland agriculture is extensive in the region today, the wetlands having been drained and the Mississippi River, as well as others, channelized. The alluvial plain area is virtually devoid of trees outside of the immediate area of the Mississippi, with Big Oak Tree State Park standing out as a sizeable continuous tract of forest in this otherwise deforested region.

The park began as a campaign in the 1930s to save a large bur oak tree and 80 acres surrounding it from logging by the timber company that owned the land. In 1938, more than 1,000 acres of land were purchased through donations and were dedicated as the park named today. The original bur oak that saved the park died in 1952, but there are many trees of impressive size remaining. Five trees rank as state champions and two as national champions for their size. Because of the significance of this park, 90 percent of it is designated as a state natural area, recognizing the significance of the bottomland forests to Missouri's ecological history.

Historically, this area of Missouri was considered unusable because the poorly drained soils could not be farmed. With improvements in technology, the 70 percent of the land that was considered unusable in 1907 dropped precipitously over three decades to only 3 percent. Virtually all the land has been logged and drained. Today, the park contains a diversity of trees typical of the mixture of trees that once covered this ecoregion: shellbark hickory (*Carya laciniosa*), pecan (*Carya illinoensis*), slippery elm (*Ulmus rubra*), sweet gum (*Liquidambar styraciflua*), persimmon (*Diospyros virginiana*), blue beech (*Carpinus caroliniana*), and swamp chestnut oak (*Quercus michauxii*). Giant cane (*Arundinaria gigantea*), a bamboo-like grass found in the park which forms canebrakes, or thickets, was the last known nesting site of Swainson's warbler (*Limnothlypis swainsonii*). This neotropical, secretive bird needs dense undergrowth and a high canopy for breeding.

The oaks that give the park its name may one day be only a memory. The oaks are very old, and no new ones are replacing them. And the open marshy pond, called Grassy Pond, which was created in 1959 to provide an artificial lake for fishing, has disrupted the natural changes in water levels. Also, drainage ditches were built encircling and through the park to reduce flooding in adjacent farm fields. By the 1980s, the swamp was dry for most of the year due to the hydrological disruptions of the past decades.

This dramatic change to the hydrology is behind a legal battle involving the U.S. Army Corps of Engineers. In 1954, Congress authorized the closure of a 1,500-foot gap in the Mississippi River Frontline Levee system and in 1986 authorized improvements to channels within the St. Johns Bayou Basin, Pump Station, and New Madrid Pump Station. This is collectively called the St. Johns Bayou and New Madrid Floodway Project. Basically, the project aims to protect the region from backwater flooding, which occurs about every three years. The alteration of The Natural ecosystem over the past 100 years has made this a viable agricultural area on which many people's livelihood depends.

Big Oak Tree State Park lies within the project boundaries and is part of the project's goals. To receive conditional approval by the Missouri Department of Natural Resources for the project, several conditions regarding the park needed to be met. A wildlife corridor would be created connecting Big Oak Tree State Park and the Tenmile Pond conservation area, buffer land would be purchased and planted, and a drainage ditch would be designed and constructed to bring floodwaters from the Mississippi to maintain the hydrology of Big Oak Tree State Park (flooding events occur about every three years). As of 2009, the St. Johns Bayou and New Madrid Floodway Project had been cancelled because of opposition from environmental groups, and more than seven million dollars of work that began on the Mississippi is being reversed. Other options are being explored.

The fate of Big Oak Tree State Park and the periodic flooding in this region of Missouri is undecided. It is contentious whether the proposed reforestation and channelizing to direct and control flooding for protection of agriculture as well as to maintain the hydrology of flood-dependent ecosystems would be successful. Big Oak Tree State Park not only houses one of the last near-virgin tracts of forest in a region now agricultural, it also stands at the heart of a struggle to balance the health of the ecosystem with healthy communities. How these issues are approached and decided are critical for how we will meet increasingly more difficult ecological, economic, and social problems ahead.

Further Reading

Flader, Susan, ed. *Exploring Missouri's Legacy: State Parks and Historic Sites.* Columbia: University of Missouri Press, 1992.

Sierra Club of Missouri. "St. Johns Bayou and New Madrid Floodway Project, Part I." http://missouri.sierraclub.org/SierranOnline/AprJune2003/05PartIofSierranFlood wayArticle_msr.HTM.

Sierra Club of Missouri. "St. Johns Bayou and New Madrid Floodway Project, Part II." http://missouri.sierraclub.org/sierranonline/JulySep2003/01PartIIofSierranArticle withmagesbyAlan_msr.HTM.

U.S. Army Corps of Engineers. "St. Johns Bayou and New Madrid Floodway Project." http://www.mvm.usace.army.mil/StJohns/overview/default.asp.

CHILTON CREEK

The 5,627-acre Chilton Creek preserve is The Nature Conservancy's largest preserve in Missouri and is located in the environmentally rich Ozark Highlands ecoregion. The preserve offers the chance to experience the diversity of this region; forests, glades, cliffs, springs, and fens are just some of the plant communities found at the preserve. In fact, more than 700 species of flowering plants are found in the preserve, making it one of the most diverse preserves in the state. The Ozark Highlands ecoregion as well is an incredibly diverse region. The diverse landscape of irregular topography, high-quality streams, and more than 60 percent of the land covered by open forest or woodlands of mainly oak and shortleaf pine has resulted in a mosaic of ecosystems. The region is characterized by deeply dissected valleys and hollows, and the preserve is rugged and relatively undeveloped, being accessible only by all-terrain vehicles. The many habitats support migratory birds such as worm-eating warblers, ovenbirds, summer tanagers, and many neotropical migratory birds that use the preserve as breeding grounds. Interestingly, half the indigenous snails of Missouri have been documented in the preserve.

The Chilton Creek preserve was created in 1991 in a partnership with the Missouri Department of Conservation (MDC), when The Nature Conservancy purchased 80,819 acres of land from the Kerr-McGee Corporation with help from the MDC. The Nature Conservancy retained the land of the present-day Chilton Creek Preserve, and the remaining acreage was incorporated into MDC lands. The same year, The Nature Conservancy launched its initiative "Last Great Places: An Alliance for People and the Environment"—an ongoing effort to protect large-scale ecosystems with an emphasis that includes people as part of the solution. Through this collaboration, The Nature Conservancy has worked with the MDC on the Missouri Ozark Forest Ecosystem Project. Started in 1990, this study observes the effects of various timber management practices on all aspects of the Ozark ecosystems, including animal, plant, soil, and water.

Before European settlement in the 1820s, fires occurred about every seven years; until the late 1920s, when the U.S. Forest Service and the MDC began fire suppression programs, fires occurred every couple of years. The last fires at Chilton Creek were during a drought in the mid-1950s. Current research is helping us understand what works and what does not work in this fire-dependent ecosystem. For instance, in 1996, 2,500 woodland acres at Chilton Creek were included in the original study area to observe the effects of managing the woodlands through prescribed burning. The results of the controlled study at Chilton Creek and other sites throughout the region are valuable for determining the best practices for managing forests for timber, recreation, and preservation in the Ozark Highlands of Missouri. Conservation land management in the Ozarks has its own challenges that may require modifications of management strategies used in other regions, even within Missouri; it is only through such studies that the best practices can be ascertained. Most importantly, conservation work links human well-being—clean water, income and resources from timber, and recreation, among other things—as integral to successful management strategies.

The educational opportunities of Chilton Creek extend beyond the scientific and economic. Area school children use the preserve as an outdoor classroom. The preserve is open to the public and affords visitors the opportunity to see an outstanding example of the diversity of the Ozark Highlands ecoregion. Visitors can also witness the results of woodland fire management in the progression toward a dynamic fire-regulated landscape.

Further Reading

Brookshire, B. L., Randy Jensen, and Daniel C. Dey. "The Missouri Ozark Forest Ecosystem Project: Past, Present, and Future." In *Proceedings of the Missouri Ozark Forest Ecosystem Project Symposium: An Experimental Approach to Landscape Research*, 1–25. USDA Forest Service General Technical Report NC-193, 1997.

Hartman, George W. "Changes in Fuel Loading as the Result of Repeated Prescribed Fires within the Ozark Forests of Missouri." In *Proceedings, 14th Central Hardwood Forest Conference*, March 16–19, 2004, 162–67. Wooster, OH: U.S. Department of Agriculture, Forest Service, Northeastern Research Station.

GRAND RIVER GRASSLANDS—DUNN RANCH AND PAWNEE PRAIRIE

Dunn Ranch's 3,680 acres and Pawnee Prairie's 910 acres are the focus of tallgrass prairie restoration efforts in the Grand River Grasslands Conservation Opportunity Area, which is part of an effort to conserve tallgrass prairie in a 70,000-acre area that spans parts of northwestern Missouri and Iowa. About half of Pawnee Prairie (476 acres) is owned and managed by the Missouri Department of Conservation; the remaining 434-acre Dunn Ranch is owned and managed by The Nature Conservancy. The area holds special significance in the Conservation Opportunity Area because Dunn Ranch contains more than 1,000 acres of prairie that have never been plowed. It is one of the best sites for conservation of a remnant tallgrass prairie in the Central Irregular Plains ecoregion.

Of the main glacial stages of the current ice age, the latest glacial advance into Missouri was in the re-Illinoian and Illinoian stage from 300,000 to about 130,000 years ago. This last glacial advance left its mark in Iowa and northern Missouri. The drift, or deposits left by the glaciers, came from limestone and shale, which make up the clay and high percentage of rock fragments in this ecoregion. The glaciers did not extend into the southern portions of this ecoregion—southwestern Missouri into Kansas; however, the topography is similarly level to rolling like the glaciated area of this region. The ecore-

Grand River Grasslands—Dunn Ranch and Pawnee Prairie. (Chase Davis)

gion is a mix of grasslands and woodlands with more woodlands along streams than in the Western Corn Belt Plains ecoregion to the north. The land is less irregular and has much less tree cover than the ecoregions to the south and east, making this a transition area from the plains to the north and the wooded Ozarks to the south. It has been determined that this intersection holds great opportunity for restoration and preservation work.

Grand River Grasslands Conservation Opportunity Area recognizes the significance of this ecoregion and the opportunities for high-quality restoration work crossing state lines. For instance, Big Creek flows through Pawnee Prairie and contains typical prairie fish such as trout perch and red shiner. There is an effort to reintroduced the federally listed Topeka shiner in local ponds. In 1999, volunteers planted more than 35 species of native prairie plants as a seed source for future restoration activities on Pawnee Prairie and Dunn Ranch. Seven thousand pounds of seed were recently harvested from this planting. Dunn Ranch is also the only public area in Missouri where people can view a booming ground of the greater prairie chicken—the prairie chicken's mating area.

Invasive woody plants and other exotics are being controlled through prescribed burns. Patch-burn grazing strategies are also being used to determine the effectiveness of spot burning and grazing for managing the prairie. A lack of baseline data on plant and animal species are challenges being met through ongoing surveys as funds and time permit. An example of this was when purple giant hyssop was discovered during a seed harvest at Pawnee Prairie; it is only the second population of this plant known in Missouri. For the conservation efforts to be successful, the vastness of the conservation area requires private landowner cooperation. Changing ownership and willingness to conduct fire management are some of the most challenging aspects of restoration activities in the area. With limited resources, only relatively small areas can be purchased outright and properly managed. Private-public partnerships are critical to the future of the tallgrass prairie, more so than in many ecosystems because of the vast expanses of land required by many of the organisms that call the prairie home.

These two preserves highlight the need to view natural areas in their context, and, in the case of particular ecosystems, it is required that preservation be viewed on a landscape scale. Because political boundaries are not the same as natural boundaries, the Grand River Grasslands provides an excellent example of private and public partnerships across local and state jurisdictions and the challenges and opportunities that are possible. All sites are open to the public.

Further Reading

Shelton, Napier. *Natural Missouri: Working with the Land.* Columbia: University of Missouri Press, 2005.
Unklesbay, A.G., and Jerry D. Vineyard. *Missouri Geology: Three Billion Years of Volcanoes, Seas, Sediments, and Erosion.* Columbia: University of Missouri Press, 1992.

Grasshopper Hollow

The 593-acre Grasshopper Hollow is significant for its natural areas and atypical ownership and management. Grasshopper Hollow is most well known for its fens, which form the largest fen complex in unglaciated North America. There are at least 15 fens and the largest known prairie fen in Missouri. Fens are areas where soils are saturated from mineral-rich groundwater. The constant cool water creates a unique wetland habitat for many plants and animals that are adapted to this particular habitat. There are four types of fens at Grasshopper Hollow. The 10-acre prairie fen, mentioned earlier, is a mixture of fen plants and dry, mesic, and wet prairie plants. Prairie fens are only found in the glaciated Midwest, with Missouri being the exception. The 10 deep muck fens consist of 15 to 40 inches of mucky soil dominated by grasses and sedges. Seep fens, which are the most common type found in the Ozarks, are boglike; they contain shallow, mucky soils found in a variety of habitats, but here, at Grasshopper Hollow, they are in the narrow valley. And last, forested fen is poorly drained and has seasonally saturated soils from rainwater and seeping groundwater; the canopy is closed. The forested fen at Grasshopper Hollow was logged in the past and is being restored. Some of the dominant trees are chestnut oak (*Quercus prinus*), green ash (*Fraxinus pennsylvanica*), and red elm (*Ulmus rubra*) with an understory of common spicebush (*Lindera benzoin*).

The diverse habitat and unique conditions of fens support an ecosystem of plants and animals endemic to the Ozark Highlands ecoregion. The fens include beavers (*Castor canadensis*) whose runs along the stony bottoms of the fens are visible; the rare four-toed salamander (*Hemidactylium scutatum*); and, most notably, it is a breeding ground for Hine's emerald dragonfly (*Somatochlora hineana*), a federally endangered species, which was first collected at this site in 1999 and not known to still live in the preserve but is found at a few sites in Wisconsin, Illinois, and Michigan. This dragonfly is closely associated with surface dolomite deposits, which is are commonly quarried. The dragonfly has been found elsewhere, often near quarries. In fact, Hine's emerald dragonflies were observed in the 10-acre prairie fen on land owned by the Doe Run Mining Company, land that is leased by The Nature Conservancy.

The dragonfly's discovery underlies the unique ownership of the natural area. The Nature Conservancy owns 223 acres and leases 80 acres from the Doe Run Mining Company. The remaining area is part of the U.S. Forest Service's Mark Twain National Forest. The mining company retains mineral mining rights on the leased land. The mining company's operations are just north of Grasshopper Hollow, and winds in winter sometimes blow dust from the lead mine tailings. Mining for lead, zinc, copper, silver, and manganese is more significant economically here than elsewhere in the ecoregion. Providing work and income for local residents, the mines are important to the regional economy, and finding a balance between environmental and economic concerns is critical for both. For instance, dye tracing, using a nonharmful dye to determine surface and subsurface water patterns, done in the early 1990s indicated that the fens are fed by springs that originated south of the natural area in Logan Creek valley. When determining the boundaries for the natural area, this was not expected. This is important because the entire fen complex was named a natural area in 1993, protecting the 2,000-acre surface watershed.

This ecosystem is dominated by water, and hydrological changes pose some of the most significant threats. Beaver dams have changed the hydrology in some areas of the fens, and The Nature Conservancy is managing the activities of beavers where their dams are significantly altering habitat. Fire management is also used not only to reduce the understory, which historically would have been more open with periodic fires, but to maintain the natural elements of the fen. By partnering with the U.S. Forest Service, The Nature Conservancy is restoring the fen watershed. Some of the best fen habitat is available through the lease with the local mining company. Open to the public, this is an important site on many levels.

Further Reading

Amon, J. P., C. A. Thompson, Q. J. Carpenter, and J. Miner. "Temperate Zone Fens of the Glaciated Midwestern USA." *Wetlands* 22, no. 2 (2002): 301–17.

Michigan Natural Features Inventory. Lansing: Michigan State University Extension, 1999. http://web4.msue.msu.edu/mnfi/pub/abstracts.cfm.

Spieles, J. B., P. J. Comer, D. A. Albert, and M. A. Kost. "Natural Community Abstract for Prairie Fen."

ONONDAGA CAVE

In a state known for its more than 5,000 caves, Onondaga Cave stands out for its size (1,317 acres), diverse cave formations, and colorful history. Onondaga Cave has been open to the public at various times since 1897. The property has changed hands several times and was the center of many lawsuits over ownership until it was eventually dedicated as a state park in 1982. The cave formed as a result of the Leasburg fault, which runs the length of the cave. The stresses on either side of the fault allowed water to run its length and carve out what would become the cave seen today. The cave is also famous for its streams, which did not form the cave but are a result of water draining into the cave.

The Onondaga Cave is best known for its colorful and varied speleothems, or cave formations. Some of the more common formations are stalactites, which are formed by dripping water and look like icicles; stalagmites, which form from water depositing calcite on the floor of the cave; columns, which form when stalagmites and stalactites meet; flowstones, which are formed by water flowing across a wall or floor; and helictites, which resemble crooked roots and are formed as water is pulled through tiny canals.

The cave's speleothems are what draw most visitors to the cave, but there is also a relative abundance of life in the caves as well. Sixty species have been documented, including frogs, bats, snails, and occasionally fish. But life is difficult in the cave, and there are many challenges to life in Onondaga Cave.

The deeper parts of the cave remain a constant temperature, with nearly 100 percent humidity. The surrounding earth regulates the cave's ambient temperature to the average temperature of region. In the case of Onondaga Cave, the temperature remains within 1° of 57° F. Not surprisingly, cave inhabitants also require a very narrow temperature range. Bats, for instance, will abandon a cave with a temperature change of as little as 2°. In the history of Onondaga Cave, nine openings have been created. This changed the movement of air in the cave, raising the temperature and making the cold-blooded cave inhabitants more active and thereby requiring more food. Drier air affected the sensitive skin of creatures such as salamanders, who breathe partially through their skin. As bat populations fluctuated because of the changes in temperature, so did the level of fresh bat guano or feces, the only source of food for many microorganisms, which in turn were food for small predators such as amphipods, which were also sources of food for organisms higher in the food chain, and so on. Several of these artificial openings have since been shut, successfully restoring microclimates in the cave.

Water is an important component of the cave for maintaining its present beauty as well as its inhabitants. For this reason, dye trace studies were conducted in 2003 to attempt to determine what surface water is entering the cave. Much of the cave's recharge area, the surface area that contributes water to the cave, lies outside the state park's boundaries. These studies have been valuable for helping to develop a management plan for protecting or purchasing above-ground areas critical to the health of the cave. Many activities can alter the recharge area of a cave such as mining; well-water draw-down; agricultural pesticides and fertilizers; and sedimentation or the accumulation of silt from logging, farming, and other development that disturbs the surface and prevents water from getting to the cave or brings excessive sediment into the cave. All these factors can dramatically affect Onondaga Cave.

Onondaga Cave is an outstanding example of Missouri's many caves and is visually one of the most spectacular caves in Missouri. Being located in the Ozark Highlands ecoregion, the cave also serves as an example of a karst feature, common in this region. The park is open for a variety of tours.

Further Reading

Aley, T. "Caves in Crisis." In *1997 Yearbook of Science and the Future*, 116–133. Chicago: Encyclopedia Britannica, 1997.

Lewis, Julian J. "The Devastation and Recovery of Caves Affected by Industrialization." *Proceedings of the 1995 National Cave Management Symposium, October 25–28, 1995, Spring Mill State Park, Indiana*, 214–27. Indianapolis: Indiana Department of Natural Resources, 1996).

Vale, Eugene, and Ronald H. Jones. "It's an Open and Shut Cave: Plugging Artificial Entrances at Onondaga Cave State Park." In *National Cave Management Proceedings, Bowling Green, Kentucky, October 23–26*, edited by Debra L. Foster, 129–31. Horse Cave, KY: 1991, American Cave Conservation Association.

PICKLE SPRINGS

Pickle Springs is a 256-acre natural area in the Ozark Highlands ecoregion and is in a transitional area between the interior of the Ozark Highlands and the adjacent Interior River Valleys and hills ecoregions of central Missouri and southern Illinois. The dissected hills and sheer bluffs are typical of this region, and Pickle Springs is known for its dramatic geology. The natural area is open to the public and is located seven miles northeast of Farmington.

The deep forested gorge that runs through the area has preserved one of the best Pleistocene (ice age) relict ecosystems in Missouri. The natural area contains a sandstone cliff, glade, canyons, savanna, talus, and forest as well as being the headwaters of a stream. The Lamotte sandstone was formed 500 million years ago and became exposed during past glaciations. This is also one of the few places in Missouri where sandstone and igneous rock are found together at the surface. The sandstone has been weathered into many unusual shapes, including hoodoo rocks, which are columns of unusually weathered rock; hoodoos are most famously found in Bryce Canyon National Park. More unusual rock formations can be seen in the two-mile trail than can be found most other places in Missouri. Also, the weathered sandstone produced the acidic soils of today evident in the abundance of the acid soil–loving wild azaleas (*Rhododendron prinophyllum*), which can be seen in full bloom in spring and are found in only a few other locations in Missouri. Other plants that prefer acidic soil include reindeer lichen (*Cladonia rangiferina*) and mosses (*Polytrichum* sp.). The soils and cool, moist air provide the conditions for this unusual habitat.

Historically, this natural area contained oaks and shortleaf pine (*Pinus echinata*), which is an important tree for lumber, wood pulp for paper, and an extract used to make turpentine. The woods were typically what would be called open woodlands—with few shrubs or understory except for herbaceous plants. The forests have now filled in because of fire suppression. Prescribed burns have been conducted at nearby Hawn State Park to restore the pine woodland habitat. This type of management may be necessary at Pickle Springs as well. The natural area protects a stream headwaters, which is important to the health of all organisms downstream that depend on it. Although development seems far away, eventually the area will see growth. Pickle Springs is currently ecologically connected to Hawn State Park through the large forests but could someday be the victim of fragmentation and become an isolated forest. This would possibly change the climatic patterns supporting the cool, humid air necessary for the survival of this relic forest. This is a real challenge for many preserves and is an important consideration in the management strategy for Pickle Springs.

The combination of unusual geology and rare and relict ecosystems makes the two-mile hike through Pickle Springs arguably one of the most fruitful and unusual in Missouri. With proper management, this relatively small area will preserve the geological and ecological past of Missouri.

Further Reading
Pielou, E.C. *After the Ice Age: The Return of Life to Glaciated North America*. Chicago: University of Chicago Press, 1991.
Unklesbay, A.G., and Jerry D. Vineyard. *Missouri Geology: Three Billion Years of Volcanoes, Seas, Sediments, and Erosion*. Columbia: University of Missouri Press, 1992.

SHELTON L. COOK MEADOW

Shelton L. Cook Meadow is significant for being one of the most diverse prairies in Missouri; it is an excellent example of the tallgrass prairie that was historically important in western and northern Missouri. Shelton L. Cook Meadow, owned and managed by The Nature Conservancy, is in the Central Irregular Plains ecoregion just west of the furthest extent of the Ozark highlands ecoregion. The Central Irregular Plains ecoregion was glaciated in pre-Illinoian time, but the Shelton L. Cook Meadow lies in an area in this ecoregion untouched by the glaciers. There are more than 400 plants in the 302-acre preserve, including the federally threatened Mead's milkweed, known to exist on fewer than 200 sites in the country. The flower is long-lived but may take as long as 15 years before it first flowers; it is therefore only found in high-quality, stable prairie ecosystems.

The very high quality of this prairie makes it an excellent source for seed to use at other restoration projects throughout the state. Because prairies are adapted to, and dependant on, fire, the use of prescribed fires is the main management strategy for preserving the Meadow. However, even with controlled burns, woody shrubs can be a problem. The prairie is much more desirable than the woody shrubs, which are continually encroaching on the preserve. Because of the prairie's rarity and the abundance of the shrub species, aggressive shrubs are being extirpated to preserve tallgrass prairie habitat.

The immediate area is mainly used for agriculture, reflecting the transition from the Ozark highlands to the tallgrass prairie of western Missouri and into Kansas. The water quality in general is more saline than the freshwater of the Ozark Highlands, and coal mining and the use of fertilizers and pesticides in agriculture have degraded the water quality. These are concerns at the Meadow. In addition, fragmentation is a general problem throughout Missouri's natural area system. Because native plant areas are isolated from one another, terrestrial animals have a much smaller habit-friendly range. If conditions in an area one year are not favorable, the organisms cannot move to another area, and if there is overpopulation of a species, individuals cannot leave the preserve because of a lack of suitable nearby habitat.

For these many reasons, as well as others, the Missouri Department of Conservation has created the Golden Grasslands Conservation Opportunity Area, an area in western Missouri comprised primarily of private land with preserves such as the Shelton L. Cook Meadow and others as anchors. One of the main goals is to increase the numbers of greater prairie chickens. However, many other goals include reducing fragmentation and increasing connectivity by educating landowners and working with ones willing to manage their grasslands, replacing woody fence rows with native shrubs to benefit wildlife such as bobwhite quail, constructing amphibian breeding areas that replicate bison wallows, and controlling invasive species.

There are many challenges to be faced. The public is not well informed and has little understanding about prairie habitat and native grassland management. There are also conflicting rules and different goals by the various management agencies. The Nature Conservancy and the Missouri Department of Conservation have had a long collaboration in the restoration and management of the natural systems of this region, and their partnership continues to this day. It will take many levels of government, private conservation groups, and, most importantly, private landowners, to maintain healthy ecosystems and preserve important habitat while developing a healthy economy and communities in the tallgrass prairie region. The Shelton L. Cook Meadow is an excellent example of a tallgrass prairie in Missouri and of conservation efforts in this region of the state.

The preserve is open to the public; the best viewing is when spring flowers are in bloom in May and June.

Further Reading

Gough, Sharron. "Grassroots Works for Grasslands." *Missouri Conservationist* 65, no. 12 (December 2004).
Manning, Richard. *Grassland: The History, Biology, Politics, and Promise of the American Prairie*. New York: Penguin Books 1997.

SHUT-IN MOUNTAIN FENS

In the Ozarks, a shut-in is a geological feature formed when a stream erodes away the soft limestone until it reaches the much harder igneous rock. At this point, the stream cuts deep, narrow channels in the rock. Unlike the shallow and broad portions of the stream, the water is constricted in the shut-in and picks up velocity. Shut-in Mountain Fens is named for the exposed igneous rock and the 15 fen types in the preserve found in three fens along Wildcat Hollow. Owned by The Nature Conservancy, the 550-acre preserve is marked by rugged terrain and dry woods of shortleaf pine (*Pinus echinata*), black oak (*Quercus velutina*), and blackjack oak (*Quercus marilandica*). The shallow soils and rock outcropping make Shut-in Mountain a very dry environment. The summit is an igneous glade, or opening with only a few stunted trees. Along the small stream and at the base of the mountain are various types of fens, saturated land fed by surface or groundwater. Being at the base of a slope, or near a stream, fens in the Ozarks are fed by constant cool water from underground. For this reason, plants normally found further north, remnants of the last glacial advance, are found in fens. The fens here are some of the most diverse in the Ozarks. More than 60 percent of the Ozark Highlands ecoregion is open forest or woodland, and Shut-in Mountain Fens is no exception. Although the immediate region of the preserve underwent intensive logging in the early 20th century, recreational activities are now an important economic activity.

The dry and wet soil regimes in the preserve and varied elevations create great ecological diversity in a small area. The geology of the region produces some of the driest and wettest habitats in Missouri, affecting the hydrology as well. The land is more irregular and generally more forested than in adjacent regions. This diverse physical landscape is also biologically diverse, and Shut-in Mountain Fens offers an excellent opportunity to see this diversity in a small place.

Past logging means that few original, or remnant, tracts remain. The rugged terrain and shallow soils have prevented crop farming, but grazing remains a concern. The Ozark Highlands ecoregion contains some of the highest-quality streams in Missouri, and runoff from grazing farm animals is a concern. Whereas the little land that is cultivated is confined to small areas in the valleys, uplands have been cleared for pasture. Waste from grazing animals runs downhill into the creeks, streams, and rivers. These patterns are easily viewed from the air, where relatively narrow strips of cleared land follow the meandering rivers.

Frequent prescribed fires are an important restoration tool at the preserve to reduce the woody plants and stimulate herbaceous plants. This is particularly important in the fens, which benefit greatly from the reduction of woody growth and rejuvenation provided by fire, which reduces dead leaves and other debris and exposes the soil and seeds. The ample water in the fens encourages woody plant growth, which must be controlled, otherwise succession would take place. Because of the biological diversity and rare plants and animals that the fens support, it is more desirable to preserve them than allow the fens to convert to forest. The restoration work is being monitored to record the plants' and animals' response to these frequent fires. The information gained will be used to better understand how to manage the unique environment of the Ozarks.

The preserve is open to the public, but visitors are restricted from walking in the sensitive fens to protect these sensitive ecosystems.

Further Reading

Dey, Daniel C., and George Hartman. "Returning Fire to Ozark Highland Forest Ecosystems: Effects on Advance Regeneration." *Forest Ecology and Management* 217 (2005): 37–53.

Haslam, S.M. *Understanding Wetlands: Fen, Bog and Marsh.* London: Taylor & Francis, 2003.

Shifley, S., and J. Kabrick. *Proceedings of the Second Missouri Ozark Forest Ecosystem Project Symposium: Post-treatment Results of the Landscape Experiment.* General Technical Report NC-227. St. Paul MN: U.S. Forest Service, North Central Forest Experiment Station, 2002.

TABERVILLE PRAIRIE

As the largest prairie in Missouri at 1,360 acres, Taberville Prairie is an invaluable ecological resource. This prairie is important nesting habitat for many birds, such as the greater prairie chicken (*Tympanuchus cupido*), once abundant over the vast prairies but now quite rare because of its preference for undisturbed prairie lands. Some plants and animals, such as the greater prairie chicken, are only found in high-quality ecosystems, so their presence, in effect, is an indication of the ecosystem's health. The organisms are thus called indicator species. The bobwhite quail (*Colinus virginianus*), Henslow's sparrow (*Ammodramus henslowii*), upland sandpiper (*Bartramia longicauda*), loggerhead shrike (*Lanius ludovicianus*), a predatory bird that impales its prey on thorns or barbed wire before eating it, and the crawfish frog also inhabit Taberville Prairie.

Hydrology is an often-overlooked element of midwestern prairies. Streams, ponds, and groundwater provide important habitat for both plants and animals. Wet prairie plants are adapted to soils that are saturated for part or all of the year. The dense vegetation at the water's edge provides habitat for birds, animals, and insects in addition to stabilizing soils and purifying water. Prairie wetlands had been high-quality wetland habitats. However, throughout the region, pollution to streams and the groundwater from industry, agriculture, and development puts increasing pressure on natural habitats such as prairies in addition to potable water supplies. The Baker Branch on Taberville Prairie has been recognized as a high-quality waterway, an indicator of the equally high-quality surrounding ecosystem. One way such high-quality waterways in Missouri are being protected is to designate them as an Outstanding State Water Resource. By receiving such a designation, activities upstream are prohibited or restricted with much tighter regulations. Damming, or diverting the upstream portion, for instance, is prohibited, and activities such as subdivision development are more closely scrutinized to determine the impact such development would have on the waterway farther downstream. Successful management and protection of a habitat such as the Taberville Prairie, therefore, goes beyond the boundaries of the prairie itself. Designation of the Baker Branch as an Outstanding State Water Resource, therefore, is an important tool in protecting the prairie wetland habitat as well as the greater prairie chicken and its inhabitants.

Taberville Prairie. (Alan Hahn)

Taberville Prairie is also managed through burning and haying to replicate the natural disturbance of the prairie ecosystem. Without disturbance such as fire, shrubs and trees gradually encroach upon the prairie, shading and outcompeting the prairie forbs, or nongrass flowering plants.

Conservation efforts are also underway on the state level to increase the numbers of the greater prairie chicken in Missouri. The greater prairie chicken is numerous enough in other states (Kansas, for example) to be hunted. In Missouri, however, as of 2008, only 500 of the birds remain. Increasing land use pressures in Missouri have greatly reduced and fragmented the greater prairie chicken's habitat. The Nature Conservancy and the Missouri Department of Conservation are collaborating on introducing the birds to Wah'Kon-Tah Prairie, which is 12 miles from Taberville Prairie. Birds have been taken from Taberville to Wah'Kon-Tah in the hopes that the two populations will eventually intermingle. Males and females were released in the early 1990s without success. This time, males are being released first at a lek, or gathering place for prairie chickens, to allow them to establish mating grounds. The females are then released about 12 weeks later, a technique that has been successful at other sites. The birds are fitted with radio collars to track their movements to determine whether they make Wah'Kon-Tah their new home. In this way, Taberville Prairie, which is the largest breeding ground for the greater prairie chicken in Missouri, is integral to the success of other prairie restoration efforts throughout the state. A private group, the Missouri Prairie Foundation, has been working with private landowners surrounding Taberville Prairie to remove trees and restore prairie to further enlarge the greater prairie chicken's habitat and reduce the effects of fragmentation.

Cooperative land management strategies through private and public partnerships are key to the successful conservation of many prairie species. The large scale required for sustainable prairie ecosystems necessitates such cooperation.

Taberville Prairie is owned and managed by the Missouri Department of Conservation. The prairie is open to the public and located two and a half miles north of Taberville on Highway H.

Further Reading

Johnson, S.R. and Aziz Bouzaher, eds. *Conservation of Great Plains Ecosystems: Current Science, Future Options.* Norwell, MA: Kluwer Academic Publishers, 1995.

Wells, Kimberly, M. Suedkamp, Joshua J. Millspaugh, et. al. "Factors Affecting Home Range Size and Movements of Post-fledging Grassland Birds." *Wilson Journal of Ornithology* (March 1, 2008): 120–30.

TUCKER PRAIRIE

Tucker Prairie is one of Missouri's few remaining remnant prairies—land that has never been plowed or altered—and the only claypan prairie of significant size in Missouri. Designated as a national natural landmark by the National Park Service, it is an excellent example of a tallgrass prairie on claypan (hardpan) soils—that is, soils that are composed of a layer of clay, resulting in poor drainage. The Tucker Prairie is at the southern end of the Central Irregular Plains ecoregion, which is an area of transition from the tallgrass prairie and croplands to the north and the more forested areas of the Ozarks to the south. Little and big bluestem (*Schizachyrium scoparium* and *Andropogon gerardii*) dominate this prairie; switchgrass (*Panicum virgatum*) and Indian grass (*Sorghastrum nutans*), two other main grasses of the tallgrass prairie, are also present. Many animals typical of the tallgrass prairie can be seen here, such as the prairie warbler. The 146-acre preserve is owned by the University of Missouri, which conducts experiments on the prairie and contributes value information on the ecology and management of prairies.

The tallgrass prairie is dominated by rhizomatic grasses, plants that grow and spread by rhizomes or typically underground rooting stems. As a result, the tallgrass prairie is a mosaic of grasses, forbs (flowers), and, to a lesser extent, trees and shrubs. The roots of prairie plants often grow many feet down and many penetrate up to 15 feet. As a result, prairie plants are able to draw nutrients and moisture from far below the surface, allowing them to live in a range of soils and to withstand extended dry periods and the vagaries of the Midwest and Western climates. But most importantly, this extensive and deep-penetrating root system is an adaptation to fire, allowing plants to survive periodic wildfires.

Many ongoing studies are investigating the effects of one-, two-, and five-year burn cycles of the prairie. Haying and other means of removing the vegetation in place of burning are also being studied. In addition, the effects of fire on insects and wildlife have been studied. The prairie is used in comparative studies with agricultural soil composition as a reference and because of its high quality. The studies have been valuable for advancing prairie ecosystem management and restoration, directly through the management practices being undertaken at Tucker Prairie and as a control for comparison with efforts to restore prairies at other sites. An increase in residential development in the area is putting greater demands on groundwater, which may affect Tucker Prairie. Tucker Prairie was reduced by 14 acres when Interstate 70 was built immediately north of the preserve. Further expansion of the interstate would further diminish its size. The site is not open to the public.

Further Reading

Reed, Catherine C. "Responses of Prairie Insects and Other Arthropods to Prescription Burns." *Natural Areas Journal* 17, no. 4 (1997): 380–85.

Trager, J.C. "Restored Prairies Colonized by Native Prairie Ants." *Restoration and Management Notes* 8, no. 2 (1990): 104–5.

TUMBLING CREEK CAVE

Tumbling Creek Cave's ecological significance goes beyond its two miles of mapped underground passages and swiftly moving groundwater-fed stream. Although it is one of many hundreds of caves in the Ozark Highlands ecoregion, it is the most ecologically rich cave west of the Mississippi River and home to some of the rarest troglobites, or cave-dwelling creatures. The cave is habitat for 112 species, including 12 troglobites, one of which, the Tumbling Creek cave snail (*Antrobia culveri*), is found only in this cave. The cave is also considered essential to the survival of the gray bat (*Myotis grisescens*), serving as its primary nesting site. In fact, it was the decline of the gray bats and the near extinction of the Tumbling Creek cave snail that prompted much of past 10 years of restoration work.

Ownership of the 2,550 acres of land surrounding the cave entrance is by the Ozark Underground Laboratory, a private organization; the entrance to the cave is held in trust. The organization opens the cave and surroundings to student groups and scientists. Forty years of research at Tumbling Creek has been valuable in providing benchmarks to monitor the health of the cave.

Located in southern Missouri, Tumbling Creek Cave is part of the Ozark Highlands ecoregion in a landscape known as karst. Karst topography, both above and below ground, is formed by slightly acidic water gradually eroding the surface and subsurface limestone or other carbonate bedrock. This erosion creates crevices, sometimes visible, that allow surface water to quickly drain, carving out a maze of underground crevices, channels, sinkholes, losing streams, and caves. These features are typical of karst regions.

Being isolated, almost completely closed ecosystems, caves are naturally vulnerable to change. The stream in Tumbling Creek Cave, having no upstream source, is fed entirely from surface water percolating through the cave's walls and ceiling. The land surface that feeds Tumbling Creek Cave, called the recharge area, was recently determined to be roughly 5,800 acres. Around 1,350 acres of the recharge area are in the Mark Twain National Forest, and the rest is held in private hands. This discovery provided possible answers to the cave inhabitants' decline and the enormous challenges that lay ahead.

More than 20 farm dumps were identified on private land in the recharge area. Many of these farm dumps were in sinkholes and gullies. With a grant from the National Park Service and U.S. Fish and Wildlife Service, cavers and Missouri volunteer groups removed tons of household chemicals, petroleum products, and empty farm pesticide containers from the private dumps. Residents were not aware of the impact these common practices had on the cave and groundwater. When the open-sewage lagoon of nearby Mark Twain School was discovered to be losing about 88 percent of its contents into the groundwater feeding Tumbling Creek Cave, residents were at first angry at cave researchers who discovered the problem; the state of Missouri was requiring the school to clean the lagoon or close. However, the situation was turned into an opportunity. With the help of the school children, a grant was obtained to clean up the lagoon and build a new, healthy sewage system, which has become a demonstration site in proper sewage management.

In the past 10 years, the population of the Tumbling Creek cave snail has declined from the thousands to only 40. The cave's creek had begun to fill up with sediment, possibly from overgrazed pastures that allow additional waste and sediment to enter the groundwater which would otherwise be trapped by vegetation. A nearby farm was purchased and is being restored through reforestation. The placement of terra-cotta tile by the Missouri Department of Conservation has also helped by providing new habitat for the Tumbling Creek cave snail. Research is being undertaken to better understand the cave snail's ecology. Bat populations have also dropped, possibly from disturbance by intruders. Bat droppings provide an important energy or food in the closed ecosystem of a cave. A chute gate was constructed in 2005 at the cave entrance to control access to the cave while allowing the bats to move freely.

The site has been named a Conservation Opportunity Area by the Missouri Department of Conservation. Management strategies are being developed in cooperation with the Ozark Underground Laboratory to provide incentives and education to private landowners, reforest streams and banks, monitor the cave inhabitants, and inventory the surrounding karst features such as losing streams and sinkholes. Tumbling Creek Cave is valuable not only for its biological diversity but for more than 40 years of research and monitoring. This research is revealing new insights into cave ecology and management. The health of Tumbling Creek Cave has been an indicator of the health of the surrounding groundwater in this karst landscape.

Further Reading

Elliott, William R., and Thomas J. Aley. *Karst Conservation in the Ozarks: Forty Years at Tumbling Cave.* Albany, NY: National Cave and Karst Management Symposium, 2005.

Hildreth-Werker, Val, and Jim C. Werker. *Cave Conservation and Restoration.* Huntsville, AL: National Speleological Society, 2006.

Klimchouk, Alexander B., Derek C. Ford, Arthur N. Palmer, and Wolfgang Dreybrodt, eds. *Speleogenesis: Evolution of the Karst Aquifers.* Huntsville, AL: National Speleological Society, 2000.

VICTORIA GLADE

One of the more unusual natural places in Missouri lies just south of St. Louis and not 10 miles from the Mississippi River. For all the natural diversity in Missouri, the 101-acre Victoria Glade is atypical. The shallow soils, exposed dolomite, and south- and west-facing slopes parch the landscape, leaving the rocky and mainly treeless preserve hot and dry. It is only because of an annual rainfall that is double that of the southwestern U.S. desert that Victoria Glade is not barren. Nevertheless, its inhabitants make it seem very much like the Southwest. There is the collared lizard (*Crotaphytus collaris collaris*), which depends on the rocky glades for its survival, and scorpions, tarantulas, and southern black widow spiders (*Latrodectus mactans*) are also found here. Although these animals and the hot, parched landscape remind one of the desert, the plants and animals are native to this region of Missouri, depending on the dry glade for survival. Drought-tolerant plants such as blue wild indigo (*Baptisia australis*), American aloe (*Agave americana*), and Missouri black-eyed Susan (*Rudbeckia missouriensis*) are also part of the rich landscape of Victoria Glade. The only shrubby-type clematis native to Missouri, Fremont's leather flower (*Clematis fremontii*), grows in abundance along with more than 300 other plants. Victoria Glade is a species-rich preserve, considering its size and the extreme conditions of the landscape.

A glade is an opening in the forest caused by disturbance such as a fire or for more permanent reasons such as poor soils. Victoria Glade is the result of having shallow soils where exposed bedrock—in this case dolomite—makes growing conditions for trees and shrubs difficult. Most of the dolomite glades face west or south and thus are exposed to the harshest of the day's sun. Other glades in the Ozarks are igneous, chert, sandstone, and limestone glades. The dolomite glades are the most biologically diverse, however. The dolomite glades are only found in east-central Missouri and along the Kansas-Nebraska border. Victoria Glade is one of the highest-quality examples of this rare community. Across the road is the Victoria Glades Conservation Area, 239 acres managed by the Missouri Department of Conservation. It is biologically an extension of Victoria Glade, but it is not as actively managed as The Nature Conservancy property.

From an aerial view, the sinuous patterns of exposed rock can clearly be seen with eastern red cedar (*Juniperus virginiana*) following the edges of the exposed rock. In fact, eastern red cedar, or red cedar, is one of the few trees that can grow in the glade. Red cedar is native to the eastern United States, ranging from Canada to Florida, west to the Dakotas and Texas. Red cedars are seen most often in the Midwest in prairie landscapes, because they are able to tolerate dry, gravelly soils and shade when young. This is the tree from which cedar furniture, pencils, and closet linings are made.

The Ozarks glades are not true cedar glades like those found in the southeast, which are permanent. In the Ozarks, glades are dependent on fire. Red cedar in the Ozarks traditionally has had difficulty completely covering the glades in the past because periodic natural or manmade fires controlled its spread. After more than a century of fire suppression, the glades are beginning to become a red cedar forest, threatening the plants and animals that depend on the open glade for survival. In fact, over 70 percent of the glades in Missouri are now cedar forests. Prescribed burning has been used to renew the glade as well as keep the cedars in check. However, although fire was natural to the glades, it occurred intermittently and most likely not completely. It has been discovered that managed fire has been detrimental to fire-sensitive invertebrates at the glades, so fire is being used on a rotational basis. Cedars are the main threat to the survival of Victoria Glade today; however, throughout Missouri, glades face other threats as well.

During the 1980s, the preserve was used for all-terrain vehicle recreation. Since, then, all-terrain vehicles have been fairly successfully prohibited from the preserve, but their tracks are still visible. The shallow soils and slow-growing plants make recovery much more difficult than in more fertile landscapes. For this reason, any disturbances have a much more long-lasting effect in this environment.

The pet trade has had a profound impact on the preserve as well. The collared lizard is a desirable animal in the pet trade and fell victim to many collectors who came to the preserve in search of the lizard. Twenty years ago, the lizard was common, and it was not unusual to see dozens on a visit. Now it is rare to see even one. Another consequence of collecting the lizard was the environmental degradation to the preserve. Collectors in search of the lizard would flip over rocks where the lizards hide during the heat of the day. These rocks were usually not put back in place. Rock flipping uncovers bare ground and covers the plants growing adjacent to the rock. It is several years before new plants grow in the exposed bare areas.

Through ongoing restoration and management efforts and better enforcement of environmentally sustainable activities, Victoria Glade will continue to be an important preserve of this rare community.

Further Reading

Anderson, Roger C., James S. Fralish, and Jerry M. Baskin, eds. *Savannas, Barrens, and Rock Outcrop Plant Communities of North America.* Cambridge, England: Cambridge University Press, 1999.

Baskin, Jerry M., and Carol C. Baskin. "Vegetation of Limestone and Dolomite Glades in the Ozarks and Midwest Regions of the United States." *Annals of the Missouri Botanical Garden* 87, no. 2 (Spring 2000): 286–94.

Ladd, D., and P. Nelson. "Ecological Synopsis of Missouri Glades." In Proceedings of the Cedar Glade Symposium, School of the Ozarks, ed. W. Davis, 1–20. Point Lookout, MO: University of Missouri—Columbia, April 23–24, 1982. Missouri Academy of Science Occasional Paper 7 (1982).

OHIO

The eastern forest, the great tall-grass prairie, and southern forests all meet in Ohio, where the east, both ecologically and socially, transitions to the Midwest. Being the ninth most populous state, urbanization is one of the great pressures facing natural places in Ohio. This is as true today and just as significant as it was 150 years ago, when settlers drained the Great Black Swamp in north-central Ohio, one of the last places to be farmed in Ohio. The natural areas in the following entries represent what Ohio's natural landscape once was. However, these places also offer hope through the partnerships, education, and research being conducted at them. Some of the preserves are in heavily populated areas and offer examples of how natural areas can be maintained and managed as the inevitable urbanization surrounds them.

The Corn Belt forms the western part of Ohio, and the Western Allegheny Plateau forms the southeastern section of the state. The effects of Lake Erie on northern Ohio, however, have created a unique environment unlike any other in the midwestern states. Several entries address this unique environment, which also happens to be one of the more heavily populated areas of the state. Natural areas in Ohio have been altered and managed in ways that reflect the growth of the United States as people expanded west. Today, partnerships and innovative approaches to ecosystem management in Ohio in many ways reflect the same concerns as in other midwestern states—agricultural impacts, invasive species, degraded streams—within a densely populated area.

BROWN'S LAKE BOG PRESERVE

Most of Ohio's wetlands have been drained for agricultural use, dramatically changing the historical hydrology of the state. Features such as swamps, potholes, bogs, and other wetlands are very rare. Brown's Lake Bog is significant because it preserves one of the few kettle hole peatlands in the state. Unlike the unglaciated area south of Brown's Lake Bog, the last glaciation left its mark on this region, and the preserve is one of the few high-quality bog sites in the region.

The preserve, owned and managed by The Nature Conservancy, has several features, remnants of its glacial past. Brown's Lake is a kettle hole lake formed by the last receding glacier. Much of the remainder of the preserve is a bog—an acidic wetland that gradually accumulates dead plants, primarily mosses, forming peat. The bog is covered by a floating sphagnum moss (*Sphagnum* spp.) mat, giving much of the area a water bed–like springy feel. There are also kames in the northeast and southern part of the preserve. A kame is a glacial mound often associated with kettles. The combination of these glacial features and the resulting hydrology allows relict boreal plant communities to thrive in the preserve. The sphagnum mat insulates the water from rapid air temperature changes, providing the unique, tempered, cool conditions needed for bog plant communities. Patches of these relict communities were more common before most of the land was drained and channelized for agriculture. In fact, the preserve is surrounded by farmland, and the possibility of runoff from fertilizers may contribute to the accelerated growth and abundance of shrubs in the preserve.

The bog has many plants typical of a boreal plant community, including large cranberry (*Vaccinium macrocarpon*), which is the cranberry grown commercially; marsh fivefinger (*Comarum palustre*); and grass-pink orchid (*Calopogon tuberosus*). There are also carnivorous plants such as the purple pitcher plant (*Sarracenia purpurea*) and round-leaved sundew (*Drosera rotundifolia*). Round-leaved sundew is extremely intolerant of shade. A recent study of the preserve showed that sundews, among other bog plants, were being shaded out by encroaching poison sumac (*Toxicodendron vernix*), speckled alder (*Alnus incana* ssp. *rugosa*), and purple chokeberry (*Aronia* x *prunifolia*). This presents an important challenge to the preserve. The advance of these invading plants may be stimulated by agricultural runoff; nonetheless, the natural succession of a bog is eventually to become a swamp forest. The natural accumulation of plant material, primarily sphagnum moss, sows the seeds of its own gradual destruction by creating an environment where shrubs and trees can thrive, thereby shading out the sun-loving bog plants. Because of the now-rare occurrence of this type of ecosystem in Ohio and its high-quality hydrology, it is more desirable to maintain the boglike quality of the preserve than allow the succession of the ecosystem, because the successional species are much more common and less ecologically important. For this reason, The Nature Conservancy maintains the open areas as well as clears areas where shrubs have encroached; the aim is to expand the bog mat around Brown's Lake. Boardwalks allow visitors to see this rare habitat in Ohio.

Unlike many preserves under threat from invasive nonnative plants, urbanization, and altered water regimes, Brown's Lake Bog has remained relatively untouched. Natural processes are the greatest threat to this glacial relict.

Further Reading

Aldrich, John Warren. "Biological Survey of the Bogs and Swamps in Northeastern Ohio." *American Midland Naturalist* 30 (1943): 346–402.

Armstrong, Richard C., and Katherine Heston. "Control of Woody Invasion of a Kettle Bog (Ohio)." *Restoration and Management Notes* 1, no. 2 (April 1982): 1–18.

Dysart Woods Laboratory

Dysart Woods Laboratory is a 50-acre old-growth forest within the 455-acre Dysart Woods. It is owned and managed by Ohio University, which uses the woods primarily for research; however, the woods are also open to the public. Located in the Western Allegheny Plateau ecoregion in eastern Ohio, the woods are in the unglaciated part of the state—a rugged, wooded region, where much of the land is too steep for crop farming. Dysart Woods is between the more forested area of southeastern Ohio and West Virginia and the open crop agricultural land to the west. The bedrock consists primarily of Permian shale, sandstone, and coal seams, which run from the surface to a few hundred feet below ground. Dysart Woods is a mixed oak and mesophytic forest; mesophytic forests need moderate amounts of moisture. The dominant trees in Dysart Woods are the 300-year-old white oaks that are 4 feet in diameter and 140 feet tall. Although the forest is often called old growth, it is not virgin because it has been selectively logged in the past. This is typical for Ohio, where it is unlikely to find any sizeable tract that has never seen the logger's axe or saw. However, the age of the trees and mix of vegetation—especially American beech (*Fagus grandifolia*) and sugar maple (*Acer saccharum*), are typical of the dominant trees in the unglaciated southeastern region of the state and, for this region, make this one of the few remaining tracts exemplary of this region's natural forests.

The cool, moist ravines and drier upland slopes of Dysart Woods create conditions for a great variety of plant and animal life. There are many opportunities for scientific research. The Department of Environmental and Plant Biology at Ohio University, for instance, has been researching the dynamics of oak forest ecosystems—in particular, investigating the regeneration of oaks in a mature oak forest. Throughout the eastern and midwestern states, scientists have observed that many oaks in mature oak forests are not regenerating. The trees produce acorns, but there are no oak trees beyond seedling. In Dysart Woods, for instance, one finds some of the largest white oaks in Ohio, but only a few are more than three feet tall. This is an almost 300-year gap between the youngest and oldest trees. The forest floor is shaded by the mature trees, and shade-tolerant trees such as sugar maples, American beech, and elm (*Ulmus* spp.) dominate the middle-age group of trees. When oaks have fallen because of storms or disease, they have been replaced by the larger shade-tolerant trees and not the oaks. Ohio University's research may shed light on the possible reasons and dynamics of this phenomenon and assist park managers in managing their aging oak woods.

Agricultural runoff is a potential problem, though not as pronounced as it is in the more heavily farmed central and western parts of the state. Invasive species have not yet been a serious problem in Dysart Woods, though they are present at the margins of Dysart Farm. Dysart Woods has been managed with basically a hands-off approach, being left in its natural state. The most recent and significant threat to the future health of the woods, however, has not come from above but from below ground.

In 1967, Ohio University took over ownership of Dysart Woods from The Nature Conservancy. In the late 1990s, the Ohio Valley Coal Company applied for a permit to mine the coal seam under Dysart Woods. Over the next decade and many legal battles later, the coal company eventually won the right in 2007 to mine near and under Dysart Woods. Environmentalists won a small victory by preventing longwall mining directly under the woods, which potentially could do the most harm. Longwall mining consists of removing coal parallel to the seam and allowing the open cavity created behind the mining process to collapse as the wall of coal is removed. This can lead to subsidence, which is the settling of land. Subsidence is commonly seen naturally in karst regions, where the limestone bedrock wears away, resulting in the land collapsing and creating a sink hole. By requiring room and pillar mining under the woods, this hazard is reduced. However, changes to groundwater levels and the eventual collapse of the land are still possible threats to the health of the woods. The value of the fossil fuel weighed against the unique and scientifically and historically valuable woods typifies the challenges faced in regions where the desire to preserve biological resources is weighed against the need for natural resources. The consequences of coal mining beneath Dysart Woods may not be known for years to come but will nevertheless be an important aspect of ongoing research at the woods. For its role in research on oak forest regeneration or the effects of coal mining on ecosystems, Dysart Woods is an important part of Ohio's biological and geological history.

Further Reading

Brown, J.E., B.C. McCarthy, and C.J. Small. "The Relationship between the Soil Seed Bank and Aboveground Vegetation in Dysart Woods, an Old-Growth Mixed Mesophytic Forest." *Ohio Journal of Science* 99 no. 21(1999).

Crowell, Douglas L. "The History of Coal Mining in Ohio." *GeoFacts* no. 14 (May 2005). Ohio Department of Natural Resources, Division of Geological Survey. www.ohiodnr. com/geosurvey.

McCarthy, Brian C., Christine J. Small, and Darrin L. Rubino. "Composition, Structure and Dynamics of Dysart Woods, an Old-growth Mixed Mesophytic Forest of Southeastern Ohio." *Forest Ecology and Management* 140, nos. 2–3 (January 2001): 193–213.

Edge of Appalachia Preserve

The Edge of Appalachia Preserve is a place of incredible diversity covering 13,500 acres in southern Ohio. The preserve is located in the Interior Plateau ecoregion, which extends from northern Alabama to just over the border of Ohio and into south-central Indiana. Being on the northernmost edge of this ecoregion, the preserve is also between the plains to the west and the Western Allegheny Plateau ecoregion of the east; it is located in a region that transitions from the plains of the central midwestern states to the forests of the east. The land is unglaciated, and streams have exposed the bedrock of two types: calcareous limestone and noncalcareous shale. This area at the intersection of disparate ecoregions is of great diversity, and the Edge of Appalachia Preserve is representative of that diversity. The preserve is one of the most ecologically diverse protected areas in the Midwest and contains the greatest number of rare plants and animals of any preserve in Ohio.

The Edge of Appalachia Preserve is also the largest privately owned preserve in Ohio, being jointly managed by The Nature Conservancy and the Cincinnati Museum of Natural History. The partnership takes full advantage of each organization's expertise combining ecological management with high-quality educational resources. For instance, school children participate in science camps where they learn about the biology of the preserve while also collecting biological information that is used in ongoing research at the preserve. Adults become directly involved through workshops and college courses investigating the preserve's unique natural history. This partnership is collaborative and mutually beneficial: the Cincinnati Museum has the opportunity to provide real-world experiences, and The Nature Conservancy is able to fulfill its mission of conservation and environmental education through outreach programs. From helping with the biological monitoring program to collecting data for ongoing research projects to assisting in ecosystem management, the benefits of collaboration have added tremendous value beyond the boundaries of the Edge of Appalachia Preserve by bringing people back to nature and introducing them to the rich natural history of the region.

The preserve benefits from its huge size. It is made up of 11 contiguous smaller preserves, each of which is unique. Four are registered as national natural landmarks. Restoration efforts—particularly in the prairie and glades, or forest openings—are improving the biological quality of these areas of the preserve by removing invasive species and woody plants. Fragmentation, the isolation of habitats, is a significant threat. Nevertheless, land acquisition is ongoing and an important goal. Sustainable timber management practices are being explored in relation to local economic development. To this end, The Nature Conservancy is working with local public and private groups finding innovative solutions to economic development compatible with the surrounding ecosystems. Although the preserve is located in a rural area, development will continue.

It is difficult to grasp the vast diversity contained in the preserve and the possibilities still in the surrounding areas. The biological diversity of the Appalachian forests can be glimpsed in this small region that touches the southern tip of Ohio. The collaborative efforts of The Nature Conservancy and the Cincinnati Museum of Natural History may have the most far-reaching effects, primarily on people's attitudes about conservation. The preserve, through its research, outreach, collaboration, and education, can have a great impact on how the region chooses to develop.

Further Reading

Bolgiano, Chris. *Living in the Appalachian Forest: True Tales of Sustainable Forestry*. Mechanicsburg, PA: Stackpole Books, 2002.

Stritholt, J.R. and R.E.J. Boerner. "Applying Biodiversity Gap Analysis to a Regional Nature Reserve Design for the Edge of Appalachia, Ohio." *Conservation Biology* 9, no. 6 (1995): 1492–1505.

GLADE WETLAND

Glade Wetland, a 292-acre preserve owned and managed by The Nature Conservancy, is most significant for its diverse wetland community, which is home to numerous plants and animals and an important site for the wintering habitat of many raptors, such as hawks, kestrels, and owls, as well as grassland birds. The preserve is located in an abandoned valley of the preglacial Teays River. The Teays River was an enormous preglacial river that flowed north and west from West Virginia, through Ohio, and into Indiana and Illinois. After repeated glacial advances of the last two million years, the river was buried under many feet of sand and gravel in the glaciated portions of Ohio and flat-bottomed valleys such as the valley in which Glade Wetland is located, in the unglaciated southern part of Ohio. A glacier eventually dammed and diverted the Teays River, creating the Ohio River. The remnants of the Teays River valley where Glade Wetland is located in Pike and Jackson Counties and south of Chillicothe, can still be seen today, quite strikingly, in aerial photos. Aquifers created when the river was buried supply clean water for people today. Glade Wetland is in an unglaciated portion of the ancient Teays River Valley, and its wetland ecosystems are unique in Ohio, preserving a snapshot of preglacial-era wetland habitat. It is located in the western Allegheny Plateau ecoregion, an area not leveled by glaciation.

The preserve is an exceptional example of present-day Teays Valley wetland habitat represented by sedge and grass meadows and pin oak–red maple woods. The lacustrine silty soils from when the Teays River was dammed to form a glacial lake support a variety of rare wetland habitats. These wetland habitats are dependent on high-quality water systems, and the hydrology of the surrounding area has been dramatically changed over the years, primarily by ditching. In partnership with the Natural Resources Conservation Service, The Nature Conservancy's restoration efforts are centered on restoring the natural hydrology of the preserve to increase wetland habitat and quality. Prescribed fires play an important role in controlling invasive species such as Japanese honeysuckle (*Lonicera japonica*) and maintaining the grassland communities. Although the preserve is located in a rural area relatively far from development pressures, it is on Ohio Route 124 and surrounded by farmland. Nonpoint pollution must be monitored closely.

The variety of habitats and diversity of species of Glade Wetland offer valuable insights into this region's past. Although the footprint of the valley's preglacial past is still visible at a landscape scale, the surrounding ecosystems of the Teays Valley have been dramatically altered through the draining of the low-lying, rich soils for agriculture. Glade Wetland is one of the most intact relicts from this area's recent and geological past. Wetlands in general are uncommon in southeastern Ohio. The ongoing management and restoration efforts are important not only for the preservation of the living organisms of the preserve but for the historical ecological significance this site holds for the region.

Vistior access to Glade Wetland is limited.

Further Reading

Hansen, Michael C. "The Teays River." *GeoFacts*, no. 10 (November 1995). Ohio Department of Natural Resources, Division of Geological Survey. www.ohiodnr.com/geosurvey.

Sibbing, Julie M. *Ohio Wetlands*. Columbus: National Audubon Society, Ohio Chapter, 1995.

Spooner, David M. "Wetlands in Teays-Stage Valleys in Extreme Southeastern Ohio: Formation and Flora." Symposium on Wetlands of the Unglaciated Appalachian Region, West Virginia University, Morgantown, May 26–28, 1982.

GOLL WOODS

Goll Woods is located in northeastern Ohio in a region commonly called the Great Black Swamp, an area extending from north-central Ohio and just into Indiana in the Huron/Erie Lake Plains ecoregion. The area was formed during the last glacial retreat, leaving the area with low, poorly drained soils dominated by deciduous swamps. The swamps persisted until the mid-19th century, when the area was drained and converted into farmland. Today, less than five percent of the original Great Black Swamp remains. Goll Woods is one of few remaining remnant forests in northwestern Ohio as well as being exemplary of what the Great Black Swamp forest looked like before it was converted to farmland. Goll Woods is known for its oaks towering 120 feet tall, 4 feet in diameter, and 200 to 400 years old. Bur oak (*Quercus macrocarpa*), white oak (*Quercus alba*), and chinquapin oak (*Quercus muehlenbergii*) comprise some of the largest specimens. Ashes (*Fraxinus* spp.), cottonwood (*Populus deltoides*), American elm (*Ulmus americana*), and other water-tolerant trees dominate in the wettest areas.

Goll Woods is a 321-acre state nature preserve. Looking at the vast farm fields that now dominate the landscape, it is difficult to envision the expansive swamp that covered this area for thousands of years. The Great Black Swamp was one of the last areas in Ohio to be settled because of the environmental difficulties encountered by early settlers. But the rich soils, once drained, now support some of the most productive grain farming in Ohio. Goll Woods is an important part of the natural history of the area, connecting the present and the past. The preserve is the least disturbed woods in this region and transports visitors back to the early nineteenth century before the land was drained and the forests cut for farmland. The preserve's location in the Great Black Swamp places the woods in the greater geological context. The last receding glaciers left behind saturated soils, and the dominant vegetative type was deciduous swamp forests. Being surrounded by farmland, Goll Woods is thus a relict from Ohio's geological past and a reminder of the agricultural development that so dramatically changed the region. Visiting Goll Woods in the summer, when the mosquitoes are in full fury, gives one a sense of the challenges faced by those who eventually succeeded in draining the Great Black Swamp.

Like many remnant woods throughout the country, Goll Woods faces many challenges. The few high-quality sites left in private ownership in the populated areas are under enormous pressures of development; with rising property values and taxes, owners may eventually sell their land for subdivision and development. Places that have had only minor disturbances and are now protected, such as Goll Woods, have survived the most prevalent threat but nonetheless face many more. Invasive species are threatening the ecological balance, and regular maintenance is necessary to keep these species in control. Groundwater contamination from surrounding farmland must be closely monitored, especially in the saturated soils of the Great Black Swamp region. Deer, whose numbers were kept in check by fluctuating seasonal food supplies and natural predators, have grown considerably because of regulated hunting and more food from agricultural fields. Their increased numbers are destroying plant communities in Goll Woods. As a result, the preserve is sometimes open for controlled hunts to reduce the deer population to manageable numbers.

Some things can never be preserved. Although the preserve is an excellent example of what the last area to be settled in Ohio once looked like, the hydrology of this swamp region has been dramatically changed. The ditching that drained this region has resulted in leaving only pockets of remaining areas that resemble what the region once was. The continued loss of nearby habitat will continue to further isolate the species in Goll Woods. Groups such as the Black Swamp Conservancy, a land trust, are working to preserve the remaining land of this region while educating the public about the ecosystem that dominated this area for the past thousands of years. Efforts by groups such as this may help restore and preserve the remaining land in northwestern Ohio. The more people are aware of the significance and importance of their ecological past, the more likely they are to be partners in its protection and preservation.

The preserve is located just northwest of Archbold and is open to the public.

Further Reading

Boerner, Ralph E., and Do-Soon Cho. "Structure and Composition of Goll Woods, an Old-growth Forest Remnant in Northwestern Ohio." *Bulletin of the Torrey Botanical Club* 114, no. 2 (1987): 173–79.

Mollenkopf, Jim. *Great Black Swamp Woods & Wanders: Nature's Jewels in Northwest Ohio*. Toledo, OH: Lake of the Cat Publishing, 2005.

Prince, Hugh. *Wetlands of the American Midwest: A Historical Geography of Changing Attitudes*. Chicago: University of Chicago Press, 1997.

Highbanks Natural Area

Highbanks Natural Area is one of 15 parks in the Columbus and Franklin County Metropolitan (Metro) Parks system. The Metro Parks consist of 23,500 acres of natural areas around Columbus, one of the most populated areas of Ohio. The main focus of the park system is the conservation of land and restoration of wildlife habitat. However, unlike many nature preserves, which provide only passive recreational opportunities, the Metro Parks also have many active recreational opportunities such as playgrounds, picnicking, sledding hills, biking and horse trails, and golf courses. The park balances these two sometimes competing interests with active educational programming.

Highbanks Natural Area, in Metro Parks, is the most visited park, with over 650,000 visitors each year. It is so named for its exceptional geological formations, namely its 100-foot-high shale bluffs overlooking the Olentangy Scenic River. Ohio Shale Concretions, large carbonate spheres, are a curious formation found embedded in the bluffs and at their base. There are a variety of birds, animals, plants, and fish within Highbanks as well as Native American archeological sites. The 1,159 acres of Highbanks are just north of Columbus, which is on the eastern edge of the eastern Corn Belt plains ecoregion. This ecoregion extends from central Ohio to the western border of Indiana. The rolling till plains are composed of glacial deposits from the latest glacial advances whose rich soils supported natural tree cover greater than the Central Corn Belt Plains with its extensive prairies to the west. Today, most of the Eastern Corn Belt Plains consists of extensive crop and livestock production with little of the original forests remaining. Farming has affected the turbidity and chemistry of most streams and rivers in the region. Highbanks, however, allows the opportunity to glimpse the forests that once covered much of this region and to experience exposed geological history and ancient cultures. There are excellent examples of oak-hickory, beech-maple, and floodplain hardwood forests, particularly along the bluff of the river. The Olentangy River also supports more species of fish than many of the surrounding streams.

The diversity and quality of the park is set against the pressures of urbanization. The expansive park and natural area are entirely encircled by subdivisions, shopping, and manufacturing. The park educators have turned this situation into an advantage by reconnecting people with nature, hosting numerous educational classes, field trips, and opportunities for the many school children and adults in the area. For instance, naturalists held a gym class for nearby students with activities such as hiking, map reading, and using a global positioning system device. There is a streamside study area along the Olentangy River where park naturalists show school children the river's rich aquatic life. The Edward F. Hutchins Nature Preserve contains a constructed wetlands used to demonstrate this habitat. The two Native American burial mounds and remnants of an embankment are important cultural features that demonstrate the effect humans have on shaping the environment, from ancient cultures to the present.

Highbanks Natural Area has many significant environmental, geological, and cultural features. But it is the extensive and varied educational programming that makes most use of the resources of the park. By actively engaging the community, particularly school children, the staff are educating the public about central Ohio's environmental and cultural history and connecting people to the area's past and informing them about the challenges of the present. The many miles of trails offer a chance to explore the geology, culture, and environment of central Ohio. The success of the programming reconnects people to the environment, as can be seen in the thousands of visitors who come each year.

Further Reading

Hansen, Michael C. "Ohio Shale Concretions." *GeoFacts*, no. 4 (October 1994). Ohio Department of Natural Resources, Division of Geological Survey. www.ohiodnr.com/geosurvey.

Lepper, Bradley T. *Ohio Archaeology: An Illustrated Chronicle of Ohio's Ancient American Indian Cultures.* Wilmington, Ohio: Orange Frazer Press, 2005.

Sanders, Randall, ed. *A Guide to Ohio Streams.* Columbus: Streams Committee, Ohio Chapter of the American Fisheries Society, 2001.

HUESTON WOODS

The 200-acre Hueston Woods is located in Hueston Woods State Park near Ohio's border with Indiana in the Eastern Corn Belt Plains ecoregion. The ecoregion is covered by glacial deposits from the latest glaciation; beech forests dominated the drier soils of what today has been converted to extensive cropland and livestock production. These activities, in turn, have affected the chemistry and turbidity of streams. Of the remaining beech forests in this ecoregion and throughout the state, virtually none is virgin, having never been logged or even only selectively cut. Hueston Woods is remarkable for having been only lightly and selectively cut and because this recognized old-growth forest is located within a very active park.

Hueston Woods State Park covers a total of 3,596 acres, with a 625-acre artificial lake at its center. The park is considered a premier resort park and has a 96-room lodge; campgrounds; hiking, biking, and equestrian trails; a public beach; boating; hunting; and an 18-hole golf course that borders the nature preserve. Nonetheless, the woods have remained intact and have not been impacted by the active use of the remainder of the park. Most nature preserves are located away from and separate from active recreation, permitting only passive recreation such as hiking and bird-watching. Hueston Woods has been maintained by clearly separating active and passive recreation, allowing only hiking and no dogs within the preserve in stark contrast to the remainder of this heavily used state park. The preserve has not experienced the human impact that other natural areas have, partly because it is damp and remote from the more popular trails. It is also clearly designated as a sensitive preserve and enforced as such.

Hueston Woods is a classic beech-maple climax forest typical of this region. American beech and sugar maple are the dominant trees in this forest type, and here many are more than 200 years old. It was partly because the sugar maples were tapped for maple syrup that the land was spared, as well as the fact that it never changed ownership, remaining in the same family from the 18th century until the early 20th century. Beech-maple is one of the most important and widespread deciduous forest plant associations in the eastern temperate forests of North America. The wood of beech and maple has many uses and was harvested for these reasons as well as to clear the land for agriculture. It is now extremely rare to find near-virgin forests of any type in Ohio, and no such pure tracts probably exist that have not at least been selectively cut in the past 200 years. Hueston Woods offers a unique opportunity to see one of the few remaining large tracts of old-growth beech-maple forests as well as to experience how the preserve has been effectively integrated into a very active state park. As population growth and urbanization reach more and more remote places, multiple-use preserves such as Hueston Woods State Park will become more common. It will become even more crucial that we find appropriate and compatible uses surrounding and within natural areas.

In addition to nearby recreational activities, Hueston Woods has other environmental issues and challenges. The woods is adjacent to the lake, so shoreline water quality and recreational activities may affect the many migrating birds and waterfowl that use the woods. Garlic mustard (*Alliaria petiolata*) is a serious invasive species taking over woods from the Atlantic to the Midwest. It forms monoculture stands, smothers all herbaceous plants, and is extremely difficult to remove. Garlic mustard was first sighted in Hueston Woods in the 1970s and has spread ever since. Various methods including using herbicide are being used to control this noxious weed. Hueston Woods is important to neotropical migratory birds as well as nesting waterfowl. Balancing human activity such as boating and wildlife is always difficult and needs to be carefully monitored. The woods has a bird banding station to take advantage of the opportunity to band the many birds migrating through the site. Being near Miami University in Oxford, among other nearby universities, the woods have been the subject of a variety of studies.

This is an important preserve that allows people to experience, on a very small scale, what the once-vast eastern forests may have looked like 200 hundred years ago. It is also a rare example of integrating important natural habitat with active recreational multiuse facilities.

Further Reading

Bonnicksen, Thomas M. *America's Ancient Forests: From the Ice Age to the Age of Discovery*. New York: John Wiley, 2000.

Hunter, Malcolm L. Jr. *Maintaining Biodiversity in Forest Ecosystems*. New York: Cambridge University Press, 1999.

Medley, Kimberly E., Christine M. Pobocik, and Brian W. Okey. "Historical Changes in Forest Cover and Land Ownership in a Midwestern U.S. Landscape." *Annals of the Association of American Geographers* 93, no. 1 (2003): 104–20.

KITTY TODD NATURE PRESERVE

The Huron/Erie Lake Plains ecoregion is a nearly flat, fertile plain with relict sand dunes and moraines. Early settlers drained and cleared the land, and now most of the ecoregion has been converted to highly productive crop and livestock agriculture. Also within this ecoregion is a gem: the Oak Openings ecoregion. This is a sub-ecoregion found in only two small parts of northern Ohio and northern Indiana. This subregion is distinguished by low, usually wooded, sand dunes that originally supported mixed oak (*Quercus* spp.) forests and oak savanna, with occasional poorly drained depressions of wet prairies. The Oak Openings ecoregion is 130 square miles in northeastern Ohio. The sand and clay soils are the result of deposits by glacial Lake Warren, which predates Lake Erie. This unique environment is becoming increasingly rare because of fire suppression, development, changes to the hydrology such as draining land and channelization, pollution of surface and ground water, and disturbance. Kitty Todd Nature Preserve consists of 750 acres owned and managed by The Nature Conservancy. It is one of the best examples of this ecosystem of oak savanna and wet prairie with over 585 native plants, 90 state rare plants, and 21 rare animal species.

Oak savannas have adapted to, and are dependent upon, fire to reduce shrub undergrowth and to stimulate growth of native grasses and forbs (primarily prairie plants).

Kitty Todd Nature Preserve. (John Hartsock)

Of current concern with the introduction of nonnative plants, fire also helps to control invasive species that are not fire tolerant. Black oak (*Quercus velutina*) is the dominant oak in the oak savanna at Kitty Todd Preserve, and proper management techniques are helping the oaks and associated plants and animals to thrive.

The wild lupine (*Lupinus perennis*), which is found only on sandy, often sterile sand prairies, has responded well to restoration efforts. This is an important plant because it is the only source of food for the larvae of the federally endangered Karner blue butterfly (*Lycaeides melissa samuelis*). As recently as the late 1980s, the Karner blue butterfly was believed to be extirpated from Ohio. A reintroduction program began in 1993, first, by restoring the wild lupine habitat at Kitty Todd and, in 1998, the releasing of hand-raised Karner blue butterflies. The restoration has also improved the habitat for birds and mammals as well. However, an early spring warm spell followed by cold temperatures dramatically set back the Karner blue butterfly numbers, reinforcing the need to have diverse populations that may better withstand such dramatic events.

The success of these and other restoration and management efforts at Kitty Todd are in part the result of planning and partnering with other groups and agencies. As can be seen from the vulnerability of the Karner blue butterfly. one preserve alone cannot protect and sustain the natural systems of this ecoregion. Success depends on conservation efforts on a landscape scale. One such grassroots effort is the Green Ribbon Initiative, whose mission is to preserve the Oak Openings Region by protecting land to create a biological corridor. Through land acquisition, conservation easements, and zoning and other regulation, impact on the remaining oak savanna can be protected by reducing the impact of development and restoring the remaining high-quality sites. The group's Conservation Plan Committee, comprised of members of various local and national conservation organizations and government officials and scientists, developed a conservation plan in fall 2008. The goals of the plan were to increase public awareness, gather data on conservation efforts and scientific research in the Oak Openings region, promote communication between the diverse conservation initiatives, and protect the long-term viability of natural areas while balancing urban growth.

The restoration efforts at Kitty Todd Nature Preserve have been very successful. However, the preserve is located just west of Toledo, and, like many natural areas, development pressures are fragmenting the remaining natural areas and areas with the potential for restoration. The successes at Kitty Todd serve as a model for conservation efforts being undertaken in the ecoregion. Conservation planning is critical to the success of balancing growth with preservation of the remaining natural resources in the Oak Openings region.

The preserve is open to the public and offers frequent educational programs and volunteer opportunities.

Further Reading

Gray, Susan Heinrichs. *Karner Blue Butterfly (Road to Recovery)*. Ann Arbor, MI: Cherry Lake, 2007.

Grove, Noel. *Earth's Last Great Places: Exploring The Nature Conservancy Worldwide*. Washington DC: National Geographic Society, 2004.

Pickens, Bradley A. *The Consequences of a Management Strategy for the Endangered Karner Blue Butterfly.* Master's thesis. Bowling Green, OH: Bowling Green State University, 2006.

MENTOR MARSH

Covering 691 acres, Mentor Marsh is one of the largest marshes on Lake Erie; Ohio's first state nature preserve (dedicated in 1971); and an important area for migratory birds, particularly waterfowl. The preserve is also significant because marshes are uncommon in northeastern Ohio and because it is just northeast of Cleveland and situated in one of the most heavily populated areas of Ohio. The preserve's location affords many educational opportunities to see a marsh ecosystem and witness seasonal migratory birds, as well as the many challenges from urban pressures. The preserve is located in the Eastern Great Lakes and Hudson Lowlands ecoregion, which occupies a narrow strip along Ohio's Lake Erie shore, the remainder of the ecoregion occupying much of northern New York State.

Mentor Marsh is jointly owned and managed by the Cleveland Museum of Natural History and the State of Ohio Division of Natural Areas and Preserves. This partnership allows the preserve to draw on the experience of museum and DNR staff and scientists for wide-ranging educational programming for students and families.

Mentor Marsh has gone through many changes. The marsh was probably an open body of water up to the early 1800s, until a dense swamp forest developed over time in the eastern portion of the marsh, eventually covering 80 percent of the swamp by 1951. However, in 1959, the swamp forest began to die off due to salt leakage into the swamp from surrounding salt mining operations. Other plants and many of the animals were also killed by salt contamination. Most importantly, the dramatic change in water quality allowed the salt-tolerant invasive exotic plant, common reed, also known as phragmites, to invade the marsh. Currently, almost all open areas of the marsh are covered by phragmites. Blackbrook Creek was rerouted in the late 1990s to try to lower salinity levels with mixed results. Some areas have somewhat recovered, whereas salinity in other areas, particularly in the dry summer months, have remained high. Eutrophication has impacted the marsh and further reduced biodiversity. Eutrophication is a natural process of a lake filling in to become a swamp and eventually a forest. Eutrophication, in this case, though, is the result of excessive growth and decay of phragmites, which has led to the buildup of decaying plant material and a reduction of oxygen in the shallow waters. Here an extremely aggressive and prolific exotic species has unnaturally and dramatically increased the eutrophication process and reduced the biodiversity.

The most recent environmental change to Mentor Marsh has been the in the frequency of fire. Since 1979, there have been a number of fires, some intense. Most were set by juveniles and some were accidental. These frequent fires have played an important role in the dynamics of the swamp. In addition to be tolerant of salt, phragmites is also tolerant of fire. Phragmites recovers quickly from fire, but many of the marsh species are not. The high combustibility of phragmites has contributed to the occurrence of fires, which, in turn, has contributed to the spread of phragmites; it is a relentless cycle. In some areas, trees were cut down to create a fire break between the marsh and the uplands. However, a long-term solution to reducing fires would be the return of the swamp forest. Since phragmites is intolerant of shade, an increased tree canopy would shade out phragmites and in the process reduce the fuel supply.

To address these and other environmental challenges, the Marsh Area Regional Coalition, a group consisting of all levels of government, private and nonprofit groups, museums, schools, and concerned citizens, created a Special Area Management Plan in 2004. This comprehensive plan provides a framework for the management of the land and water in, surrounding, and impacting Mentor Marsh and the Lake Erie coastal areas. It attempts to balance environmental and economic issues facing the area. It is the first Special Area Management Plan to be developed in Ohio and is an important step toward not only the restoration of the marsh but also the coordination of different levels of government, organizations, educational institutions, and private citizens and businesses.

Further Reading

Fineran, Stacey A. "Assessing Spatial and Temporal Vegetative Dynamics at Mentor Marsh, 1796 to 2000 A.D." Ph.D. dissertation, University of Ohio, Columbus, 2003.
Fleischman, John. *The Ohio Lands*. San Francisco: BrownTrout, 1995.

MORGAN SWAMP

Morgan Swamp is approximately 2,000 acres of wetland habitat in what was once part of a glacial lake bed, now forming an important part of the Grand River lowlands and one of the largest undeveloped interior wetlands in Ohio. The Grand River is a major river flowing into Lake Erie, and the surrounding wetlands are an important source of freshwater. The Nature Conservancy protects 1,015 acres, half of Morgan Swamp, and in 2006, opened the preserve to the public. Many wetlands in the region have been drained for agriculture and logging. Nearly half of Morgan Swamp was historically a hemlock swamp (*Tsuga canadensis*) that was cut down for timber in the mid 1800s; the remaining wetland was devastated by massive fires. The swamp has recovered with very little human intervention over the past 100 years; however, the habitat composition has changed from its once-dominant hemlock swamp-shrub composition.

Morgan Swamp is a diverse wetland complex that supports many rare organisms and provides critical habitat for nesting and migratory birds such as the yellow-bellied sapsucker (*Sphyrapicus varius*) and cerulean warbler (*Dendroica cerulea*) as well as other animals such as beavers (*Castor canadensis*) and the North American river otter (*Lontra canadensis*). Beavers were once an integral component of wetland communities in this region, damming streams and creating ponds. At Morgan Swamp, beavers are an important part of wetland succession from open water to forest. Beavers play an important role in aiding the development of a variety of mixed emergent marshes, which are wetland communities dominated by herbaceous emergent vegetation. This type of vegetation lives in a perennial wet habitat consisting of grasses, broad-leaved, floating, and submersed plants. They also create impoundments, or areas where water collects. By flooding the surrounding land, beavers create or extend wetland habitat. Morgan Swamp once had the largest hemlock swamp in the state, and the beavers are credited with helping to bring back this habitat type. Morgan Swamp is recovering in part because of natural disturbance in the swamp, which is an important factor in sustaining the mosaic of wetland habitats that are in various stages of succession.

The Nature Conservancy's efforts directly protect half of the swamp, which is also within two square miles of the Grand River's 712-square-mile watershed. Morgan Swamp is a critical component to the health of the watershed—changes to the swamp have consequences further down the watershed. Likewise, activities upstream have impacts beyond Morgan Swamp because of the important beneficial aspects the swamp has on the ecosystem, acting as a filter for pollutants and a buffer for water quality downstream in the watershed. Activities such as forestry have increased runoff, adding sediment to streams and affecting the water-holding capacity of the soils. Cattle and other livestock grazing near streams has increased potential runoff due to overgrazing and fecal matter in open bodies of water. Likewise, gas and oil wells are of special concern because of the possibility of contaminating groundwater. Invasive species have been an ongoing battle at Morgan Swamp. Monocultures of nonnative plants such as common reed reduce diversity, displace the natural vegetation, and reduce habitat for native animals. Volunteers remove and spray invasive plants to control and reduce their spread. Common reed, in particular, can quickly take over emergent habitat, so its control is critical to the biodiversity and health of Morgan Swamp. The effort to control this invasive wetland species at Morgan Swamp is part of a larger effort to document potential methods of eradicating this destructive plant and, as such, has important implications for its control at other preserves.

The Erie/Ontario Drift and Lake Plain ecoregion is the most industrialized part of Ohio. Despite this, the Grand River is currently in good condition and has high biodiversity. The Nature Conservancy, Grand River Partners, the Ohio Division of Wildlife, and Lake Metroparks work together on issues facing the Grand River such as habitat loss, invasive species control, and protecting wetland and other natural habitat. Great efforts are being made at Morgan Swamp to preserve this important ecologically rich place, and without targeted intervention the swamps would decline due to invasive species. However, pressures from the surrounding unprotected areas and from the upstream Grand River and Grand River watershed can have serious consequences as well. Partnerships are invaluable to the protection of Morgan Swamp through education, stewardship, and enforcement.

Further Reading

Environmental Law Institute. *Ohio's Biological Diversity: Strategies and Tools for Conservation*. Washington DC: Environmental Law Institute, 1998.

Keddy, Paul A. *Wetland Ecology: Principles and Conservation*. Cambridge, England: Cambridge University Press, 2000.

Marks, Marianne, Beth Lapin, and John Randall. *Element Stewardship Abstract for Phragmites australis Common Reed*. Arlington, VA: The Nature Conservancy, 1993.

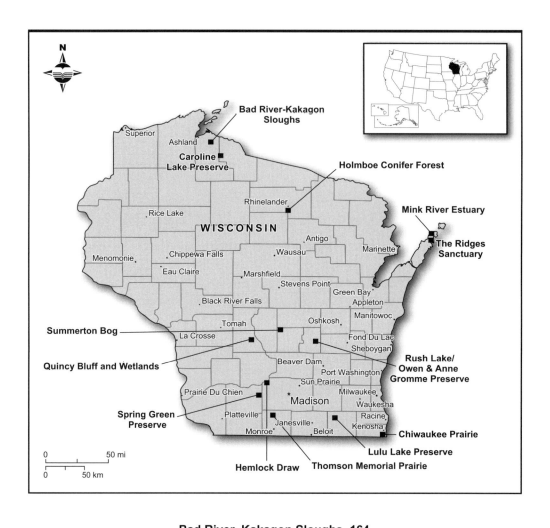

WISCONSIN

Wisconsin is a state rich in its diversity of natural ecosystems. Bordered by two great lakes, Lake Superior on the north and Lake Michigan on the east, with the Mississippi River running along most of its western boundary, the state also has over 6,000 named lakes (more than 15,000 total lakes). Many of these lakes were created by the last glaciation, which ended around 10,000 years ago. Although all midwestern states have been affected to one degree or another by glacial advances, no other state has been so dramatically shaped by the latest glacial advance than Wisconsin. Evidence can be seen in the many lakes, rolling hills, and other topographic features. The soils and rock debris from the glaciers are evident in the pink, sandy soils of northwestern Wisconsin and the glacial till of the many farm fields. Where the glacier was virtually absent, in the southwestern part of the state, one finds large, rugged outcroppings and shallow soils where bedrock at the surface is not uncommon.

The water, vegetation, soils, climate, and animal life are extremely varied, exhibiting almost all of the broad ecosystems seen in the other midwestern states combined. Wisconsin is where the boreal forest meets the hardwood forests of the southern and eastern states and the grasslands, or prairies, of the west. From the pine barrens of the northwestern part of the state to the shoreline habitats of Lake Superior and Lake Michigan, Wisconsin's ecological diversity is impressive. So, too, are the numerous environmental initiatives and many unique approaches being taken to preserve natural places. The following entries give a sample of what the state has to offer and the ways in which the natural areas are being protected. Readers are encouraged to view aerial photography of these places at any mapping Web site. Many of the patterns of vegetation, hydrology, and geology of Wisconsin can only be truly grasped on a landscape scale, and the view from several thousand feet to several miles above will greatly enhance readers' understanding the natural places and the challenges that they face.

BAD RIVER–KAKAGON SLOUGHS

The Bad River–Kakagon Sloughs is a 16,000-acre wetland located on the Lake Superior shore and protected from harsh storms and waves by Long Island–Chequamegon Point, a dune-studded coastal barrier that stretches across Chequamegon Bay in northern Wisconsin. A slough, in the eastern United States, is a type of swamp formed by the backwater of a large waterway, similar to a bayou, with trees being present. The Bad River–Kakagon Sloughs is a large estuarine wetland complex that lies on calcareous red clays deposited during the last glaciation, along with organic deposits in the swampy areas. This area is typical of the Lake Superior Clay Plain ecoregion, which is in the Northern Lakes and Forests ecoregion. The Bad and Kakagon rivers run through this area, and the extensive and diverse mosaic of coastal and wetland communities are among some of the least disturbed of their types and rank among the most significant in the Great Lakes. The sloughs are an important habitat for migratory and nesting waterfowl in addition to spawning fishes. The sloughs are within the Bad River Band of Lake Superior Chippewa Reservation and are accessible only by request.

The Bad River Band acquired 21,322 acres in September 2003 in a land acquisition negotiated by The Nature Conservancy. This put almost one-fifth of the total area of the reservation into tribal hands, protecting more than 24 miles of streams within the sloughs and other critical habitat, especially vast wild rice beds. *Manoomin* is the Ojibwe (Chippewa) word for northern wild rice, and, at 400 acres, the sloughs contain the largest natural rice beds in the Great Lakes basin. Wild rice is important economically and culturally for the Chippewa (the anglicized name given to the Ojibwe, most commonly used in the United States). The protection of the watershed, therefore, is of critical importance to the wild rice habitat as well as the mosaic of wetland habitat found in the sloughs.

Lands along the rivers that run north through the sloughs into Lake Superior are at threat for contamination from fecal matter from septic systems on and off the reservation and cattle that are allowed in streams. Clear-cutting logging practices along the stream have increased runoff from the unstable clay soils, increasing turbidity and flow of the streams. Sedimentation is necessary for the sloughs, but deforestation has increased stream flow. Sedimentation builds Chequamegon Point, which protects the sloughs and feeds the aquatic life throughout the sloughs. Dramatic changes to this system may have unforeseen consequences. Invasive species also have become a serious problem. Significant infestations of plants such as purple loosestrife (*Lythrum salicaria*) have been reported in recent surveys of rivers in the watershed. The seeds float and quickly colonize disturbed soil downstream by natural processes and deforestation; colonies further upstream have now taken hold within the sloughs.

The Bad River Reservation was established by the Treaty of La Poine in 1854 and held in trust 125,000 acres. Over the years, land was sold to non-Indians, and, by 1992, about 51 percent remained in tribal ownership. This means that land in the area is held in federal, tribal, state, and local jurisdictions, making management, land planning, and water protection difficult. This is why the recent acquisition of over 21,000 acres by

The Bad River twists around Copper Falls State Park. (Jonah Westrich)

the tribe was so critical. The Bad River tribe has been working with the state Department of Natural Resources, the Environmental Protection Agency (EPA), The Nature Conservancy, and other agencies to survey and assist in the management of the sloughs. Walleye (*Sander vitreus*), otters (*Lontra canadensis*), and other animals are being collected to monitor and analyze contamination in the Kakagon and Bad rivers as part of the Lake Superior fish contaminant monitoring program. The EPA is working with the Bad River Band to monitor federally permitted wastewater treatment plants in the Lower Bad River watershed to ensure public health and environmental standards are being met.

This high-quality area faces many future challenges from a variety of sources, and the disparate ownership means that state, federal, and tribal laws and regulations are not evenly enforced. However, the collaboration at this stage between the various government agencies, private landowners, and groups shows promise. Water and environmental quality are being carefully monitored to obtain a baseline for understanding the dynamics of this high-quality ecosystem as well as to provide valuable data for responding to changes to this wetland system.

Further Reading

Harkin, Michael E., ed. *Native Americans and the Environment: Perspectives on the Ecological Indian*. Omaha: University of Nebraska Press, 2007.

Johansen, Bruce E. *Indigenous Peoples and Environmental Issues*. Westport, CT: Greenwood Press, 2003.

Waters, Thomas F. *The Superior North Shore*. Minneapolis: University of Minnesota Press, 1988.

CAROLINE LAKE PRESERVE

The 1,044 acres of Caroline Lake Preserve are located in an area of the Northern Lakes and Forests ecoregion, which transitions from the boreal forests to the north and the mixed hardwood conifer forests to the south. The more than 12,000 lakes in Wisconsin are a result of the last glaciation, and most of the lakes are located in northern Wisconsin. The beauty and serenity of the lakes has meant that virtually all of them have been developed with one or more private homes. The Caroline Lake Preserve allows visitors to see what the northern woods of Wisconsin might have looked like before settlement.

The surrounding forests are mainly balsam fir (*Abies balsamea*), aspen (*Populus* spp.), Canadian hemlock (*Tsuga canadensis*), and yellow birch (*Betula lutea*), with a variety of maples (*Acer* spp.), and pines (*Pinus* spp.). Large mammals such as gray wolves (*Canis lupus*), coyotes (*Canis latrans*), and black bears (*Ursus americanus*) are typical of this area. The wetlands and three lakes—Caroline Lake, Twin Lake–East and Twin Lake–West—are important nesting and migratory stopover habitat for North American and neotropical birds. Besides the wildlife and habitat protected in the preserve, the site is important because Caroline Lake is the headwaters of the Bad River, whose clear, high-quality water flows into the Kakagon/Bad River Sloughs, which is the largest and highest-quality functioning estuarine system remaining in the upper Great Lakes region. The continued health of this river and wetland complex depends upon the quality of the waters flowing from Caroline Lake.

The land was purchased by The Nature Conservancy in 1997 from the Georgia-Pacific Corporation paper company. In 1999, the state of Wisconsin purchased most of the remaining shoreline of Caroline Lake and has been managing the property as a state natural area. The preserve is used by Northland College to study the effects of deer and hare browsing and the regeneration of conifer trees. However, the most unusual and unlikely current use of the preserve is as a managed forest.

As part of what it calls an adaptive management framework, The Nature Conservancy is using silviculture—which is the study, development, and management of forests—to further the group's conservation efforts. As a science-based organization that tries to balance human needs with the protection of natural habitat, the conservancy is applying an active forest management program to Caroline Lake Preserve. Trees are being selectively harvested by The Nature Conservancy for various lumber needs. Harvesting is based on the natural patterns of disturbance, maintaining biodiversity while ensuring a sustainable rate of economic return, managing the forests at an appropriate scale, and considering the cumulative impact and landscape context. The preserve was purchased to be managed under the state's Managed Forest Law, and 860 acres are being managed as productive working forests.

The transitional northern hardwood ecosystem of the preserve has historically adapted to small-scale natural disturbances. Understanding the dynamics of such disturbances is critical to proper forest management, and silviculture can be used to aid natural processes. Trees of various ages are harvested, and the canopy is not reduced by more than one-third during each cutting. With this approach, the pattern of natural disturbance processes is replicated. However, more research is needed on these natural processes for the different ecosystems present in order to best manage habitat. In this sense, the preserve is being managed not only for habitat conservation and sustainable timber harvest but also as a living laboratory in the dynamics of small-scale northern woods habitat disturbance. Too often, conservation efforts are not compatible with economic goals. The forest management plan for Caroline Lake Preserve is an example of how ecological and economic goals can be compatible in the right conditions.

Further Reading

Knight, Richard, and Kevin Gutzwiller. *Wildlife and Recreationists Coexistence through Management and Research.* Washington, DC: Island Press, 1995.

Palik, Brian, and Louise Levy, eds. *Proceeding of the Great Lakes Silviculture Summit.* St. Paul, MN: North Central Research Station, U.S. Forest Service, 2004.

Wisconsin Woodland Owner's Association. *100 Years of Wisconsin Forestry, 1904–2004.* Black Earth, WI: Trails Media Group, 2004.

CHIWAUKEE PRAIRIE

Located in two sections along the shores of Lake Michigan in southeastern Wisconsin on the Illinois border, Chiwaukee Prairie is one of the largest remnant prairies (an intact and unplowed prairie) and the most intact coastal wetland in Wisconsin. Covering a total of 410 acres, the main tract is the 226-acre contiguous southern section managed by The Nature Conservancy and co-owned by the University of Wisconsin–Parkside. The northern section, owned by the Wisconsin Department of Natural Resources, is fragmented by roads and private property. The northern section has limited access, while the southern section is open to the public with undeveloped hiking trails.

Chiwaukee Prairie is noted for its exceptional diversity consisting of more than 475 species of vascular plants (plants with strands of cells that form a system for transporting fluids throughout its various parts—distinct from algae, fungi, liverworts, and mosses); few prairies of this size have such diversity (200 or fewer species of plants are typically found in a prairie this size). Although only a remnant of the vast presettlement prairie that once covered southern Wisconsin and the southern shores of Lake Michigan, the site boasts a variety of both upland and wetland plant communities, including southern sedge meadow and wet and wet-mesic to dry-mesic prairie. Mesic prairies are sites dominated by prairie plants with soils that have ample moisture but are well-drained.

Such diversity is a result of the topography. Glacial Lake Michigan receded in a series of stages over several thousand years, leaving behind sandy ridges. The Toelston

Ridge forms the western boundary of the prairie, which is also the raised bed for the railroad tracks that border the preserve. Smaller sandy ridges several feet high were also produced, and they support mesic and more drought-tolerant plant communities. Because of poor drainage and a high water table, the swales, or low areas between the sandy ridges, support hydric, or wet-loving, plants. As a result, this prairie has a myriad of microhabitats where dry- and wet-adapted plants exist, sometimes within a few feet of one another. Portions of the site have been classified as a rare calcareous fen. A fen is a type of wetland that is primarily supported by groundwater discharge, while a calcareous fen contains calcium and magnesium. The high pH, or measure of the acidity or alkalinity of soil or water, coupled with the constant supply of groundwater, creates a unique environment that supports not only the typical wet prairie plants but also species found growing only under these distinct conditions. These indicator plants, or obligated plants, are found only in the presence of distinct environmental conditions that indicate a high-quality natural environment. Chiwaukee Prairie has a many obligated wetland plant species.

This unique site is protected today as the result of over 25 years of work by concerned citizens, The Nature Conservancy, and the state of Wisconsin. In the early 1920s, the land was purchased and plated for subdivision development; however, with only a few roads and homes built, the economic downturn of the Great Depression put an end to this project. Over the intervening years, the land changed hands and several houses were built on scattered parcels, primarily nearer Lake Michigan. Attempts were made by the Wisconsin Department of Natural Resources to purchase the area for conservation, but the idea encountered difficulty as a result of the scattered ownership and lack of funds. In 1965, a group of citizens concerned about further development on sites not yet built formed a committee under the auspice of The Nature Conservancy. With a loan from The Nature Conservancy, they purchased an initial 15-acre parcel and were able to bring more attention and conservation efforts to this unique natural area. By 1990, over 200 acres of contiguous land had been acquired through donations by landowners and the purchase of additional parcels. As further recognition of the environmental importance of the area, Chiwaukee Prairie was designated a national natural landmark by the National Park Service in 1973. This program identifies and recognizes the best examples of biological and geological features in both public and private ownership.

But the prairie remains under threat. In 1994, a proposal was put forward to construct a limestone quarry a little more than a half-mile northeast of Chiwaukee Prairie. The construction of an open pit had the potential to draw down and drastically interrupt the shallow water tables of the Pike Creek watershed (an area in which all the water drains to a river or creek), of which the prairie, and in particular the fens, are an integral part. Quarrying activities, even though almost a mile away, could dry up the prairie. The measure was defeated by petitions, letters, and phone calls.

Chiwaukee Prairie is exemplary of the interconnectedness of natural systems. It offers visitors the chance to experience the diversity of the coastal prairies that once stretched for miles along Lake Michigan.

Further Reading

Hoffman, Randolph M. *Wisconsin's Natural Communities: How to Recognize Them, Where to Find Them.* Madison: University of Wisconsin Press, 2002.

Muir, John. *The Story of My Boyhood and Youth.* Boston, MA: Houghton Mifflin, 1913.

Van Hise, Charles Richard. *The Conservation of Natural Resources in the United States.* New York: Macmillan, 1910.

HEMLOCK DRAW

Hemlock Draw derives its name from the Appalachian term, *draw*, meaning a valley. The preserve is owned by The Nature Conservancy and is one of several governmental and Nature Conservancy preserves in the Baraboo Hills Range, an ancient mountain range extending for 25 miles through Wisconsin's Driftless Area ecoregion. As a result, the Baraboo Hills, and in particular Hemlock Draw, exhibit some of the best geological and ecological wonders of this ecoregion. The last glacial advance 12,000 years ago missed this area, so many plants and animals typical of more northern areas today live in the preserve's cool, moist valleys. Though atypical for southern Wisconsin in general, these relics are not unusual in this unglaciated region.

Hemlock Draw is 994 acres of incredible geological and biological diversity. Sea stacks, or narrow pillars of rock, located in the preserve are remnants from when the Baraboo Hills were mere islands in a vast sea. The one-and-a-half-billion-year-old Baraboo quartzite in the Baraboo Hills is, in fact, among the oldest exposed geological features on earth. Along Honey Creek, a narrow gorge of sandstone supports species typically found further north, such as Canadian hemlock (*Tsuga canadensis*), yellow birch (*Betula alleghaniensis*), and several species of club moss (*Lycopodium* spp.). Further from the banks, northern species such as sugar maple (*Acer saccharum*) and big-tooth aspen (*Populus grandidentata*) are common, with red oak (*Quercus rubra*) dominating the drier bluff tops at the north and south end of the draw. These forests shelter many state-threatened or endangered plants and create an important breeding and migratory habitat for many birds. More than 40 breeding birds and four woodpeckers depend on Hemlock Draw for breeding habitat and food. Most notable is the worm-eating warbler (*Helmitheros vermivorus*).

The porous sandstone has a high capacity to hold water. The water is slowly released, creating a humid, cool environment preferred by hemlocks—though other northern species are also present. These unique conditions have allowed Canadian hemlock to survive much further south. These relict stands of hemlock remnants are disjunct from their usual northern Wisconsin range and thus form rare plant communities here. Periglacial relics—plants that lived on the edges of glacial areas—were left behind when the last glaciers retreated, surviving in pockets not generally found elsewhere in this part of the state. These plants and animals left behind have become habitat specialists; they are not

Hemlock Draw. (Peter Patau)

able to survive in the conditions of surrounding areas. As a result, Hemlock Draw and many of these specialized relict habitats are at great risk.

Disruptions to the factors responsible for maintaining these special microclimates, such as the hydrology and deep shade, can adversely affect the health of the hemlocks and their associated plants and animals. Recreational use such as horses, all-terrain vehicles, and animal grazing can quickly erode the steep slopes, and invasive species such as garlic mustard can threaten the natural communities. Because the stands are isolated, it can be difficult or impossible for species to recolonize a site. Currently, hemlock seems to be reproducing well, but its leaves are a favorite of white-tailed deer, and heavy browsing needs to be monitored.

,. The Nature Conservancy's acquisition of the larger and ecologically significant landscape of the Baraboo Hills Range and other land beginning in the early 1960s began as a quest to save important sites. However, The Nature Conservancy, along with other conservation groups, realized the importance of the goal of protecting ecological landscapes and not just areas for a single species or a unique feature. The land, water, plants, birds, animals, and insects are interconnected, and the associations are critical to the survival of all; no organism lives independent of others. The management strategy of many environmental agencies and organizations has thus changed over the years to think on a landscape scale. For instance, from 2003 to 2006, the Wisconsin Department of Natural Resources convinced 32 families to sign away development rights through conservation easements to protect more than 2,100 acres in the Baraboo Range. One farm family put its 323-acre farm in Hemlock Draw into a conservation easement, thus expanding the area protected. Because of the work of The Nature Conservancy and Sauk County's Baraboo Range Protection Program, many of these landowners were already familiar with the conservation easement program when the Department of Natural Resources approached them. Educational efforts can have long-reaching effects.

Located just north of Leland, the preserve is open to the public but is undeveloped.

Further Reading
French, Hugh. *The Periglacial Environment.* West Sussex, England: John Wiley, 2007.
Lange, Denneth I. *A Postglacial Vegetational History of Sauk County and Caledonia Township, Columbia County, South Central Wisconsin (Technical Bulletin No. 168).* Madison: Wisconsin Department of Natural Resources, 1990.

HOLMBOE CONIFER FOREST

The Holmboe Conifer Forest is a 39-acre woodland preserve just south of Rhinelander on the Pelican River. It is notable for its diverse old-growth forest that has never been logged. It was one of the earliest preserves managed by The Nature Conservancy in Wisconsin, being managed since 1965. In 2007, the ownership was transferred to the Northwoods Land Trust, a nonprofit group committed to the conservation of Wisconsin's north woods. The high visibility of this preserve makes it a showcase for the efforts of the Northwoods Land Trust in northern Wisconsin.

The preserve is an excellent example of many of the Northern Lakes and Forests ecoregion forest types in one small space. The rolling landscape contains swamps and uplands on a mix of soils from river sediment, to loam, to sand, which is the predominant soil type in northern Minnesota, Wisconsin, and Michigan. An esker—a sinuous ridge formed from sand and rocks deposited by rivers running through a glacier—runs along the western boundary. Typical of the well-drained, acidic, sandy soils of this region are upland species such as white pine, (*Pinus strobus*), red pine (*Pinus resinosa*), paper birch (*Betula papyrifera*), and sugar maple (*Acer saccharum*). A stand of quaking aspen (*Populus tremuloides*) is located where gravel was once dug. Being a pioneer species, it quickly filled in the area after being abandoned. The swamps between the ridges contain tamarack (*Larix laricina*) and white cedar (*Thuja occidentalis*) stands as well as swamp hardwoods yellow birch (*Betula alleghaniensis*), black ash (*Fraxinus nigra*), and swamp alder (*Alnus incana*), typical of lowland areas of this region. The American yew (*Taxus canadensis*), an extremely rare tree in the wild in Wisconsin because it is a favorite winter food of white-tailed deer (*Odocoileus virginianus*), grows in Holmboe. Three species of club moss

(*Lycopodium* spp.), Labrador tea (*Ledum groenlandicum*), wintergreen (*Gaultheria procumbens*), and many other lowland species native to these acidic soils are also found here. Seeping springs that drain into the Pelican River provide a moist, humid environment where white cedar and Canadian hemlock (*Tsuga canadensis*) thrive. The proximity to the river and diverse terrain provide a glimpse of many of the plant communities found throughout the northern midwestern states.

The diverse vegetation also provides habitat for the green-backed heron (*Butorides virescens*), spotted sandpiper (*Actitis macularia*), and purple martin (*Progne subis*); at least 23 bird species make Holmboe their home. The wide range of tree species supports this diversity of animals, offering a glimpse of the variety of northern forest associations in a very small space.

Holmboe Conifer Forest has been designated a wildlife sanctuary, which provides additional protection to the plants and animals in the preserve. Invasive species, such as honeysuckle (*Lonicera* spp.) and buckthorn (*Rhamnus cathartica*), are becoming more common in all areas of Wisconsin, and volunteers at Holmboe work annually to remove them. The small size of the preserve also is a challenge. There are development pressures to the south and east of the preserve, and the water quality of the Pelican River and the springs in the preserve will become increasingly important issues. The preserve is used for educational purposes and has given the Northwoods Land Trust more visibility. The trust works with landowners to protect lands through stewardship in one of the fastest-growing regions of the state. Having many of the diverse northern forest habitats in an easily accessible area, Holmboe Conifer Forest will become an increasingly important tool in educating and informing people in the need to manage and develop wisely an area that will see vast growth in the coming decades.

Further Reading

Gretz, Jocelyn, ed. *In Their Own Words: Landowners' Stories of Protecting Their Land.* Madison, WI: Gathering Waters Conservancy, September 2003.

Newton, Adrian C. *Forest Ecology and Conservation: A Handbook of Techniques.* Oxford, England: Oxford University Press, 2007.

LULU LAKE PRESERVE

Lulu Lake preserve contains one of the best collections of diverse high-quality habitats in Wisconsin. The glacial topography is exemplary of the area, and the preserve reflects the diversity of the Southeastern Wisconsin Till Plains ecoregion—a mosaic of vegetation types in a region that is a transition between the hardwood forests and oak savannas to the west and the tall-grass prairies to the south. Although there are fewer lakes in this ecoregion than are typically found in northern Wisconsin, this area in the ecoregion contains more lakes than is typical because of past glacial activity. When two glacial lobes collided during the last glacial advance, they left behind kettle lakes and moraines, hence the area is called the Kettle Moraine region. Kettle lakes are remnants of the last glacial advance, when a retreating glacier left behind a block of ice that formed a depression, which filled when the ice melted. These kettles are often found in moraines—accumulations of unconsolidated glacial debris such as sand, rocks, and clay left behind from a melting or retreating glacier. Lulu Lake, the preserve's principal feature, is a 95-acre, 40-foot-deep clear alkaline lake. The lake and Mukwonago River, which feeds the lake, support diverse populations of fish and other animals that require clear, high-quality aquatic habitat, such as the long-ear sunfish, a fish that is intolerant of turbid waters and agricultural runoff. The long-ear sunfish's presence, therefore, indicates the quality of the lake.

The topography of the 1,805-acre preserve provides excellent examples of glacial landforms particular to this region. In addition to Lulu Lake, moraines in the preserve provide both wetland and upland habitat such as oak openings, calcareous fen, shrub carr, sedge meadow, and bogs. In fact, there are 14 different natural communities in the preserve. Most notable are the drier gravel upland ridges of the moraines, which contain 50 to 80 acres of oak openings, a community dominated by bur, white, and black oaks (*Quercus macrocarpa, Q. alba, Q. velutina*). Less than half of the land is shaded in oak openings, with the understory comprised of prairie grasses, flowers, and some shrubs. This savanna-type landscape once covered five and a half million acres in Wisconsin. Currently, only 500 acres are intact within the state, 10 percent of which are in Lulu Lake Preserve.

The quality of the aquatic life is no less impressive. Fifty-nine of the 150 fishes in Wisconsin have been documented in Lulu Lake and the Mukwonago River which feeds the lake. The lake contains glacial relics—or animals that thrived in glacial conditions and now exist further south only in isolated areas of similar conditions—such as the black-chin shiner (*Notropis heterodon*) and Iowa darter (*Etheostoma exile*). These fish require clear, deep lake waters typically found further north, but they survive in Lulu Lake and the Mukwonago River because of the condition of the waters.

The incredible diversity is the result of varied topography as well as high-quality water sources. More species may yet be discovered, because the preserve has not been fully inventoried. Scientific research is ongoing, particularly on the oak openings, the hydrology of the meadows and fens, and the rare species in the preserve. This information is critical to better understanding the complex associations and requirements of the organisms and communities in the preserve.

The Nature Conservancy owns 505 acres of the preserve, and the rest is owned by the Wisconsin Department of Natural Resources. Adjacent privately owned land is also being protected. More than anything else, the long-term health of the organisms and natural communities of Lulu Lake Preserve depend on the hydrology of the surround lands. Lulu Lake and the Mukwonago River have each been classified as an exceptional water resource by the Department of Natural Resources. This designation entails greater oversight and restrictions on activities adjacent to and within the lake and river. Because of the importance of the surrounding hydrology to the preserve, The Nature Conservancy works to protect the entire Mukwonago River Watershed as part of its management of Lulu Lake Preserve. This includes partnering with public and private groups and individuals to preserve and maintain the health of the preserve while balancing human needs. For instance, motorized boats are allowed on Lulu Lake but at reduced speeds to preserve the lake shoreline and to not disturb nesting birds. However, enforcement is difficult. The battle with invasive species both in the lake and within the preserve is ongoing. Invasive plants are pulled or killed with herbicides by volunteer work parties. Prescribed fires are used to control invasive plants and maintain habitats such as the oak openings, which depend on and have adapted to periodic fires, and prevent other fire-sensitive native plants, such as sugar maples, from slowly replacing the oak groves. With the incorporation of the Mukwonago River Watershed into the long-term planning and management of the preserve, the incredible diversity of aquatic and terrestrial species and habitats can be maintained.

The preserve is open to the public with access on both The Nature Conservancy's and Department of Natural Resources' property.

Further Reading

Morgan, Neville C., and Peter S. Maitland. *Conservation Management of Freshwater Habitats—Lakes, Rivers and Wetlands.* Norwell, MA: Kluwer Academic Publishers, 2002.

Sabatier, Paul A., Will Focht, and Marty Matlock. *Swimming Upstream: Collaborative Approaches to Watershed Management (American and Comparative Environmental Policy).* Cambridge, MA: MIT Press, 2005.

MINK RIVER ESTUARY

The Mink River Estuary is one of the few high-quality estuaries remaining in the United States. An estuary is an area where a freshwater river meets the ocean. Salt water and fresh water mix in this area, and the rising and falling tide likewise draw salt water temporarily upstream, flooding the low-lying areas. Barrier islands and peninsulas protect estuaries from the full force of the ocean's waves, winds, and storms. A place of hydrological transition, estuaries are some of the most highly productive and diverse places on earth. In the United States, estuaries provide 75 percent of the commercial fish catch. Healthy estuaries are critical to economic and ecological prosperity.

The Mink River Estuary is a special kind of estuary called a freshwater estuary. Freshwater estuaries occur where a drowned river mouth, the lower end of the river that is periodically submerged by lake water, meets a very large freshwater lake, such as one of the Great Lakes. Freshwater estuaries are influenced not by tides but by seiches or wind tides. A seiche is a natural phenomenon occurring on very large bodies of water. The Great Lakes are subject to a back-and-forth movement much like shaking water in bowl. The movement results from atmospheric disturbances such as winds or a change in pressure. In this sense, freshwater estuaries are similar to coastal estuaries because the drowned river mouth is inundated by lake water at the peaks of the seiche, which, in the case of the Mink River Estuary, can last from minutes to eight hours. Unlike tides, however, this movement is not periodic, and estuaries can have extended dry and wet periods. Rather than saline water mixing, the lake water can be of a different temperature and chemical composition and can create turbidity in the estuary.

This pristine freshwater estuary is fed by alkaline spring-fed wetlands on the Door Peninsula, which terminates less than two miles downstream into Lake Michigan at Rowley's Bay. Currently, The Nature Conservancy protects 1,757 acres of the estuary. Including the adjacent Newport State Park, over 13 miles of contiguous shoreline is protected. Access to the estuary is best made by canoe from the Wagon Trail Resort on Rowley's Bay on County Route ZZ, because the surrounding marshland is impossible to traverse by foot. Canoeing up the estuary into the Mink River is like stepping back in time. In spring, the estuary is a major spawning habitat supporting aquatic life for much of the peninsula area. The wetlands support white cedar swamps, (*Thuja occidentalis*) which edge the wild rice marshes. These habitats are an important site for migrating birds, of which more than 200 species have been recorded. They include black-crowned night herons (*Nycticorax nycticorax*), common loons (*Gavia immer*), great blue heron (*Ardea herodias*), wood ducks (*Aix sponsa*), and sandhill cranes (*Grus canadensis*). Beavers (*Castor canadensis*), porcupine (*Erethizon dorsatum*), and muskrat (*Ondatra zibethicus*), among other mammals, inhabit this fertile area. Among the many insects found here, the federally endangered Hine's emerald dragonfly (*Somatochlora hineana*), which breeds only in spring-fed shallow alkaline waters, inhabits this area.

Estuaries are internationally threatened, because limited shoreline is of great value for residential development and an excellent location for shipping and industry. Upstream, estuaries are vulnerable to the impact of residential and commercial land uses, which introduce pollutants and change the hydrology of the estuary's watershed. Fortunately, because of the lack of industry and heavy commercial activity on the Door Peninsula, the Mink River Estuary is relatively free from upstream problems. However, invasive species and loss of habitat are concerns.

Protection of the estuary has been primarily through the acquisition of land. Partnering with the Wisconsin Department of Natural Resources, The Nature Conservancy recently received a grant from the U.S. Fish and Wildlife Service to purchase additional land including shoreline. Landowner incentive programs such as conservation easements have not only increased protected land by preventing future development, they have also increased the public's awareness of coastal and estuary ecosystems and the need for protection. These efforts have slowed the introduction of new invasive aquatic species and the spread of existing ones and have reduced detrimental recreational activities such as all-terrain vehicles and human disturbance of nesting birds. Because most of the Great Lakes coastlines are privately owned, public and private partnerships are critical to preserving shoreline habitat.

Further Reading

Restore America's Estuaries and the National Oceanic and Atmospheric Administration. *A National Strategy To Restore Coastal and Estuarine Habitat.* Arlington, VA: Restore America's Estuaries, April 2002.

Epstein, Eric, Elizabeth Spencer, and Drew Feldkirchner. *A Data Compilation and Assessment of Coastal Wetlands of Wisconsin's Great Lakes.* Madison: Wisconsin Department of Natural Resources, June 2002.

QUINCY BLUFF AND WETLANDS

Quincy Bluff and Wetlands is in the Glacial Lake Wisconsin Sand Plain ecoregion—a transitional area between the northern forested lake region of northern Wisconsin and the agricultural regions to the south. The transition is reflected in the mosaic of land cover and uses consisting of forests, wetlands, cropland, and pasture. Quincy Bluff and Wetlands lies in what was Glacial Lake Wisconsin 15,000 years ago. The low-relief sandy lake plain of today is dominated by wetland habitat in the low areas with uplands consisting of fast-draining, sandy, gravelly soils with pine and oak barrens vegetation. The region is a contrast to other regions in this transitional area as a result of the glacial lake. The 4,870 acres of Quincy Bluff and Wetlands contain the diverse habitats of this region before settlement.

Quincy Bluff and Wetlands is owned and cooperatively managed by The Nature Conservancy and the Wisconsin Department of Natural Resources. The natural area is, for the most part, a contiguous protected area, and there are plans to acquire additional land connecting the remaining fragments. A diversity of rare plants and animals can be found, including prickly pear cactus (*Opuntia fragilis*), the federally protected Karner blue butterfly (*Lycaeides melissa samuelis*), and a host of mammals and birds. Particular to this region, one finds wetland habitat adjacent to pine and oak barrens, which are some of the driest habitats.

Quincy Bluff is the main feature of the preserve. It is a sandstone outcrop that rises 200 feet above the surrounding, mostly flat, landscape. The bluff extends for two miles north to south and contains dry forests and barrens and cliff communities. Lone Rock is a sandstone mesa that features Cambrian (over 5500-million-year-old) sandstone cliffs. These features were once islands in the bed of Glacial Lake Wisconsin 15,000 years ago. These sandy ridges support barrens natural communities of jack pine and northern pin oak, with prairie species found in the bluff openings. The unique geology of this region strongly influences the natural communities.

This large state natural area is the result of The Nature Conservancy acquiring 1,564 acres from farmers and landowners in 1990 and two years later acquiring an additional 1,663 acres from a paper company and other private landowners. The northern 1,663-acre section was transferred to the Department of Natural Resources to establish

Quincy Bluff and Wetlands. (Mary Fairchild)

the area as a state natural area. These large acquisitions made it possible to manage this area on a landscape scale. For instance, the pine-oak barrens is a habitat that has adapted to, and is dependent on, fire. These plants have adapted to being able to survive periodic fires. They are not, however, able to compete with forest trees and shrubs that over time gradually encroach upon the barrens. When natural fires and those set by Native Americans occurred, the woodland plants were killed and the grasslands and barrens quickly reclaimed the land. More than a half a century of fire suppression has threatened these increasingly rare communities and the insects, birds, reptiles, and mammals that depend upon them. The Nature Conservancy is reintroducing fire to bring back the natural balance to these areas. Fire breaks have been installed to better manage the fires, making them safer and protecting surrounding properties. Coincidentally, the reduction of fuel assists in managing unintended fires by reducing the strength at which fires can burn.

Restoration activities have been taking place for a relatively short time, but the large scale of the preserve allows management of the land on a truly landscape scale. This is important to being able to maintain a gradient of communities, from open wetland to oak opening and oak woodland in order to preserve the greatest diversity of habitat. Old logging roads run through the natural area, which is open to the public.

Further Reading

McShea, William J., and William M. Healy, eds. *Oak Forest Ecosystems: Ecology and Management for Wildlife.* Baltimore, MD: Johns Hopkins University Press, 2002.

Nielsen, S., C. Kirschbaum, and A. Haney. "Restoration of Midwest Oak Barrens: Structural Manipulation or Process-only?" *Conservation Ecology* 7, no. 2 (2003): 10. www.consecol.org/vol7/iss2/art10/.

THE RIDGES SANCTUARY

The Ridges Sanctuary is located in Door County, on a peninsula in Lake Michigan just north of Baileys Harbor. The preserve is open to the public. The 1,600 acres of the Sanctuary contains 30 crescent-shaped sandy ridges. The ridges were formed by changing water levels of Lake Michigan, each ridge being once a former beach line and thus running parallel to the lake. The ridges date back to 1,400 to 1,500 years ago, with successive ridges forming over periods of 30 to 50 years. The ridges, in effect, are a chronology of Lake Michigan's water levels in which the oldest plant communities lie furthest from the present-day shoreline. Biologically, the ridges have created an incredibly diverse habitat. In fact, according to the Wisconsin Department of Natural Resources, the area has more rare plants than almost anywhere in the Midwest. The narrow sandy ridges contain dry soil habitat with trees typical of the boreal forest such as black spruce (*Picea mariana*), white spruce (*Picea glauca*), balsam fir (*Abies balsamea*), and white pine (*Pinus strobus*). The swales between the ridges are often open to the sky and contain swamp conifers as well as marsh and bog flora such as sedges (*Carex sp.*) just feet from upland habitat. A total of 28 species of orchids have been found as well as the rare dwarf lake iris (*Iris lacustris*), which is found only in the Great Lakes region and primarily on old beach ridges. Also, the largest discovered population of the federally endangered Hine's emerald dragonfly (*Somatochlora hineana*) resides in the Sanctuary.

The great variation in terrain, from wet to dry, in a relatively small area, as well as Lake Michigan moderating and cooling the air, allows many plants to survive that would normally be found further north in northern Wisconsin and Canada. Proceeding from the present-day shoreline north away from the bay one can observe the succession of plant communities from the pioneer dune grass species on the first ridge to the more mature forests inland. Diversity comes from the variation in soil moisture, temperature, and age of the ridges creating the conditions for the tremendous floristic variety and animal habitat within a relatively small area. There are 475 plant species, 63 breeding bird species, and 12 state-threatened or -endangered species in the Sanctuary—a level of diversity seldom found in any area of this size.

The Ridges Sanctuary is owned by The Ridges Sanctuary, Inc., a nonprofit group. It is the oldest nonprofit nature preserve in Wisconsin (formed in 1937) and the first preserve in the state created for the purpose of protecting native plants. Earlier preserves had an emphasis on preserving animals and not specifically plants. To better fulfill the organization's mission of protecting the Sanctuary, providing education and outreach, and offering research opportunities, the group adopted a five-year strategic plan for 2008 to 2012. This is an important tool for meeting the challenges that lay ahead and ensuring the continued health of The Ridges Sanctuary. Some of the goals and objectives are to monitor the ecosystem to determine a baseline for developing proper management policies for the sanctuary; continue to aggressively control invasive species and partner with neighboring landowners to do the same; acquire additional land as a conservation buffer to the watershed of the Sanctuary; partner with and be a resource for businesses, government, and the community in local environmental issues; develop educational programs for school children and adults; assist landowners in protecting water quality and biodiversity on their lands; and encourage and support research by collaborating with other organizations and scientists to inventory the flora and fauna to be able to better monitor changes and variations within The Ridges Sanctuary.

The importance of a strategic plan cannot be overemphasized. It provides preserve managers both general and specific directions on how to meet present, future, and unforeseen challenges. The Ridges Sanctuary is continuing its mission of the protection and preservation of the preserve thorough education, stewardship, and research.

Further Reading

Burton, Frances, and Aurelia Stampp. *101 Wildflowers of the Ridges Sanctuary: A Field Guide for the Curious*. Madison, WI: Ridges Sanctuary, 2003.

Johanson, Tezz C., and Ronald D. Stieglitz. "Age and Paleoclimatic Significance of Lake Michigan Beach Ridges at Baileys Harbor, Wisconsin." in *Late Quaternary History of the Lake Michigan Basin*, eds. Allan F. Schneider and Gordon S. Fraser, 67–74. Boulder, CO: Geological Society of America, 1990.

Lichter, J. "Primary Succession and Forest Development on Coastal Lake Michigan Sand Dunes." *Ecological Monographs* 68, no. 4 (1998): 487–510.

Rush Lake/Owen
& Anne Gromme Preserve

At 3,200 acres, Rush Lake is the largest prairie pothole lake east of the Mississippi River. It is also a drainage lake, a lake with an inlet (Henderson Creek), an outlet (Waukau Creek), and at least 12 significant intermittent and perennial steams. The watershed of Rush Lake and the Upper Waukau Creek has historically been one of the most productive waterfowl areas in the Midwest. The lake has an average depth of only 18 inches, with several small areas up to about seven feet deep. Water level historically varied with the season, but a dam at its northern outlet, Waukau Creek, was added in the late 1940s to artificially raise and maintain the water level. The Nature Conservancy owns and manages 439 acres at the Rush Lake/Owen & Anne Gromme Preserve. The preserve was named after the Wisconsin wildlife artist Owen Gromme, who painted many scenes of Rush Lake.

The low water levels allow marsh conditions, with the historically dominant emergent vegetation being cattails (*Typha latifolia* and *angustigolia*) and hardstem bulrush (*Scirpus acutus*), after which the lake is named. Rare nesting birds such as the red-necked grebe (*Podiceps grisegena*), Forster's tern (*Sterna forsteri*), and black-crowned night herons (*Nycticorax nycticorax*) are found here. However, over the past 70 years, and particularly the last 40, there has been a precipitous decline in the water quality, vegetation, and wildlife in and around the lake. Comparisons of aerial photographs from the late 1930s with recent photos show a lake with a heavy cover of vegetation compared to a lake of virtually none. Several reasons have been given for the changes, including artificially stable and high water levels preventing the growth of vegetation; agricultural runoff; and the introduction of carp (*Cyprinus carpio*) in the late 1800s, which degrades aquatic habitat and water quality by uprooting vegetation and suspending sediments during feeding, thereby reducing water clarity, which further reduces light levels, causing die-off of aquatic vegetation.

Because of the varying water levels, there has been an attempt to dam the lake since European settlement in the early 1800s. Dams were built for power or to raise the lake level only to flood surrounding farms and lands. As a result, Rush Lake has seen periods in which the lake level was stabilized from damming and the subsequent removal of the dams, allowing nature to control lake levels. Since the 1950s, the lake had been held at a static water level. In the late 1960s, ecologists noticed that damming, or stabilizing the lake water levels, was changing the lake's ecology. However, public opinion kept the dam in place.

Other factors have also affected Rush Lake. Development—including residential, urban, commercial, and agricultural—has affected the hydrology of the watershed and the water entering Rush Lake. Chemicals, fertilizers, and animal waste from agricultural activities contaminate the surface and groundwater. Increased urban development means more impervious surfaces and poor-quality runoff carrying oil, chemicals, and other non-point pollution as well as additional sediment. These issues have all exacerbated the problems at Rush Lake.

Because of the rich waterfowl habitat, Rush Lake has been prime hunting grounds as well. The amount of lead shot discovered from surveys completed in 1994 attest to this. An average of 8.3 shots per square foot were found. This means that nearly four million shells have been fired over Rush Lake, or the equivalent of 150 tons of lead shot. Unfortunately, many waterfowl ingest lead shot from sediment on the bottom of the lake when feeding, which may cause lead poisoning.

To address the many issues facing Rush Lake, the Rush Lake Steering Committee was formed in June 2000. Composed of local, county, and state officials, the committee sought public involvement in setting goals for Rush Lake. To assist in developing a strategic plan, the committee hired an environmental firm to help inventory habitat, assist in public participation, and develop a plan for restoration and management of Rush Lake. An important product of this work was an extensive report completed in April 2002 of the inventory and history of management practices on Rush Lake. This intensive analysis of past and present practices assisted the group in identifying problems in order to be able to make sound recommendations for the restoration and management of Rush Lake. A major recommendation was to reduce the lake water level to expose 50 percent of the lake bottom for two growing seasons. This would allow revegetation of emergent and submergent vegetation with the intent of improving habitat and increasing hardstem bulrush. The rhizomes, or horizontal-running rootlike stems, of the bulrush would cover the lead shot. Reducing the lake level would also promote winter kill of the carp. In August 2007, after two years of lower water levels, dam gates were raised and there has been significant vegetative growth.

Farmers and residents in the watershed are being educated about better practices to reduce runoff, which introduces chemicals and sediment into the lake from upstream. Most importantly, the entire process, from forming the committee to commissioning the study and report, was to generate stakeholder interest in the management of Rush Lake and its watershed. No project of this scale can succeed without public education and involvement. Although much work and expense lies ahead, the importance of having a short- and long-term management plan that involves all stakeholders is invaluable in protecting and managing the many resources of Rush Lake for the diverse interests of today and tomorrow.

The Nature Conservancy's 439-acre property on Rush Lake does not contain trails but is open to the public. It is located three and a half miles north of Ripon, on County Route E. There are also two public access points on the north end and one on the south of Rush Lake.

Further Reading

Deming, Tricia L. *Rush Lake/Upper Waukau Creek Resource Inventory and Strategic Planning Project, April 2002*. Report prepared for Rush Lake Steering Committee. Waupau, WI: Northern Environmental, 2002. http://www.northernenvironmental.com/projects/Rush%20Lake/Rush%20Lake%20Report/Rush%20Lake%20Report.html.

Heinen, Elizabeth B., B. Baeten, and T. O'Brien. "Glacial and Environmental Geology of Rush Lake: Geology of the Upper Fox River Basin: Guidebook for the 24th Wisconsin Undergraduate Geologic Field Conference." University of Wisconsin–Oshkosh,: 2-1–2-9, September 24, 1994.

Landis, Wayne G., and Ming-Ho Yu. *Introduction to Environmental Toxicology: Impacts of Chemicals upon Ecological Systems*, 3rd ed. Boca Raton, FL: CRC Press, 2004.

SPRING GREEN PRESERVE

Located in the unglaciated area of Wisconsin—the Driftless Area—Spring Green is unique in its assemblage of dry communities such as sand prairie, dry bluff prairie, and black oak (*Quercus velutina*) barrens. The preserve is situated on a bluff just off the Wisconsin River. The characteristic hilly topography reflects a region that was bypassed by the last glacial advance and little affected by prior ones. However, the quality and scale of the sandy dunelike landscape at Spring Green Preserve are now extremely rare in Wisconsin. With surface soil temperatures in summer reaching 140° F and desertlike plants such as prairie fame-flower (*Phemeranthus rugospermus*) and prickly pear cactus

(*Opuntia fragilis*) the preserve has been called the Wisconsin Desert. Communities such as these covered thousands of acres of Wisconsin, but grazing and fire suppression have led to their disappearance.

The preserve is an example of the transition from forest to plains and dunes. An oak forest covers the ridge of the bluff, with steep bluff vegetation leveling off into dry prairie with dunes and several sand blowouts—or sandy depressions—as a result of wind action. This unique habitat hosts equally unusual organisms. In addition to the plants mentioned, there are pocket gophers (*Geomys bursarius*) whose digging and tunnels help to turn over the soil as well as provide habitat for animals such as the bull snake (*Pituophis catanifer*), grassland birds, and three lizard species including the state-endangered slender glass lizard (*Ophisaurus attenuatus*). The invertebrates are among the rarest and most unusual for Wisconsin. The Virginia tiger beetle (*Megacephala virginica*), which is commonly found further south, is one of seven tiger beetles. Ten species of wolf spiders have been documented, and five species of cicadas have been identified.

The Nature Conservancy acquired 480 acres in 1971 and, until recently, had managed roughly the same area. However, recent grant money has enabled The Nature Conservancy to purchase additional land, and it currently owns or manages 1,002 acres. This is critical because the dunes, sand prairies, and cliffs are easily eroded by activities such as grazing cattle. In this parched landscape, it would be difficult to imagine that a hands-off approach could have negative consequences; however, succession plants such as trees and shrubs and, in particular, red cedars are persistent invaders of these communities. Although this is the natural succession, the present communities of sand and bluff prairie at Spring Green Preserve and the birds, reptiles, and invertebrates that depend upon them are now quite rare in Wisconsin. Fire was one of the most significant elements that maintained these communities, and prescribed burns are being used to restrain invading plants while stimulating the plants adapted to the dry sandy slopes. The red cedars are removed by hand.

Cooperation with private landowners is a key aspect of conservation at the Spring Green Preserve. The Nature Conservancy and the Prairie Enthusiasts, a private organization committed to protecting and managing upper Midwest prairies and savannas, are working with landowners to purchase land, acquire conservation easements, and assist in the management and restoration of land surrounding the preserve. This cooperation has allowed private landowners to retain ownership of their land while committing to the preservation of the plants and animals and extending the protected area. Additionally, this work serves the important function of educating people about the nature of this unique ecosystem and the threats to it. For instance, to protect the 20 ornate box turtles that have been found in the preserve, a sizable habitat beyond the current boundaries of the preserve is needed to maintain a viable population of the species. Landowners might be willing to help but may be unaware of this species' importance, so The Nature Conservancy has worked to introduce adjacent landowners to this species and its importance. Cooperation is critical.

The preserve is open to the public.

Further Reading

Bowles, M., M. Jones, and J. McBride. "Twenty-Year Changes in Burned and Unburned Sand Prairie Remnants in Northwestern Illinois and Implications for Management." *American Midland Naturalist* 149 (2002): 35–45.

Tekiela, Stan. *Reptiles & Amphibians of Wisconsin Field Guide*. Cambridge, MN: Adventure Publications, 2004.

SUMMERTON BOG

The 423-acre Summerton Bog, located in the North Central Hardwood Forests ecoregion, is one of the most floristically diverse sites containing a mosaic of the landscapes for this region. The North Central Hardwood Forests ecoregion is one of transition from the forested lake region to the north and the agricultural ecoregions to the south. Summerton Bog is an excellent example of this transition. Plants typically found further north, such as some of the sedges (*Carex*), and bog trees like the tamarack (*Larix laricina*), dominant to dominate the preserve. A wide variety of wildflowers are present, including nine species of orchid. A calcareous fen whose calcium-rich water provides for a habitat in contrast to the acidic peaty bog is located on the western side of a five-acre glacial till oak/hickory island. The island supports a relatively dry habitat compared to the predominately lowland areas of the preserve. The ground is saturated because water is at the surface for most of the year, being supplied by rainwater and five artesian springs. Summerton Bog is a notable example of ecological processes that are a direct result of recent geological events. The bog, which is part of a glacial lake bed, is also an example of natural succession. Lakes created by the last glacial advances gradually fill from millennia of decaying vegetation, while semiaquatic, and later terrestrial, plant communities begin to encroach on the now relict lake.

The lush sedge meadow and fen are habitat for many nesting birds, 65 species having been documented. In addition to Nashville warbler (*Vermivora ruficapilla*), green heron (*Butorides virescens*), and song sparrow (*Melospiza melodia*), the bog is an important nesting area and migratory stop for sandhill cranes (*Grus canadensis*), which depend on open freshwater wetland habitats. The pickerel frog (*Rana palustris*), which is found in higher-quality wetlands, is also common here.

The diverse Summerton Bog and the surrounding land have undergone dramatic changes. Maps from the 1830s described the land as a predominantly sedge meadow. Now the area surrounding Summerton Bog is predominantly agricultural land in which grazing, haying, logging, and ditching has greatly disturbed or completely altered the natural landscape. Recently, one such ditch running thorough the preserve was filled in an attempt to restore the natural hydrology. The sedges growing in the bottom of the ditch were removed with a backhoe while the old ditch spoils were placed back in the bottom of the ditch. The sedges were then placed back on top of the filled ditch.

Runoff from nearby agriculture has the potential to affect the artesian springs and wetland communities of the bog. The altered surrounding landscape has also favored shrubs and trees such as black locust (*Robinia pseudoacacia*), which are invading the preserve. Black locust, historically found as far north as Missouri and southern Illinois, was planted across the country for fence posts, timber, and other uses. In northern areas, it has formed large colonies and has become an invasive species. In the Summerton Bog, it is invading the upland areas. The Nature Conservancy is working to remove invading shrubs and trees that are not native or whose number would have been kept in check naturally by wildfires. In fact, prescribed burns are one of the management techniques being used to maintain the vigor of the sedge meadow and fen. The desire is not to eliminate shrubs, as they were a component of the native vegetation, but rather to not allow them to dominate and thus reduce the diversity of plants and habitat for animals and insects.

The Summerton Bog has two parking lots for visitors, but much of the land is saturated and there is poison sumac (*Toxicodendron vernix*) throughout the sedge meadow, so waterproof boots are recommended.

Further Reading

Eastman, John. *The Book of Swamp and Bog: Trees, Shrubs, and Wildflowers of the Eastern Freshwater Wetlands*. Mechanicsburg, PA: Stackpole Books, 1995.

Kingsbury, B., and J. Gibson. "Habitat Management Guidelines for Amphibians and Reptiles of the Midwest." Midwest Partners in Amphibian and Reptile Conservation, 2002. http://herpcenter.ipfw.edu/index.htm?http://herpcenter.ipfw.edu/outreach/misc/general_reference_guide.htm&2.

THOMSON MEMORIAL PRAIRIE

The Thomson Memorial Prairie's 476 acres are owned and managed by The Nature Conservancy. The preserve is comprised of three tracts in Dane and Iowa counties, 30 miles west of Madison. The preserve is an excellent example of a xeric, or dry, prairie in a landscape where limestone bedrock lies close to the surface and exposed bedrock is common. The preserve is in a region known as the Driftless Area, because the last glacial advance bypassed this area. The Wisconsinan glaciation began about 110,000 years ago and ended about 10,000 years ago. During this period, the continental glaciers made three advances and retreats; its greatest advance was around 18,000 years ago. We are currently living in the last glacial retreat or interglacial period. The Wisconsinan glaciation is also one of many glaciations that occurred during the Pleistocene epoch, a division of geological time from almost two million years ago until 10,000 years ago. The Driftless Area is located primarily in southwestern Wisconsin but also includes parts of Minnesota, Iowa, and Illinois. The Driftless Area ecoregion encompasses roughly the same area as this geological landscape. The terrain of the region is diverse and rugged, a result of being untouched by the last glacial advances. The area is closest to what the surrounding regions might have looked like during the Pleistocene epoch, before glaciers bulldozed the rough terrain into smooth, rolling hills. It is a rugged terrain with steep valleys and crested ridges. The land is quite different from other regions in the Midwest.

Thomson Memorial Prairie thus offers a view of the past not only when dry prairies dominated the Driftless Area, but also before the glacial advances. Less than one percent of the original or remnant prairie in Wisconsin remains, most of it having been converted into agricultural land. Other areas that have not been farmed have become forests because of lack of disturbance such as fire. The Thomson Memorial Prairie is a remnant prairie because it has never been plowed; it was never plowed because the bedrock lies close to the surface, making agriculture difficult. This is true of many of the natural areas in the region and elsewhere—the areas that are most difficult and unsuitable for development have avoided development.

Typical vegetation of a dry prairie can be seen here with plants such as big and little bluestem, porcupine grass (*Stipa spartea*), bird's-foot violet (*Viola pedata*), and the rare pomme-de-prairie (*Pediomelum esculentum*), whose starchy roots were eaten by Native Americans and pioneers. Many birds and butterflies have also been observed in the preserve. Sixty-eight plant species and 34 species of birds have been recorded, making this a relatively diverse dry prairie.

Preservation and restoration of grasslands can be difficult because the plants and animals require large tracts of land for survival. The grasslands that are protected are often fragmented and isolated from other tracts of grassland. The Thomson Memorial Prairie is one such example of fragmentation, because it is composed of three separate tracts of land. The Nature Conservancy is working to restore agricultural land surrounding the preserve as well as acquiring additional land to reduce fragmentation. Streams also run through the three tracts of land, and pollution from agricultural runoff must be carefully monitored.

The preserve is within a larger area designated as the Military Ridge Prairie Heritage Area—more than 50,000 acres in southwestern Wisconsin recognized for the significant tall-grass prairies and savannas that remain. This designation means that the Wisconsin Department of Natural Resources has given its highest priority to large-scale grassland management and protection in this part of the state. The initiative promotes a greater ecological awareness among area landowners by providing tax incentives for ecologically managing and not developing their land. The Military Ridge Prairie Heritage Area also assists in partnering private, public, and nonprofit groups to work toward the preservation and restoration of this ecosystem.

Further Reading

Henderson, R. A. *Plant Species Composition of Wisconsin Prairies*. Technical Bulletin No. 188. Madison: Wisconsin Department of Natural Resources, 1995.

Renfrew, R. B., and C. A. Ribic. "Multi-scale Models of Grassland Passerine Abundance in a Fragmented Ecosystem." *Landscape Ecology* 23 (2008): 181–93.

GLOSSARY

ALGIFIC TALUS SLOPE   A rare natural habitat created by the seepage of air through fissures in the earth's surface, which is cooled over ice in underground passages and exits down a talus, or loose rock, slope. The cool air allows northern organisms to survive much farther south than usual. Algific means cold producing.

BOG   A type of wetland that receives all its water from precipitation rather than groundwater. A bog is an acidic wetland that gradually accumulates dead plants (primarily mosses), and forms peat.

BOREAL FOREST   The nearly continuous circumpolar northern forest and largest terrestrial biome in the world. The boreal forest is characterized by predominantly cold-tolerant conifers growing over nutrient-poor, acidic soils. North of the boreal forest is the tundra.

CONIFER   A tree with needlelike leaves. The tree's needles may be evergreen, such as a pine, or deciduous (dropping its needles every fall), such as a tamarack or larch.

DISSECTED   In a geological context, divided by peaks and valleys.

DRAW   An Appalachian term meaning valley.

DRIFTLESS AREA   Region in southeastern Minnesota, northeastern Iowa, northwestern Illinois, and southwestern Wisconsin that was virtually untouched by the last glaciation, which ended about 9,000 years ago. The Driftless Area region is characterized by terrain that is more rugged than the surrounding land, which was sheared by past glaciers to form the plains and rolling hills typical of much of the Midwest. The Driftless Area has many unique ecosystems because of the region's recent geological history. The name is derived from the lack of glacial drift or unconsolidated glacial deposits in the region.

ECOREGION   A geographical area where biotic and abiotic components of terrestrial and aquatic systems exhibit relatively similar patterns to that of other areas. Ecoregions are intended to show patterns in the potential of ecological systems and are a useful tool in ecosystem management. In this sense, ecoregions are most useful in defining regions where there is a similarity in the diversity of the ecosystems and their components. There are many definitions of ecoregions, some with specific purposes and not intended to address ecosystems in the broadest sense.

ECOSYSTEM   A unit of interdependent organisms functioning in a similar biotic and abiotic environment. The features of an ecosystem are varied and unpredictable, and, in many ways, an ecosystem is more of a conceptual unit. An ecosystem is a way of grouping the living (biotic) and nonliving (abiotic) elements that appear to function as a system.

ECOSYSTEM MANAGEMENT   The management of natural systems as opposed to the management of specific ecological components such as forests, wildlife, streams, and wetlands. Ecosystem management recognizes the interrelatedness of all ecological components—biotic, abiotic, terrestrial, aquatic, and human—and the imperative to take a holistic approach to the management and preservation of natural environments.

EMERGENT VEGETATION   Plants rooted in water but growing partially in the air, as opposed to submergent plants, which grow entirely below the water's surface.

ESTUARY   An area where a freshwater river meets the ocean. In the Midwest, estuaries are rivers that meet with a drowned lake. In a process similar to an ocean estuary, the lower end of the river is periodically submerged by lake water wind tides or seiches, the back-and-forth movement of water in a large body of water. Estuaries are highly productive ecosystems because of this interaction of different temperatures and compositions of the water.

FEN   A type of wetland that is primarily supported by groundwater discharge. A calcareous fen contains calcium and magnesium.

FRAGMENTATION   The separation of a species into distinct and separate geographical areas. Often the result of human activities such as agriculture and urbanization, fragmentation separates populations of a species, making interaction of the separated populations difficult or impossible.

GLACIAL DRIFT   A general term for all unconsolidated—not clumped together—glacial deposits. Glacial deposits can include clay, silt, sand, gravel, and boulders, which can be found sorted or unsorted. Drift is an old term for sediment of various sizes thought to be deposited from drifting icebergs.

GLACIAL TILL   Poorly sorted deposits of a glacier composed of angular and rounded rocks.

GLACIATION   The process by which a glacier grows or advances. The past two million years have been marked by significant and named glaciations, or periods in which glaciers advanced and covered substantial portions of the earth for considerable geological periods. Glaciation is the period associated with the maximum glacial extent.

GLADE   An opening in the forest caused by disturbance such as fire or for more permanent reasons such as poor soils.

HABITAT   An environmental area typically inhabited by a species.

HYDRIC   Wet-loving plants.

HYDROLOGY   The study of groundwater, its movement, distribution, and chemistry.

INVASIVE SPECIES   Nonnative species disrupting and often taking over or displacing native species' habitat. Invasive species typically originate from another continent. Invasives may originate from the same continent, but they are considered invasive when they are introduced to a region from which they are historically not typical. In all such cases, introduced species are considered invasive when they displace native species because they have a biological advantage over native populations.

LOESS   Wind-blown, fine-grained, silty sediment. In North America, loess is the result of glacial activity, the process of past glaciers grinding rocks almost to a powder.

KARST TOPOGRAPHY   A landscape shaped by the dissolving of bedrock, typically limestone or dolomite. A karst landscape typically displays features such as caves, sink holes, and losing streams, to name a few. A karst region is often excessively drained because of the dissolution of the underlying bedrock leaving the surface parched.

MARSH   A wetland dominated by grasses and other emergent plants.

MESIC   Moist but well-drained soil. The term describes the moisture gradient of a habitat. A mesic prairie, for example, is an ecosystem with plants typical of a moderately moist prairie.

NATIONAL NATURAL LANDMARK   A designation administered by the National Park Service to recognize and encourage the conservation of natural biological and geological features, both public and private. The goal of the program is to bring attention to outstanding natural features and not for the purpose of public acquisition.

PATCH-BURN GRAZING   Management of grasslands, particularly prairies, by a combination of alternate grazing and burning to maintain species diversity and ecosystem vigor. Cattle prefer to graze on land with fresh grass growth, the result of a spring burn, and will leave unburned areas nearly untouched. This allows flowering plants more light, thereby increasing their numbers. In succeeding years, the patch is not burned but allowed to recover. After three or more years, the same patch of land is burned again. The concept comes from mimicking the grazing of bison and frequent prairie fires of the pre-European American landscape.

PEAT   A type of soil in which plant material is still visible. Peatlands are formed because of low-oxygen, cold temperatures, and a short growing season, which prevent complete decomposition of decaying plants.

pH   A measure of the acidity or alkalinity of a solution. On a scale of 0 to 14 with 7 being neutral, below 7 is acidic, above 7 is alkaline. Plants that prefer acidic soil, such as most conifers, blueberries, and azaleas, grow in soils that have a low pH.

PIONEER SPECIES   A plant that is the first to colonize a disturbed area or area that lacks vegetation. Over time, the landscape changes as a succession of later plants replaces the pioneer species.

PRESCRIBED FIRE   Intentionally set and controlled fires for the purpose of ecosystem management.

RECHARGE AREA   The surface area of the land that supplies water to the aquifer or underground layer of water-bearing rock or gravel.

RELICT   A species or ecosystem from an earlier time that has survived in an environment that has undergone considerable change. An ecosystem and its inhabitants that are found much further south than usual would be a relict from the last glaciation, when the climate was considerably colder and the glaciers retreated north. A relict has thus become geographically isolated from present-day populations.

RELIEF   The difference in elevation in the landscape.

REMNANT   In an ecological sense, an area that has not been altered by humans and retains most of its prehuman ecological characteristics.

SHUT-IN   A geological feature formed by a stream eroding away soft limestone until much harder igneous rock is reached. At this point, the stream cuts deep and narrow channels in the rock.

SLOUGH   A type of swamp in the eastern United States formed by backwater of a large waterway. In this respect, a slough is similar to a bayou, with trees being present.

SPELEOTHEM   Cave formation such as stalactite, stalagmite, or flowstone.

SUBSIDENCE   The settling of land. Subsidence is commonly seen in karst regions where the limestone bedrock erodes away, resulting in the land collapsing and creating a sink hole.

SUCCESSION   The predictable change in the composition and structure of an ecosystem. Successional plants are typically pioneer species that are the first to colonize a disturbed area, eventually giving way to more stable species.

SWAMP   A wetland in which temporary or permanent shallow water floods large forested areas. Marshes and other types of wetlands have much more sun reaching the ground and are thus more open, whereas a swamp is dominated by woody vegetation, a true swamp being dominated by trees with much more open surface water as well.

TROGLOBITE   Cave-dwelling creature.

BIBLIOGRAPHY

Allerton Park and Retreat Center. University of Illinois at Urbana-Champaign. http://www.allerton.uiuc.edu/.

Benke, Arthur C., and Colbert E. Cushing, eds. *Rivers of North America.* Burlington, MA: Elsevier Academic Press, 2005.

Benson, Lorna. "Forest Changes Linked to Global Warming." Minnesota Public Radio, March 8, 2006. http://minnesota.publicradio.org/display/web/2006/03/03/globaltrees/.

Bettendorf, Elizabeth. "Land Lovers." *Illinois Issues,* July 1995. http://www.lib.niu.edu/1995/ii950710.html.

Bloom, Phil. *Hiking Indiana.* Guilford, CT: Globe Pequot Press, 2000.

Bonnicksen, Thomas M. *America's Ancient Forests: From the Ice Age to the Age of Discovery.* New York: John Wiley, 2000.

Border Route Hiking Trail. http://www.borderroutetrail.org/.

Broll, Gabriele, and Beate Keplin, eds. *Mountain Ecosystems: Studies in Treeline Ecology.* New York: Springer, 2005.

Cadillac Forest Management Unit. "Compartment Review Presentation." Department of Natural Resources. August 26, 2002, http://www.michigandnr.com/PUBLICATIONS/PDFS/ForestsLandWater/DoNotUpdate/Cmpt_Reviews/Cadillac/2004/Cmpt076.pdf.

Carlson, Don. *Forest Management Plan for the Davis Purdue Agricultural Center.* Purdue University, December 2004. http://www.fnr.purdue.edu/research/properties/mgmtplan/davis.pdf.

City of Murphysboro, Illinois. "Little Grand Canyon." http://www.murphysboro.com/index.php?p=71.

Cohen, J.G. "Natural Community Abstract for Dry-Mesic Northern Forest." Michigan Natural Features Inventory, Lansing, MI, 2002. http://web4.msue.msu.edu/mnfi/abstracts/ecology/Dry-mesic_northern_forest.pdf.

Cooperative Conservation America. "Case Study: Restoration at Kankakee Sands." http://www.cooperativeconservation.org/viewproject.asp?pid=528.

Corcoran Hill, Elizabeth, and Kate Corcoran. *Hiking Iowa*. Guilford, CT: Globe Pequot Press, 2005.

Davis, Mary Byrd. *Eastern Old-Growth Forests: Prospects for Rediscovery and Recovery*. Washington, DC: Island Press, 1996.

Detroit Free Press. "Deep in the Forest, the White Pines Whisper." *Celebrate Michigan: Our State Symbols*. http://www.michigan.gov/documents/hal_mhc_mhm_whitepine_63867_7.pdf.

Dodds, Walter K. *Freshwater Ecology: Concepts & Environmental Applications*. San Diego, CA: Academic Press, 2002.

Dorney, J. "Impact of Native Americans on Vegetation." *Wisconsin Academy of Sciences, Arts and Letters* 69 (1981): 26–35.

Earlham College. "Indiana's Geologic Processes." http://www.earlham.edu/~scottna/GeologicProcesses.htm.

Edwards, Victoria M. *Dealing in Diversity: America's Market for Nature Conservation*. Cambridge, UK: Cambridge University Press, 1995.

Elpel, Thomas J. *Botany in a Day: The Patterns Method of Plant Identification*. Silver Star, MT: HOPS Press, 2004.

Elzinga, Caryl L., Daniel W. Salzer, and John W. Willoughby. *Monitoring Plant and Animal Populations*. Malden, MA: Blackwell Science, 2001.

Encounter Lee County, Illinois. "Nachusa Grasslands." http://www.encounterleecounty.com/?q=content/nachusa-grasslands.

Encyclopædia Britannica. "Wyandotte Cave." *Encyclopædia Britannica Online*. http://www.britannica.com/EBchecked/topic/650130/Wyandotte-Cave.

Environment News Service. "Bison Return to Iowa's Native Prairie." October 20, 2008. http://www.ens-newswire.com/ens/oct2008/2008-10-20-095.asp.

"Establishment Record of the Pioneer Mothers Memorial Research Natural Area within the Hoosier National Forest." Unpublished report, Northern Research Station, Rhinelander, 1943. http://nrs.fs.fed.us/rna/documents/establishment/in_hoosier_pioneer_mothers_memorial.pdf.

"Establishment Report for the Dukes Research Natural Area within the Hiawatha National Forest." Unpublished report, Northern Research Station, Rhinelander. http://www.nrs.fs.fed.us/rna/documents/establishment/mi_hiawatha_dukes.pdf.

Evansville Audubon Society. "Gibson County Hotspots: Hemmer's Woods State Nature Preserve." http://www.evvaudubon.org/gibson.htm#Hemmer%E2%80%99s%20 Woods%20State%20Nature%20Preserve.

Fedora, Mark. "Ecosystem Analysis of the Sand Lake/Seven Beavers Project Area, in the Upper St. Louis Watershed, Minnesota." U.S. Forest Service and The Nature Conservancy. May 12, 2005. http://www.nature.org/wherewework/northamerica/states/ minnesota/files/slsb_ecosystem_analysis.pdf.

Fliege, Stu. *Tales & Trails of Illinois*. Champaign: University of Illinois Press, 2002.

Forrest, Sharita. "Deer Dilemma: Increase in Deer Population Causes Concern at Allerton." *Inside Illinois* 24, no. 1 (July 1, 2004). University of Illinois at Urbana-Champaign. http://news.illinois.edu/II/04/0701/deer.html.

Friends of Highland Recreation Area. "Haven Hill." http://www.friendsofhighlandrec. org/index_files/FriendsofHighlandRecreationAreaHavenHill.htm.

Great Lakes Indian Fish & Wildlife Commission. "Tribal Wildernesses, Tribal Research Areas, and Tribal Vehicle Permit Areas on National Forests." August 1998. http:// www.fs.fed.us/r9/cnnf/cnnf-old/mou/tribal_wild_rna.pdf.

Greenberg, Joel. *A Natural History of the Chicago Region*. Chicago: University of Chicago Press, 2002.

Grese, Robert. "Ecological Restoration Plan: Detroit Edison Trespass, Haven Hill Natural Area, Highland Recreation Area." University of Michigan, Ecosystem Management Initiative. http://www.snre.umich.edu/ecomgt/restoration/research.htm.

Hardwood Forest Foundation. "Central Hardwood Notes: Central Hardwood Forest Types." http://www.hardwoodforest.org/learn/pdfs/ForestFacts/CentralHardwood ForestTypes.pdf.

Harker, Donald. *Landscape Restoration Handbook*, 2nd ed. New York: United States Golf Association, 1999.

Herzberg, Ruth, and John Pearson. *The Guide to Iowa's State Preserves*. Iowa City: University of Iowa Press, 2001.

Hill, John R. "Landscapes of Indiana." Indiana Geological Survey, Indiana State University, 1998. http://igs.indiana.edu/geology/topo/landscapes/index.cfm.

Hoffman, Randy. *Wisconsin's Natural Communities: How to Recognize Them, Where to Find Them*. Madison: University of Wisconsin Press, 2002.

Houghton Lake Area. "Canoeing." http://www.visithoughtonlake.com/canoe.html.

Howell, Kevin, "Indiana's Natural Wonder." *Forest Magazine*. Fall 2006. http://www. fseee.org/forestmag/ivot/fall06ot.shtml.

Illinois Department of Natural Resources. http://dnr.state.il.us/.

Illinois Department of Public Health. "Wabash River: Species and Meal Frequency." Illinois Fish Advisory. http://www.idph.state.il.us/envhealth/fishadv09/wabashriver. htm.

Illinois State Museum. http://www.museum.state.il.us/.

Illinois Wesleyan University. "Community Action." Environmental Studies. https://www.iwu.edu/environ/activities/community.shtml.

Indiana Audubon Society. "Spring Mill State Park." *Online Birding Guide*. http://www.indianaaudubon.org/Sites/sprngmil.htm.

Indiana Department of Natural Resources. http://www.in.gov/dnr/.

"Indiana Dunes National Lakeshore." *Midwest Living*. http://www.midwestliving.com/travel/destination/indiana/indiana-dunes-national-lakeshore/.

Indiana Outfitters. "Pioneer Mothers Memorial Forest Trail." http://www.indianaoutfitters.com/Destinations/Pioneer_Mothers.htm.

Indiana University. "Effect of Structure and Rock Type on Karst Features." *Indiana Geological Survey*. http://igs.indiana.edu/geology/karst/karstInIndiana/karstInIndiana03.cfm.

Indiana University–Purdue University, Department of Earth Sciences. "Indiana Geography and Geology Facts." http://www.geology.iupui.edu/Resources/Students/Geology_Resources/indiana_geology_facts.htm.

Indiana University Southeast. "General Site Description of the Blue River." Blue River Darter Project, 1999. http://homepages.ius.edu/SPECIAL/darters/gensd.htm.

Indiana University Southeast. "Harrison Springs Info Table." Blue River Darter Project, 1999. http://homepages.ius.edu/Special/Darters/HSDescr.htm.

Iowa Department of Natural Resources. "Hayden Prairie State Preserve." http://www.iowadnr.gov/wildlife/wmamaps/maps/hayden_prairie.pdf.

Iowa Department of Natural Resources. "Landform Regions of Iowa." *Geological Survey*. http://www.igsb.uiowa.edu/Browse/landform.htm.

Iowa Department of Natural Resources, Education Division. "People and Wildlife: Who Is Responsible for Wildlife?" http://www.iowadnr.gov/education/wldppl.html.

Iowa Natural Heritage Foundation, Central Iowa Prairie Rescue Locations. "Ames High Prairie State Preserve." http://www.inhf.org/centraliowarescue2003.htm#Ames%20High%20Prairie%20Preserve.

Iowa Natural Heritage Foundation, Eastern Iowa Prairie Rescue Locations. "Hayden Prairie State Preserve." http://www.inhf.org/eastiowarescue2003.htm#Hayden%20Prairie.

Iowa State University Extension. "Managing Iowa Habitats: Restoring Iowa Woodlands." http://www.extension.iastate.edu/Publications/PM1351I.pdf.

Jackson, Marion T. "Forest Communities and Tree Species of the Lower Wabash River Basin." *Proceedings of the Indiana Academy of Science*. February 12, 2007. http://goliath.ecnext.com/coms2/gi_0199-6578478/Forest-communities-and-tree-species.html.

Johnston, Isabel. "Those Darn Multifloras." *Nachusa Grasslands ECO*, no. 1 (May 1989). http://www.nachusagrasslands.org/PSmoke/Issue1May1989.pdf.

Karns, Daryl R. "BioBlitz at the Fall IAS Meeting." *Indiana Academy of Science Newsletter,* no. 136 (June 2008). http://www.indianaacademyofscience.org/136%20June%20 2008.pdf.

Keddy, Paul A. *Wetland Ecology: Principles and Conservation.* Cambridge, UK: Cambridge University Press, 2000.

Kleitch, Matt, and Patrick Doran. "Lake Michigan Dune Restoration Project Summary— 2007 Field Season Report." The Nature Conservancy. November 2007. http://www. nature.org/wherewework/northamerica/states/michigan/files/dune_restoration_ report.pdf.

Kost, M. A. "Natural Community Abstract for Dry Sand Prairie." *Michigan Natural Features Inventory.* 2004. Lansing, MI. http://web4.msue.msu.edu/mnfi/abstracts/ecology/ Dry_sand_prairie.pdf.

Kost, M. A., et al. 2007. "Natural Communities of Michigan: Classification and Description." Michigan Natural Features Inventory, Report No. 2007–21, Lansing, MI. http://web4.msue.msu.edu/mnfi/abstracts/ecology/Coastal_plain_marsh.pdf and http://web4.msue.msu.edu/mnfi/communities/community.cfm?id=10679.

LandScope America. "Iowa Conservation Summary." http://www.landscope.org/iowa/ overview/.

LaPorte County. "Mount Baldy Indiana Dunes National Lakeshore." http://www.laporte county.net/sites/mountbaldy.html.

Larson, Chris. "Into the Wild: Watch Migrating Birds, Hike and Camp Near Dunes, and Swim at Popular State Park." *Chicago Wilderness Magazine,* Winter 1998. http:// www.chicagowildernessmag.org/issues/winter1998/IWillinoisbeach.html.

Lewis, Julian J. "Conservation Assessment for Golden Cave Harvestman (*Erebomaster flavescens*)." U.S. Forest Service, Eastern Region, October 2002. http://www.fs.fed. us/r9/wildlife/tes/ca-overview/docs/invertebrate_Erebomaster_flavescens-Golden CaveHarvestman.pdf.

Lucas, Marty. "Kankakee Sands." *Chicago Wilderness Magazine,* Summer 2005. http:// www.chicagowildernessmag.org/issues/summer2005/weekendexplorer.html.

Lyons, Stephen J. "Return of the Native: Forest and Tallgrass Prairie Preserved in Allerton Park in Illinois." *Sierra,* November 1998. http://findarticles.com/p/articles/ mi_m1525/is_6_83/ai_54233011/.

McAuliffe, Bill. "Minnesota's Peat Bogs 'Wild Card' in Global Warming." *Minneapolis Star Tribune,* January 9, 2008. http://www.startribune.com/local/13581681.html.

McClain, William E., Richard L. Larimore, and John E. Ebinger. "Woody Vegetation Survey of Beall Woods Nature Preserve, Wabash County, Illinois." *Proceedings of the Indiana Academy of Science,* January 1, 2001. http://www.highbeam.com/doc/1G1- 83518033.html.

McCormac, James S., and Gary Meszaros. *Wild Ohio: The Best of Our Natural Heritage.* Kent, OH: Kent State University Press, 2009.

McLaren, George. "Nature Conservancy Buys Land To Protect Indiana's Lost River Caves." *Indianapolis Star*, February 21, 2003. http://www.citizenreviewonline.org/feb_2003/nature_conservancy.htm.

Meffe, Gary, Larry Nielsen, and Richard L. Knight. *Ecosystem Management: Adaptive, Community-Based Conservation.* Washington DC: Island Press, 2002.

Meyerson, Howard. "Black Bear May Be Record for Wyoming Hunter." *Grand Rapids Press*, October 24, 2008. http://www.mlive.com/outdoors/index.ssf/2008/10/black_bear_may_be_record_for_w.html.

Michigan Department of Natural Resources. http://www.michigan.gov/dnr.

Michigan State University, Campus Planning and Administration. "Toumey Woodlot." http://www.cpa.msu.edu/nat_area/toumey.htm.

Michigan State University, Pesticide Safety Education. "Forest Types in Michigan." http://www.pested.msu.edu/Resources/bulletins/pdf/Category2/Chap5.pdf.

Michigan State University Extension. "Michigan's Natural Communities: Northern Bald." *Michigan Natural Features Inventory.* http://web4.msue.msu.edu/mnfi/communities/community.cfm?id=10695.

Mineralogical Society of America. "Virtual Field Trip to the Keweenaw Peninsula, Michigan." http://www.minsocam.org/MSA/collectors_corner/vft/mi2a.htm.

Minnesota Department of Natural Resources. http://www.dnr.state.mn.us/index.html.

Minnesota Pollution Control Agency. "Upper Minnesota River Watershed." http://www.pca.state.mn.us/water/basins/mnriver/uppermn.html.

Minnesota State Parks. "Itasca State Park." http://www.stateparks.com/itasca.html.

Minnesota State University. "Minnesota River Valley Formation." Minnesota River Basin Data Center. http://mrbdc.mnsu.edu/mnbasin/fact_sheets/valley_formation.html.

Mohlenbrock, Robert H. "Little Grand Canyon." *Natural History*, June 1997. http://findarticles.com/p/articles/mi_m1134/is_n5_v106/ai_19752779/.

Montz, Gary R. "Aquatic Macroinvertebrates of the Pigeon River, Minnesota." Minnesota Department of Natural Resources, Ecological Services Section. November 1993. http://files.dnr.state.mn.us/eco/nongame/projects/consgrant_reports/1993/1993_montz.pdf.

Mottl, Eric, Lisa Schulte, and Brian Palik. "Effects of Invasive Shrubs on Oak Forest Dynamics in Southeastern Minnesota: Implications for Forest Management." Iowa State University and U.S. Forest Service, Northern Research Station. 2007. http://www.nrem.iastate.edu/landscape/projects/oak_ecosystem/oak.html.

Nachusa Grasslands Friends, Franklin, Illinois. http://www.nachusagrasslands.org/.

National Audubon Society. "Indiana's Important Bird Areas Program." http://iba.audubon.org/iba/viewState.do?state=US-IN.

National Audubon Society. "Kankakee Sands Project and Surrounding Natural Areas." Important Bird Areas. http://iba.audubon.org/iba/profileReport.do?siteId=2172&navSite=search&pagerOffset=0&page=1.

National Park Service. http://www.nps.gov/index.htm.

The Nature Conservancy. http://www.nature.org/.

Neumann, David, and Georgia Peterson. "Northern Hardwood Forest Management." *Michigan State University Extension Bulletin* E2769. August 2001, http://forestry.msu.edu/extension/extdocs/E2769.pdf.

North American Native Fishes Association. "Wabash River Fishes." http://www.nanfa.org/convention/99Wabash.shtml.

North Woods Wilderness Recovery. "An Afternoon at Dukes Forest." http://www.northwoodswild.org/projects/forest-watch/103-an-afternoon-at-dukes-forest.

Omernik, James M. "Perspectives on the Nature and Definition of Ecological Regions," *Environmental Management* 34, Suppl. 1 (2004): S27–S38.

Pullin, Andrew S. *Conservation Biology*. Cambridge, UK: Cambridge University Press, 2002.

Purdue University. "Purdue Agricultural Centers." http://www.agriculture.purdue.edu/arp/pacs/Davis.html.

Purdue University, Purdue Agriculture, Forestry & Natural Resources. "Davis Purdue Ag Center." http://www.ag.purdue.edu/fnr/Pages/propdavis.aspx.

Pure Michigan: Michigan's Official Travel and Tourism Site. "Nan Weston Preserve at Sharon Hollow." http://www.michigan.org/Property/Detail.aspx?p=B4982.

Quinn, Bowden. "Lost River." *Indiana Sierran*, Summer 2005. http://indiana.sierraclub.org/Sierran/05-3/lost.asp.

Ramsar Convention on Wetlands. "Ramsar Sites in Order of Addition to the Ramsar List of Wetlands of International Importance." http://www.ramsar.org/sitelist_order.pdf.

Randall, Carolyn. "Forest Types in Michigan." *Forest Pest Management*, Manual no. E-2045. Michigan State University Pesticide Safety Education. 2000. http://www.pested.msu.edu/Resources/bulletins/pdf/Category2/Chap5.pdf.

Reemts, Charlotte, Darin Ellair, and Peter Murphy. "Edge Effects in Old-Growth Forests." Ecological Society of America. Michigan State University. East Lansing. http://abstracts.co.allenpress.com/pweb/esa2004/document/36410.

River Raisin Watershed Council and The Nature Conservancy. "Upper River Raisin Conservation Plan." October 2002. http://riverraisin.org/reports/tnc_raisin_2002.doc.

Robertson, Kenneth R., Mark W. Schwartz, Jeffrey W. Olson, Brian K. Dunphy, and H. David Clarke. "50 Years of Change in Illinois Hill Prairies." *Erigenia: Journal of the Illinois Native Plant Society*. no. 14 (January 1996): 41–52.

Sargent, M.S., and K.S. Carter, eds. "Managing Michigan Wildlife: A Landowners Guide. Dry Mesic Conifers (White Pine)." Michigan United Conservation Clubs,

East Lansing. 1999. http://www.michigandnr.com/publications/pdfs/huntingwildlife habitat/Landowners_Guide/Habitat_Mgmt/Forest/Dry_Mesic_Conifers.htm.

Sargent, M.S., and K.S. Carter, eds. "Managing Michigan Wildlife: A Landowners Guide. Lowland Conifers (Tamarack, Black Spruce & White Cedar)." Michigan United Conservation Clubs, East Lansing, MI. 1999. http://www.michigandnr. com/publications/pdfs/huntingwildlifehabitat/Landowners_Guide/Habitat_Mgmt/ Forest/Lowland_Conifers.htm.

Savage, Candace. *Prairie: A Natural History.* Vancouver, BC: Greystone Books, 2004.

Scheuering, Rachel White. *Shapers of the Great Debate on Conservation.* Westport, CT: Greenwood Press, 2004.

Schoon, Kenneth J. *Calumet Beginnings: Ancient Shorelines and Settlements at the South End of Lake Michigan.* Bloomington: Indiana University Press, 2003.

Simon, Thomas P., ed. *Biological Response Signatures: Indicator Patterns Using Aquatic Communities.* Boca Raton, FL: CRC Press, 2003.

Society for Ecological Restoration International, Peter H. Raven, James Aronson, and Suzanne J. Milton. *Restoring Natural Capital: Science, Business, and Practice (The Science and Practice of Ecological Restoration Series).* Washington, DC: Island Press, 2007.

Somme Prairie Grove. "Trees and Shrubs of Somme Prairie Grove." http://www.sommep reserve.org/treesshrubs.html.

Southern Illinois University, Department of Plant Biology. "Botany in the Natural Areas of Southern Illinois." http://www.plantbiology.siu.edu/information/natural.html.

Southern Indiana Education Center. "Wondrous Wyandotte Caves." http://www.siec. k12.in.us/cannelton/wyandotte/wonders.htm.

Southern Indiana Trails. "Hemmer Woods Nature Preserve." http://southernindiana trails.awardspace.com/graphics/hemmer/hemmer.htm.

Spading, Kenton. "Browns Valley Dike, Browns Valley, Minnesota: Lake Traverse Project: History and Potential for Interbasin Flow." U.S. Army Corps of Engineers. January 2000. http://www.mvp-wc.usace.army.mil/projects/docs/BrownsValleyDike.pdf.

StateParks.com. "Volo Bog Nature Preserve." http://www.stateparks.com/volo_bog.html.

Stein, Bruce A., Lynn S. Kutner, and Jonathan S. Adams, eds. *Precious Heritage: The Status of Biodiversity in the United States.* Oxford, England: Oxford University Press, 2000.

Sullivan, Janet. "Mosaic of Bluestem Prairie and Oak-Hickory Forest." *Fire Effects Information System,* U.S. Department of Agriculture, Forest Service, Rocky Mountain Research Station, Fire Sciences Laboratory (Producer). 1995. http://www.fs.fed.us/ database/feis/kuchlers/k082/all.html.

Sullivan, Janet. "Northern Floodplain Forest." *Fire Effects Information System,* U.S. Department of Agriculture, Forest Service, Rocky Mountain Research Station, Fire

Sciences Laboratory (Producer). 1995. http://www.fs.fed.us/database/feis/kuchlers/k098/all.html.

Suloway, Liane, Mark Joselyn, and Patrick W. Brown, "Inventory of Resource Rich Areas in Illinois: An Evaluation of Ecological Resources." Lower Wabash River RRA. Center for Wildlife Ecology, Illinois Natural History Survey. 1996. http://www.inhs.uiuc.edu/cwe/rra/site24.html.

Tauke, Paul. "The Oak Forest Resource in Iowa: An Overview of Iowa's Oak Forest Resource." Iowa Department of Natural Resources, Bureau of Forestry. http://www.iowadnr.gov/forestry/pdf/Oakdoc.pdf.

Thompson, Paul Woodward. "Vegetation of Haven Hill, Michigan." *American Midland Naturalist* 50, no. 1 (July 1953): 218–23.

United Way for Southeastern Michigan. "Highland Recreation Area Stewardship Volunteer." http://volunteer.united-e-way.org/uwsem/org/opp/10248693257.html.

University of Illinois at Springfield. "The Emiquon Field Station Project." http://www.uis.edu/emiquon/about/index.html.

University of Illinois at Urbana-Champaign. "Deer Management." Allerton Park and Retreat Center. http://www.allerton.uiuc.edu/deer.html.

University of Illinois at Urbana Champaign. "History." Allerton Park and Retreat Center. http://www.allerton.uiuc.edu/history.html.

University of Illinois, University Outreach & Public Service. "Robert Allerton Park and Visitor Center." http://ness2.uic.edu/UI-Service/programs/UIUC301.html.

University of Minnesota. "Cedar Creek Ecosystem Science Reserve." http://www.cedarcreek.umn.edu/about/.

University of Missouri–St. Louis. "Shawnee Forest–Heron Pond in the Cache River Natural Area, Southern Illinois." *Biology 440: Ecological Research in Temperate Zones (Fall 2000)*. http://www.umsl.edu/~loiselleb/Biol440/Shawnee/Introduction.html.

University of Southern Indiana. "Historic Southern Indiana: Physical Features." http://www.usi.edu/hsi/trivia/features.asp.

University of Wisconsin Aquatic Sciences Center, Sea Grant Institute. "Gifts of the Glaciers." http://seagrant.wisc.edu/glaciers/.

Unterreiner, Gerald A. "Hydrogeology of Harrison County, Indiana." Indiana Department of Natural Resources, Division of Water. 2006. http://www.in.gov/dnr/water/files/5361.pdf.

Upham, Warren. "The Glacial Lake Agassiz: Chapter II, Topography of the Basin of Lake Agassiz." U.S. Geological Survey. 1896. http://www.lib.ndsu.nodak.edu/govdocs/text/lakeagassiz/chapter2.html.

U.S. Department of Agriculture, Natural Resources Conservation Service. "Restoring and Managing Habitat for Reptiles and Amphibians." February 2005. http://www.ia.nrcs.usda.gov/news/brochures/ReptilesAmphibians.html.

U.S. Fish and Wildlife Service. "Emiquon National Wildlife Refuge." http://www.fws.gov/Refuges/profiles/index.cfm?id=33654.

U.S. Fish and Wildlife Service. "Endangered Bats Using More of Wyandotte Cave Following Winter Closure." May 19, 2003. http://www.fws.gov/news/NewsReleases/showNews.cfm?newsId=999150B4-5B7B-4E18-ABCE22E3E3D54F70.

U.S. Fish and Wildlife Service. "Oak Savanna." Sherburne National Wildlife Refuge. http://www.fws.gov/midwest/Sherburne/Oak.HTM.

U.S. Fish and Wildlife Service, Midwest Region. "Habitat Management Activities at Sites Containing Federally Listed Vascular Plant Species." *Region 3 Endangered Species Report*. 2008. http://www.fws.gov/midwest/endangered/grants/2008/S6_IA_2008_plantsE15R1.pdf.

U.S. Forest Service. http://www.fs.fed.us/.

U.S. Geological Survey. http://www.usgs.gov/.

Ver Steeg, Karl, "Some Features to the Tributaries to Lake Superior in Northeastern Minnesota." *Ohio Journal of Science* 48, no. 2 (March 1948). https://kb.osu.edu/dspace/bitstream/1811/3625/1/V48N02_056.pdf.

Wesselman Nature Society. "Wesselman Woods Nature Preserve." http://wesselmannaturesociety.org/woods/index.php.

Wetland Science Advisory Group. "Recommendations of the Wetland Science Advisory Group on Rare and Ecologically Important Wetland Type Definitions." July 28, 2005. www.in.gov/idem/files/rareecowetland.doc.

Wiens, John A., Michael R. Moss, and Monica G. Turner, eds. *Foundation Papers in Landscape Ecology*. New York: Columbia University Press, 2007.

Wiggers, Ray. "Classic Prairie Restoration: Gensburg-Markham Prairie." *Chicago Wilderness Magazine*, Summer 2000. http://www.chicagowildernessmag.org/issues/summer2000/gensburg.html.

Witt, Bill. "Iowa's Wild Orchids." Iowa Natural Heritage Foundation. 2009. http://www.inhf.org/orchids.htm.

Yaffee, Steven Lewis, Ali Phillips, Irene C. Frentz, and Paul W. Hardy. *Ecosystem Management in the United States: An Assessment of Current Experience*. Washington, DC: Island Press, 1996.

Young, Chris. "A Walk through Allerton Park." *State Journal-Register*, August 3, 2008. http://www.sj-r.com/archive/x2043521498/A-walk-through-Allerton-Park.

INDEX